SOUTH ENGL[AND]
Regional Road Atlas

G000048349

CONTENTS

Key to Map Pages............ 2-3
Road Maps........................4-49
Index to Towns and Villages............50-61
Town Plans, Airport & Port Plans...62-72

REFERENCE

MOTORWAY — M2
Under Construction
Proposed
MOTORWAY JUNCTIONS WITH NUMBERS
Unlimited interchange 4 Limited interchange 5
MOTORWAY SERVICE AREA — MEDWAY
with access from one carriageway only
MAJOR ROAD SERVICE AREAS with 24 hour Facilities — PEASE POTTAGE — GRASBY
PRIMARY ROUTE — A21
PRIMARY ROUTE DESTINATION — DOVER
DUAL CARRIAGEWAYS (A & B Roads)
CLASS A ROAD — A260
CLASS B ROAD — B2011
MAJOR ROADS UNDER CONSTRUCTION
MAJOR ROADS PROPOSED
GRADIENT 1:5(20%) & STEEPER (Ascent in direction of arrow)
TOLL — TOLL
MILEAGE BETWEEN MARKERS — 8
RAILWAY AND STATION
LEVEL CROSSING AND TUNNEL
RIVER OR CANAL
COUNTY OR UNITARY AUTHORITY BOUNDARY
NATIONAL BOUNDARY
BUILT-UP AREA
VILLAGE OR HAMLET
WOODED AREA
SPOT HEIGHT IN FEET — • 813
HEIGHT ABOVE SEA LEVEL
400' - 1,000' — 122m - 305m
1,000' - 1,400' — 305m - 427m
1,400' - 2,000' — 427m - 610m
2,000'+ — 610m +
NATIONAL GRID REFERENCE (Kilometres) — 100
AREA COVERED BY TOWN PLAN — SEE PAGE 67

TOURIST INFORMATION

AIRPORT
AIRFIELD
HELIPORT
BATTLE SITE AND DATE — 1066
CASTLE (Open to Public)
CASTLE WITH GARDEN (Open to Public)
CATHEDRAL, ABBEY, CHURCH, FRIARY, PRIORY
COUNTRY PARK
FERRY (Vehicular)
(Foot only)
GARDEN (Open to Public)
GOLF COURSE — 9 HOLE — 18 HOLE
HISTORIC BUILDING (Open to Public)
HISTORIC BUILDING WITH GARDEN (Open to Public)
HORSE RACECOURSE
INFORMATION CENTRE
LIGHTHOUSE
MOTOR RACING CIRCUIT
MUSEUM, ART GALLERY
NATIONAL PARK OR FOREST PARK
NATIONAL TRUST PROPERTY (Open) — NT
(Restricted Opening) — NT
(National Trust of Scotland) — NTS NTS
NATURE RESERVE OR BIRD SANCTUARY
NATURE TRAIL OR FOREST WALK
PLACE OF INTEREST — Monument •
PICNIC SITE
RAILWAY, STEAM OR NARROW GAUGE
THEME PARK
VIEWPOINT
WILDLIFE PARK
WINDMILL
ZOO OR SAFARI PARK

SCALE

1:158,400
2.5 Miles to 1 Inch

Geographers' A-Z Map Company Ltd

Head Office : (General Enquiries & Trade Sales)
Fairfield Road, Borough Green, Sevenoaks,
Kent TN15 8PP Telephone: 01732 781000

Showrooms : (Retail Sales)
44 Gray's Inn Road, London, WC1X 8HX
Telephone: 020 7440 9500
www.a-zmaps.co.uk

Edition 6 2002

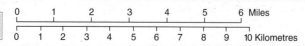

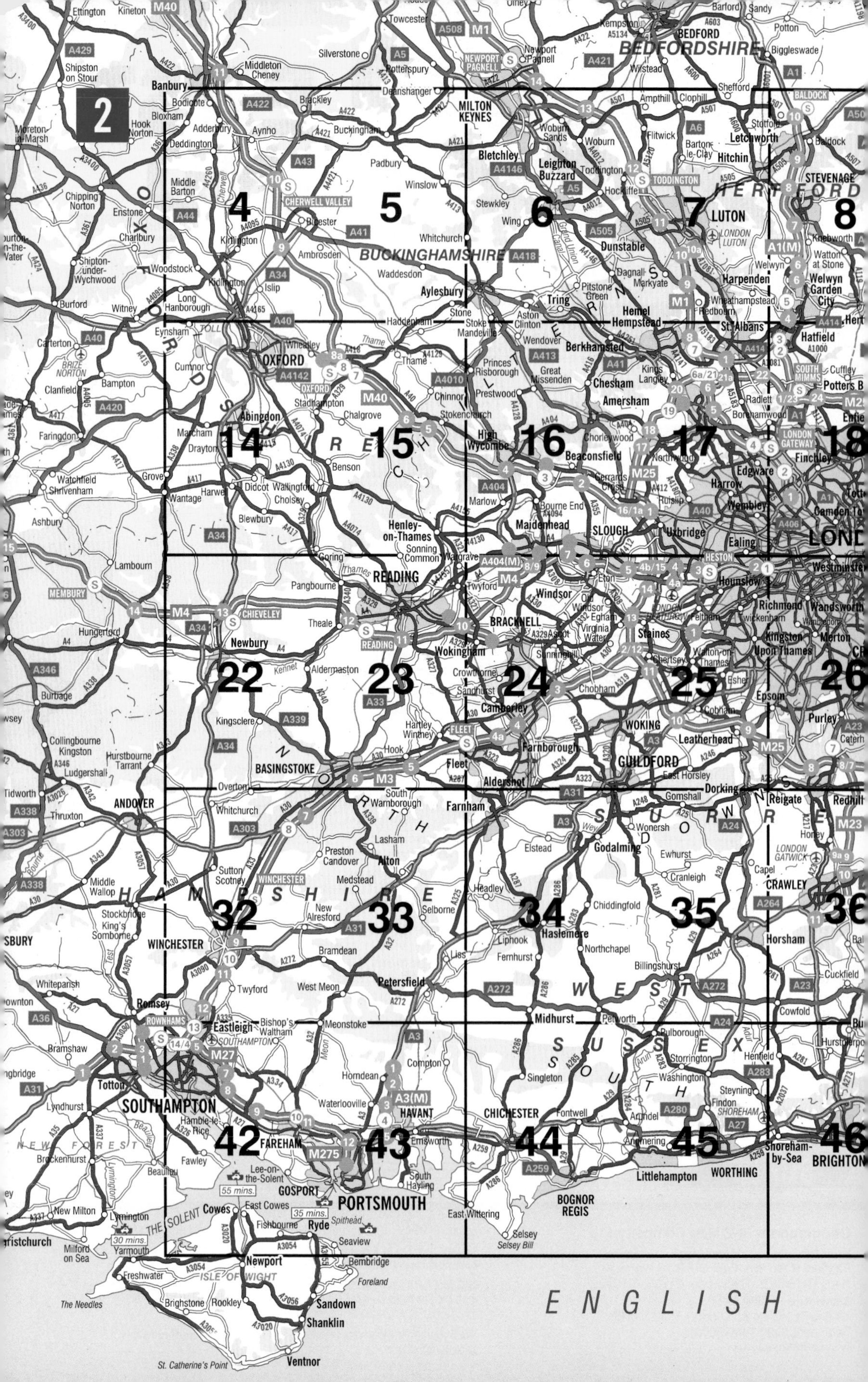

2
4
5
6
7
8
14
15
16
17
18
22
23
24
25
26
32
33
34
35
36
42
43
44
45
46
BEDFORDSHIRE
BUCKINGHAMSHIRE
HERTFORD
OXFORDSHIRE
HAMPSHIRE
NORTH
CHILTERNS
NORTH DOWNS
SOUTH DOWNS
WEST SUSSEX
ISLE OF WIGHT
NEW FOREST
THE SOLENT
Spithead
ENGLISH
Ettington
Kineton
Towcester
Olney
Kempston
Bedford
Barford
Sandy
Potton
Biggleswade
Shipston on Stour
Banbury
Middleton Cheney
Silverstone
Potterspury
Newport Pagnell
Wilstead
Deanshanger
Brackley
Milton Keynes
Shefford
Ampthill
Clophill
Baldock
Moreton-in-Marsh
Bodicote
Bloxham
Hook Norton
Adderbury
Deddington
Aynho
Buckingham
Woburn Sands
Woburn
Flitwick
Barton-le-Clay
Letchworth
Hitchin
Stotfold
Stevenage
Chipping Norton
Middle Barton
Padbury
Winslow
Bletchley
Leighton Buzzard
Toddington
Hockliffe
Enstone
Charlbury
Kirtlington
Bicester
Stewkley
Wing
Luton
Knebworth
Shipton-under-Wychwood
Woodstock
Ambrosden
Whitchurch
Dunstable
Watton at Stone
Welwyn
Welwyn Garden City
Harpenden
Burford
Witney
Long Hanborough
Kidlington
Islip
Waddesdon
Aylesbury
Dagnall
Markyate
Wheathampstead
Tring
Pitstone Green
Stone
Aston Clinton
Haddenham
Stoke Mandeville
Hemel Hempstead
Redbourn
St. Albans
Hatfield
Eynsham
Carterton
Brize Norton
Cumnor
Wheatley
Oxford
Thame
Wendover
Princes Risborough
Berkhamsted
Great Missenden
Kings Langley
Chesham
Potters Bar
Cuffley
Clanfield
Bampton
Stadhampton
Chinnor
Prestwood
Amersham
Radlett
Borehamwood
Faringdon
Abingdon
Chalgrove
Stokenchurch
High Wycombe
Chorleywood
Beaconsfield
Northwood
Finchley
Marcham
Drayton
Watchfield
Shrivenham
Grove
Wantage
Harwell
Didcot
Wallingford
Cholsey
Benson
Marlow
Gerrards Cross
Edgware
Harrow
Wembley
Ruislip
Camden Town
Ashbury
Blewbury
Henley-on-Thames
Bourne End
Maidenhead
Slough
Uxbridge
Ealing
London
Lambourn
Goring
Sonning Common
Wargrave
Reading
Pangbourne
Twyford
Windsor
Eton
Old Windsor
Hounslow
Westminster
Richmond
Wandsworth
Hungerford
Newbury
Theale
Bracknell
Ascot
Egham
Virginia Water
Staines
Feltham
Twickenham
Kingston Upon Thames
Merton
Wokingham
Sunninghill
Chertsey
Walton-on-Thames
Burbage
Aldermaston
Crowthorne
Sandhurst
Camberley
Chobham
Esher
Epsom
Kingsclere
Hartley Wintney
Woking
Cobham
Purley
Collingbourne Kingston
Hurstbourne Tarrant
Basingstoke
Hook
Fleet
Farnborough
Guildford
Leatherhead
Ludgershall
Tidworth
Aldershot
East Horsley
Dorking
Reigate
Redhill
Andover
Overton
South Warnborough
Farnham
Gomshall
Thruxton
Whitchurch
Wonersh
Horley
Lasham
Elstead
Godalming
Ewhurst
Capel
Preston Candover
Alton
Cranleigh
Crawley
Middle Wallop
Sutton Scotney
Medstead
Headley
Chiddingfold
Stockbridge
King's Somborne
New Alresford
Selborne
Haslemere
Horsham
Winchester
Bramdean
Liphook
Fernhurst
Northchapel
Billingshurst
Cuckfield
Whiteparish
Twyford
West Meon
Petersfield
Romsey
Eastleigh
Bishop's Waltham
Meonstoke
Midhurst
Petworth
Cowfold
Bramshaw
Pulborough
Storrington
Henfield
Hurstpierpoint
Totton
Southampton
Horndean
Compton
Singleton
Washington
Steyning
Lyndhurst
Hamble-le-Rice
Waterlooville
Havant
Chichester
Fontwell
Arundel
Findon
Shoreham
Brockenhurst
Fareham
Emsworth
Angmering
Fawley
Beaulieu
Lee-on-the-Solent
Gosport
Portsmouth
South Hayling
Littlehampton
Worthing
Shoreham-by-Sea
Brighton
Bognor Regis
New Milton
Lymington
Cowes
East Cowes
Fishbourne
Ryde
Seaview
East Wittering
Selsey
Selsey Bill
Christchurch
Milford on Sea
Yarmouth
Newport
Bembridge
Freshwater
Foreland
The Needles
Brighstone
Rookley
Sandown
Shanklin
Ventnor
St. Catherine's Point
55 mins.
35 mins.
30 mins.
M40
M1
M4
M3
M25
M27
M275
A3(M)
A1(M)
A404(M)
Cherwell Valley
Toddington
Chieveley
Membury
Reading
Fleet
Winchester
Rownhams
Heston
South Mimms
London Gateway
Baldock
Newport Pagnell
Oxford
London Luton
London Heathrow
London Gatwick
Grand Union Canal
Thames
Kennet
Cherwell
Test
Meon
Arun
Wey

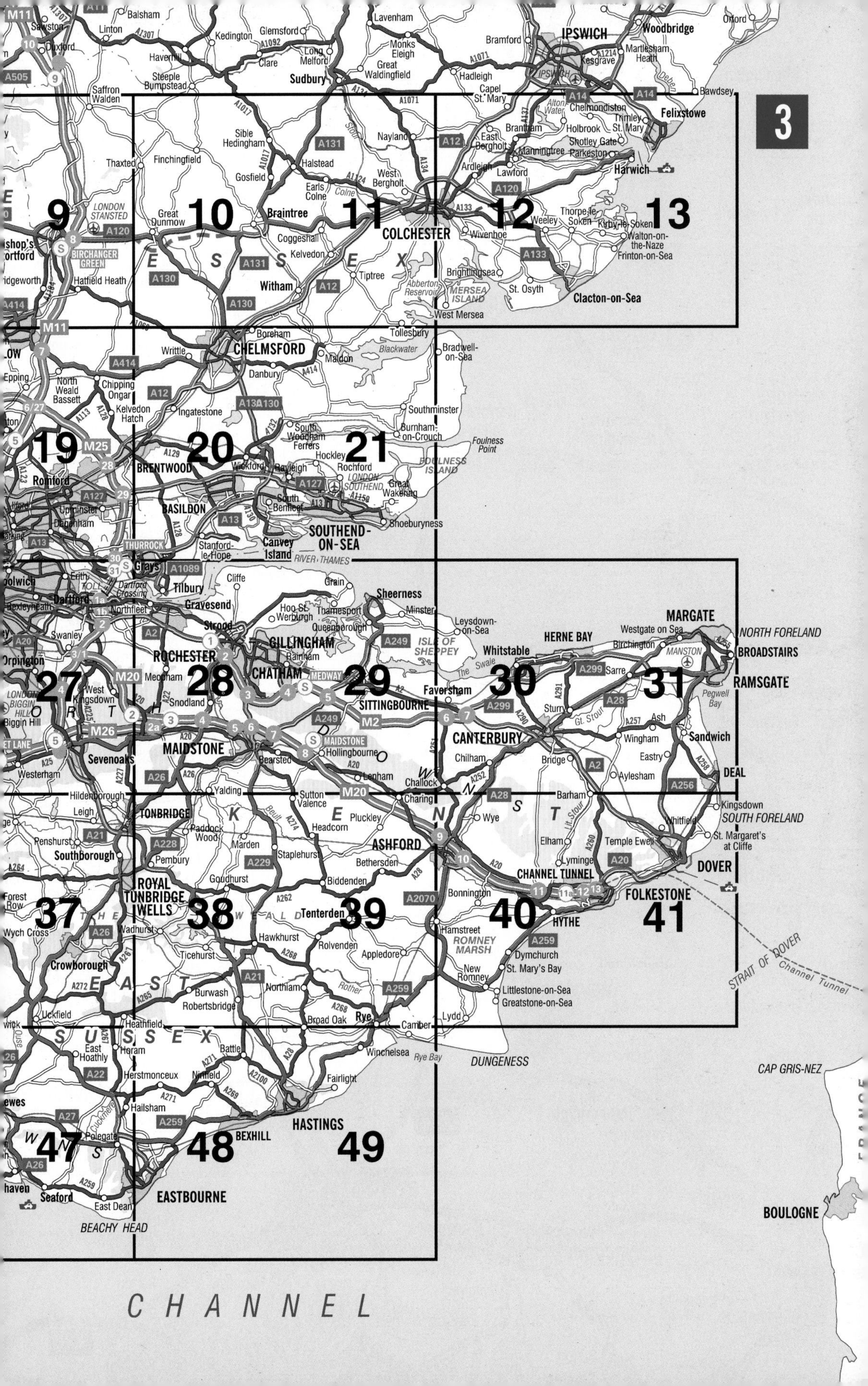

3

CHANNEL

IPSWICH · Woodbridge · Orford · Bramford · Kesgrave · Martlesham Heath
Balsham · Linton · Kedington · Glemsford · Lavenham · Hadleigh · Capel St. Mary · Bawdsey · Felixstowe
Sawston · Duxford · Haverhill · Long Melford · Monks Eleigh · Great Waldingfield · Alton Water · Chelmondiston · Trimley St. Mary · Shotley Gate · Parkeston

9 · **10** · **11** · COLCHESTER · **12** · **13**

Thaxted · Finchingfield · Sible Hedingham · Halstead · West Bergholt · East Bergholt · Brantham · Manningtree · Lawford · Harwich
Saffron Walden · Steeple Bumpstead · Gosfield · Earls Colne · Nayland · Ardleigh · Wivenhoe · Weeley · Thorpe-le-Soken · Kirby-le-Soken · Walton-on-the-Naze
Bishop's Stortford · BIRCHANGER GREEN · Great Dunmow · Braintree · Coggeshall · Kelvedon · Tiptree · Brightlingsea · St. Osyth · Frinton-on-Sea
Hatfield Heath · Witham · Mersea Island · West Mersea · Clacton-on-Sea

Boreham · Tollesbury · Blackwater · Bradwell-on-Sea
CHELMSFORD · Maldon · Southminster
Writtle · Danbury · Burnham-on-Crouch · Foulness Point

19 · BRENTWOOD **20** · **21**

Romford · Ingatestone · South Woodham Ferrers · Hockley · Rochford · Great Wakering
Upminster · BASILDON · Wickford · Rayleigh · SOUTHEND · Shoeburyness
Stanford-le-Hope · South Benfleet · Canvey Island · SOUTHEND-ON-SEA
THURROCK · Grays · RIVER THAMES

Tilbury · Cliffe · Grain · Sheerness · MARGATE · NORTH FORELAND
Gravesend · Strood · Hoo St. Werburgh · Thamesport · Minster · Leysdown-on-Sea · Westgate on Sea · Birchington · BROADSTAIRS
Dartford Crossing · ROCHESTER · GILLINGHAM · Queenborough · ISLE OF SHEPPEY · Whitstable · HERNE BAY · MANSTON
Swanley · CHATHAM · Rainham · The Swale · Faversham · Sarre · RAMSGATE
Orpington · **27** · Meopham · **28** · **29** · Faversham · **30** · **31** · Pegwell Bay
West Kingsdown · Snodland · SITTINGBOURNE · Sturry · Wingham · Sandwich
BIGGIN HILL · Sevenoaks · MAIDSTONE · Hollingbourne · CANTERBURY · Chilham · Bridge · Aylesham · DEAL
Westerham · Bearsted · Lenham · Challock · Barham · Kingsdown · SOUTH FORELAND
Hildenborough · Yalding · Sutton Valence · Charing · Wye · Elham · Whitfield · St. Margaret's at Cliffe
TONBRIDGE · Paddock Wood · Pluckley · Headcorn · Lyminge · Temple Ewell
Leigh · Pembury · Marden · Staplehurst · ASHFORD · CHANNEL TUNNEL · DOVER
Southborough · ROYAL TUNBRIDGE WELLS · Goudhurst · Biddenden · Bethersden · Bonnington · FOLKESTONE
37 · **38** · **39** · **40** · HYTHE · **41**
Forest Row · Wych Cross · Tenterden · Hamstreet · ROMNEY MARSH · Dymchurch · STRAIT OF DOVER
Crowborough · Wadhurst · Hawkhurst · Rolvenden · Appledore · St. Mary's Bay · New Romney · Littlestone-on-Sea · Greatstone-on-Sea
Ticehurst · Northiam · Rother · Lydd
Uckfield · Burwash · Robertsbridge · Broad Oak · Rye · Camber · DUNGENESS
Heathfield · Battle · Winchelsea · Rye Bay · CAP GRIS-NEZ
Lewes · Horam · Herstmonceux · Ninfield · Fairlight
East Hoathly · Hailsham · HASTINGS · FRANCE
47 · **48** BEXHILL · **49**
Seaford · East Dean · EASTBOURNE · BOULOGNE
Newhaven · BEACHY HEAD

C H A N N E L

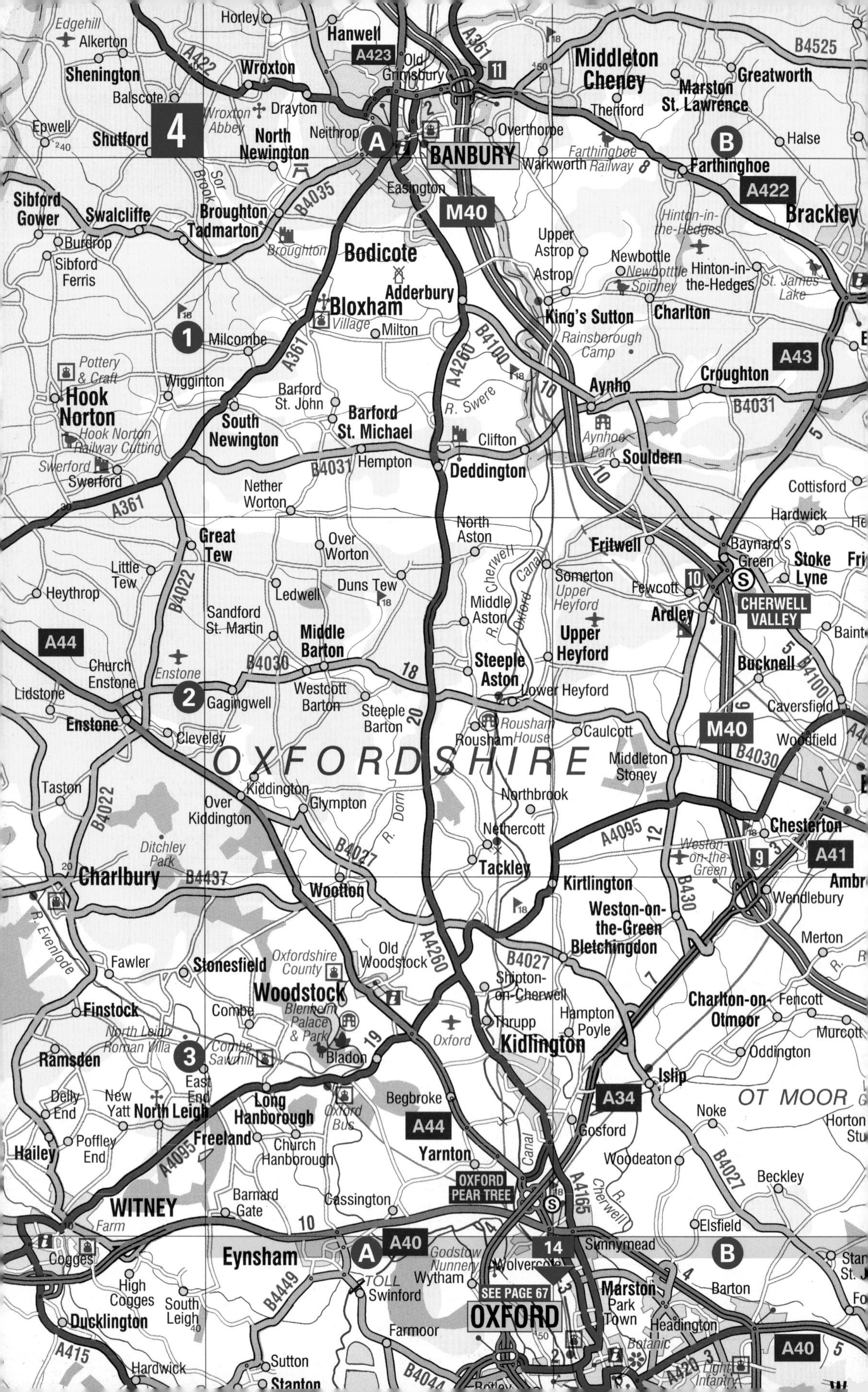

Edgehill
Horley
Hanwell
Alkerton
A422
Wroxton
A423
Old Grimsbury
A361
11
Middleton Cheney
B4525
Greatworth
Shenington
Balscote
Drayton
Marston St. Lawrence
Thenford
4
Wroxton Abbey
Epwell
Shutford
North Newington
Neithrop
A
Overthorpe
B
Halse
BANBURY
Warkworth
Farthinghoe Railway
Farthinghoe
A422
Sor Brook
Easington
Sibford Gower
Swalcliffe
Broughton
Tadmarton
B4035
M40
Brackley
Burdrop
Broughton
Bodicote
Upper Astrop
Hinton-in-the-Hedges
Sibford Ferris
Newbottle
Newbottle Spinney
Hinton-in-the-Hedges
St. James Lake
Astrop
Adderbury
Bloxham
King's Sutton
Charlton
Village
Milton
Rainsborough Camp
1
Milcombe
B4100
A43
A361
A4260
Pottery & Craft
Wigginton
Croughton
Aynho
Hook Norton
Barford St. John
R. Swere
B4031
Barford St. Michael
Aynhoe Park
South Newington
Hook Norton Railway Cutting
Clifton
Souldern
Swerford
Hempton
B4031
Swerford
Deddington
Nether Worton
Cottisford
A361
Hardwick
North Aston
Great Tew
Over Worton
Fritwell
Baynard's Green
Stoke Lyne
Little Tew
Somerton
Heythrop
Ledwell
Duns Tew
Fewcott
10
CHERWELL VALLEY
Upper Heyford
Sandford St. Martin
Middle Aston
Ardley
R. Cherwell
Oxford Canal
A44
Middle Barton
Upper Heyford
B4030
Steeple Aston
Bucknell
Church Enstone
Enstone
B4100
Lidstone
2
Gagingwell
Westcott Barton
Lower Heyford
Caversfield
Steeple Barton
Enstone
Rousham House
M40
Rousham
Caulcott
Woodfield
Cleveley
B4030
OXFORDSHIRE
Middleton Stoney
Taston
Kiddington
Northbrook
Over Kiddington
Glympton
B4022
R. Dorn
Nethercott
A4095
Chesterton
Ditchley Park
B4027
Weston-on-the-Green
A41
Tackley
Charlbury
B4437
Kirtlington
Wootton
B430
Wendlebury
R. Evenlode
Weston-on-the-Green
Bletchingdon
Old Woodstock
A4260
Merton
Oxfordshire County
Fawler
Stonesfield
B4027
Woodstock
Shipton-on-Cherwell
Finstock
Combe
Blenheim Palace & Park
Hampton Poyle
Charlton-on-Otmoor
Fencott
North Leigh Roman Villa
Thrupp
Murcott
Oxford
Kidlington
Oddington
Ramsden
3
Combe Sawmill
Bladon
East End
Islip
Delly End
New Yatt
North Leigh
Long Hanborough
Begbroke
A34
OT MOOR
Oxford Bus
Noke
Hailey
Poffley End
A4095
Freeland
Church Hanborough
A44
Gosford
Yarnton
Woodeaton
B4027
OXFORD PEAR TREE
Beckley
A4165
R. Cherwell
Barnard Gate
Cassington
WITNEY
Farm
Elsfield
A
A40
14
Sunnymead
B
Cogges
Eynsham
Godstow Nunnery
Wolvercote
TOLL
Wytham
Marston
Barton
High Cogges
Swinford
SEE PAGE 67
B4449
South Leigh
Park Town
Headington
Ducklington
OXFORD
Botanic
Farmoor
A40
A415
Sutton
A420
Light Infantry
Hardwick
Stanton
B4044

Hazelborough Wood
A43
Syresham
Brackley Hatch
Silverstone
A413
Potterspury
A5
Cosgrove
Cosgrove Park
Haversham
NEWPORT PAGNELL
Great Linford
Lillingstone Lovell
Old Stratford
5
Wolverton
A422
C
D
Whitfield
Biddlesden
Lillingstone Dayrell
Deanshanger
Wicken
Passenham
Stony Stratford
Bradwell
Dadford
Turweston
Calverton
A5
Loughton
Stowe
Akeley
Leckhampstead
Upper Weald
Shalstone
NT Stowe
Foxcote Res.
Great Ouse
Beachampton
Shenley Church End
Equestrian Centre
Chackmore
Maid's Moreton
Thornton
Shenley Brook End
Milton Keynes Bowl
A422
Buffler's Holt
River
Water Stratford
Old Gaol
Chantry Chapel NT
1
Buckingham
Nash
BLETCHLEY
Radclive
Thornborough Bridge
Thornborough
Whaddon
Finmere
Tingewick
A421
12
A421
B4034
University College
Mount Pleasant
Singleborough
Finmere
Gawcott
Great Horwood
Little Horwood
Barton Hartshorn
Newton Purcell
Padbury
Adstock
B4033
A4421
Chetwode
Norbury
Preston Bissett
A413
Addington
Drayton Parslow
Hillesden
Church
Mursley
Claydon
Winslow Hall
Winslow
Steeple Claydon
Shipton
6
Swanbourne
Stratton Audley
Twyford
Middle Claydon
Brook
Stewkley Dean
Poundon
Calvert Jubilee
East Claydon
NT
2
Hoggeston
Grebe Lake
Calvert
Granborough
Littlecote
Charndon
Claydon House
Botolph Claydon
Dunton
Marsh Gibbon
North Marston
Launton
Edgcott
Cublington
BUCKINGHAMSHIRE
Grendon Underwood
Oving
Whitchurch
Quainton
Bolebec
Pitchcott
Aston Abbots
Blackthorn
Kingswood
Hardwick
B4011
A41
Buckinghamshire Railway Centre
A418
Ludgershall
Weedon
Piddington
Westcott
Waddesdon
The Lake
Wotton House
NT
Wotton Underwood
Waddesdon Manor
Duck Decoy
Boarstall Decoy
Pushreeds Wood
Bierton
Quarrendon
Upper Winchendon
3
NT Boarstall
NT Tower
Dorton
Ashendon
Dorton House
Brill
Pollicott
AYLESBURY
Grand
Little London
Nether Winchendon House
Lower Winchendon
Stone
Oakley
Dinton Castle
County
Southcourt
Weston Turville
Cuddington
Upton
A413
B4443
Chilton
Gibraltar
Dinton
Stoke Mandeville
Westlington
Easington
Chearsley
Buckinghamshire Goat Centre
A418
Bishopstone
15
C
D
Long Crendon
Courthouse
Thame
Ford
Marsh
Nash Lee
Worminghall
Haddenham
Aston Sandford
Kimble Wick
North Lee
Terrick
M40
Ickford
A4010
B4011
Waterperry
Shabbington
Thame
Kingsey
Owlswick
Little Kimble
Ellesborough
Waterstock
North Weston
Meadle
Great

MILTON KEYNES
SEE PAGE 67
BLETCHLEY
AYLESBURY
BUCKINGHAMSHIRE
NEWPORT PAGNELL
Wolverton
Stony Stratford
Woburn Sands
Leighton Buzzard
Linslade
Tring
Wendover
BERKHAMSTED
Winslow
Haddenham
Waddesdon
Woburn
Aspley Guise
Cranfield
Stoke Mandeville
Aston Clinton
Cheddington
Ivinghoe
Wing
Soulbury
Stewkley
Swanbourne
Whitchurch
Quainton
Wingrave
Weedon
Buckland
Halton
Weston Turville
Marsworth
Wilstone
Aldbury
Wigginton
Eaton Bray
Edlesborough
Newton Longville
Stoke Hammond
Great Horwood
Little Horwood
Thornborough
Nash
Whaddon
Old Stratford
Cosgrove
Haversham
Great Linford
Moulsoe
Broughton
Salford
Wavendon
Ridgmont
Husborne Crawley
Bow Brickhill
Fenny Stratford
Little Brickhill
Great Brickhill
Heath and Reach
Hockliffe
Eggington
Tilsworth
Stanbridge
Billington
Slapton
Mentmore
Horton
Ledburn
Crafton
Hollingdon
Stewkley Dean
Mursley
Drayton Parslow
Hoggeston
Dunton
Littlecote
Burcott
Cublington
Aston Abbots
Granborough
North Marston
Oving
Pitchcott
Hardwick
Rowsham
Hulcott
Bierton
Quarrendon
Puttenham
Long Marston
Gubblecote
Pitstone
Bulbourne
New Mill
Upper Dunsley
Drayton Beauchamp
West Leith
Hastoe
Cholesbury
St. Leonards
Buckland
Kingsash
Ellesborough
Terrick
Nash Lee
North Lee
Little Kimble
Kimble Wick
Marsh
Bishopstone
Meadle
Owlswick
Aston Sandford
Ford
Westlington
Dinton
Upton
Gibraltar
Stone
Southcourt
Shipton
Calverton
Upper Weald
Beachampton
Thornton
Passenham
Loughton
Shenley Church End
Shenley Brook End
Bradwell
Willen
Milton Keynes Village
Walton
Aspley Heath
Birchmoor Green
Froxfield
Potsgrove
Battlesden
Brogborough
Milton Bryan
Tebworth
Northall
Ivinghoe Aston
Dagnall
Ringshall
Singleborough
A5
A508
A509
A421
A422
A413
A41
A418
A4146
A4012
A5130
A505
A4010
A507
A4157
A4251
B4032
B4033
B4034
B488
B489
B4443
B4544
B4009
B4506
B486
6
16
5

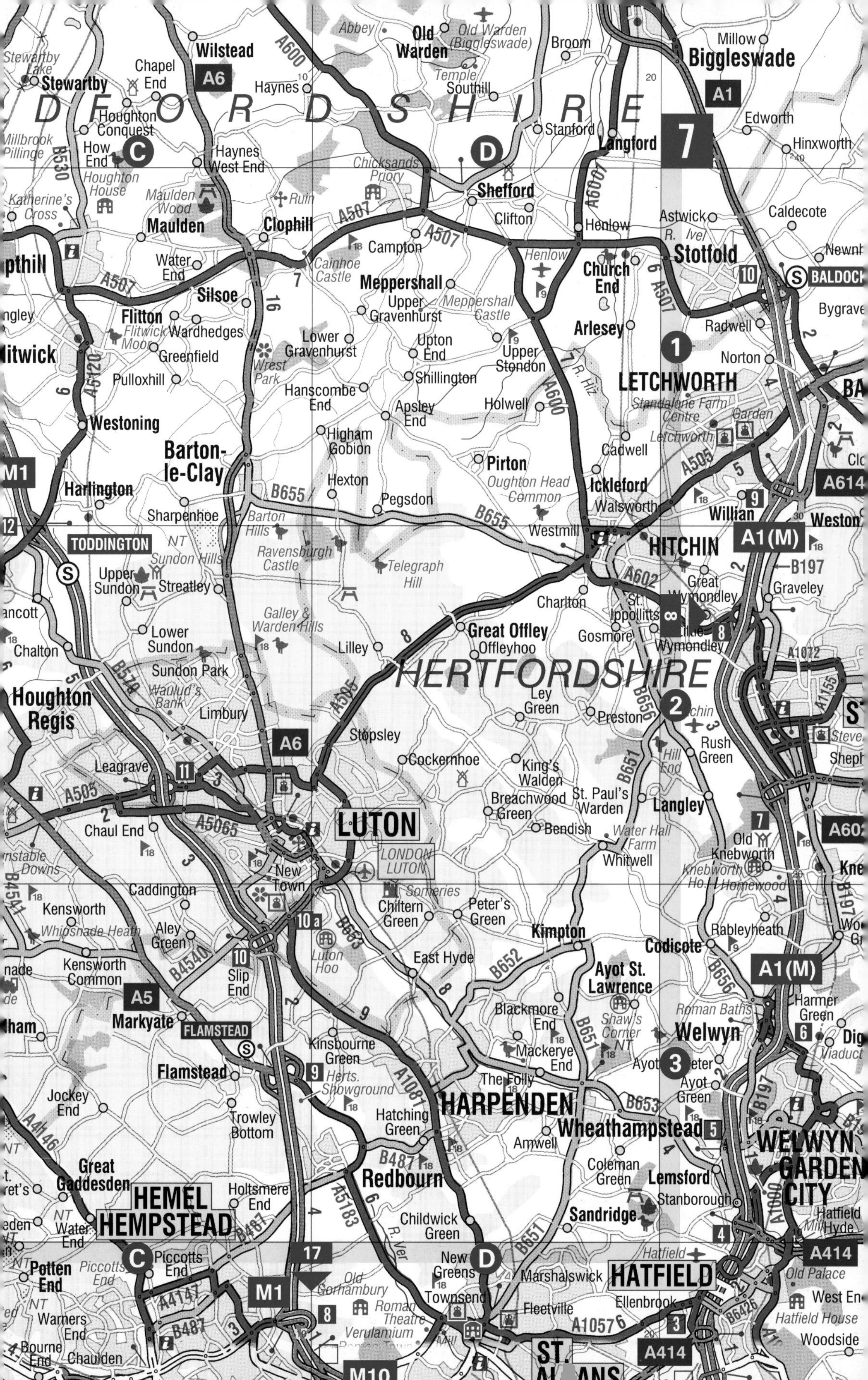

BEDFORDSHIRE
HERTFORDSHIRE
7
Stewartby Lake
Stewartby
Chapel End
Wilstead
A6
A600
Haynes
Abbey
Old Warden
Old Warden (Biggleswade)
Broom
Temple
Southill
Millow
Biggleswade
A1
Edworth
Hinxworth
Houghton Conquest
Millbrook
Pillinge
How End
C
Houghton House
Haynes West End
Stanford
Langford
D
Chicksands Priory
Ruin
Shefford
Maulden Wood
Katherine's Cross
Maulden
Clophill
A507
Clifton
A6001
Henlow
Astwick
R. Ivel
Caldecote
Newnham
Campton
Henlow
Stotfold
10
BALDOCK
Church End
Water End
Cainhoe Castle
Meppershall
Arlesey
Ampthill
Silsoe
16
Upper Gravenhurst
Meppershall Castle
Bygrave
Flitton
Wardhedges
Radwell
Flitwick Moor
Lower Gravenhurst
Upton End
Upper Stondon
1
Norton
Flitwick
Greenfield
Wrest Park
Shillington
R. Hiz
LETCHWORTH
A5120
Pulloxhill
Hanscombe End
Holwell
Standalone Farm Centre
Garden
Westoning
Apsley End
Letchworth
Higham Gobion
Barton-le-Clay
Pirton
Cadwell
A505
M1
Hexton
Oughton Head Common
Ickleford
A6141
Harlington
B655
Pegsdon
Walsworth
9
William
Weston
Sharpenhoe
Barton Hills
12
TODDINGTON
NT
Sundon Hills
Westmill
HITCHIN
A1(M)
Ravensburgh Castle
Telegraph Hill
B197
Upper Sundon
Streatley
A602
Great Wymondley
Graveley
Charlton
St. Ippollitts
Chalton
Galley & Warden Hills
Great Offley
Lower Sundon
Lilley
Offleyhoo
Gosmore
Little Wymondley
A1072
Sundon Park
Houghton Regis
Waulud's Bank
HERTFORDSHIRE
B579
Ley Green
Limbury
Preston
2
B656
A1155
Stopsley
Rush Green
Stevenage
Shephall
Leagrave
11
Cockernhoe
King's Walden
Hill End
B651
A505
Breachwood Green
St. Paul's Walden
Langley
Chaul End
A5065
LUTON
Bendish
Water Hall Farm
Old Knebworth
A602
Dunstable Downs
LONDON LUTON
Whitwell
Knebworth
New Town
Knebworth Ho.
Homewood
Caddington
Someries
Kensworth
Chiltern Green
Peter's Green
Rableyheath
Whipsnade Heath
Aley Green
10 a
B653
Kimpton
Codicote
B4541
Luton Hoo
Kensworth Common
B4540
East Hyde
Ayot St. Lawrence
B652
Slip End
Harmer Green
A5
B656
Roman Baths
Blackmore End
Shaw's Corner
Markyate
FLAMSTEAD
Kinsbourne Green
Welwyn
Digswell Viaduct
Mackerye End
Ayot St. Peter
3
Flamstead
Herts. Showground
The Folly
Ayot Green
A1081
HARPENDEN
B653
Jockey End
Trowley Bottom
Hatching Green
Wheathampstead
5
A4146
Amwell
WELWYN GARDEN CITY
Great Gaddesden
B487
Redbourn
Coleman Green
Lemsford
Holtsmere End
HEMEL HEMPSTEAD
A5183
Stanborough
Water End
Childwick Green
Sandridge
Hatfield Hyde
A1000
R. Ver
Potten End
Piccotts End
17
New Greens
Hatfield
A414
M1
Old Gorhambury
Marshalswick
HATFIELD
Old Palace
A4147
Townsend
Ellenbrook
West End
Warners End
Roman Theatre
Fleetville
A1057
Hatfield House
B487
8
Verulamium
B6426
Bourne End
Chaulden
ST. ALBANS
A414
Woodside
M10

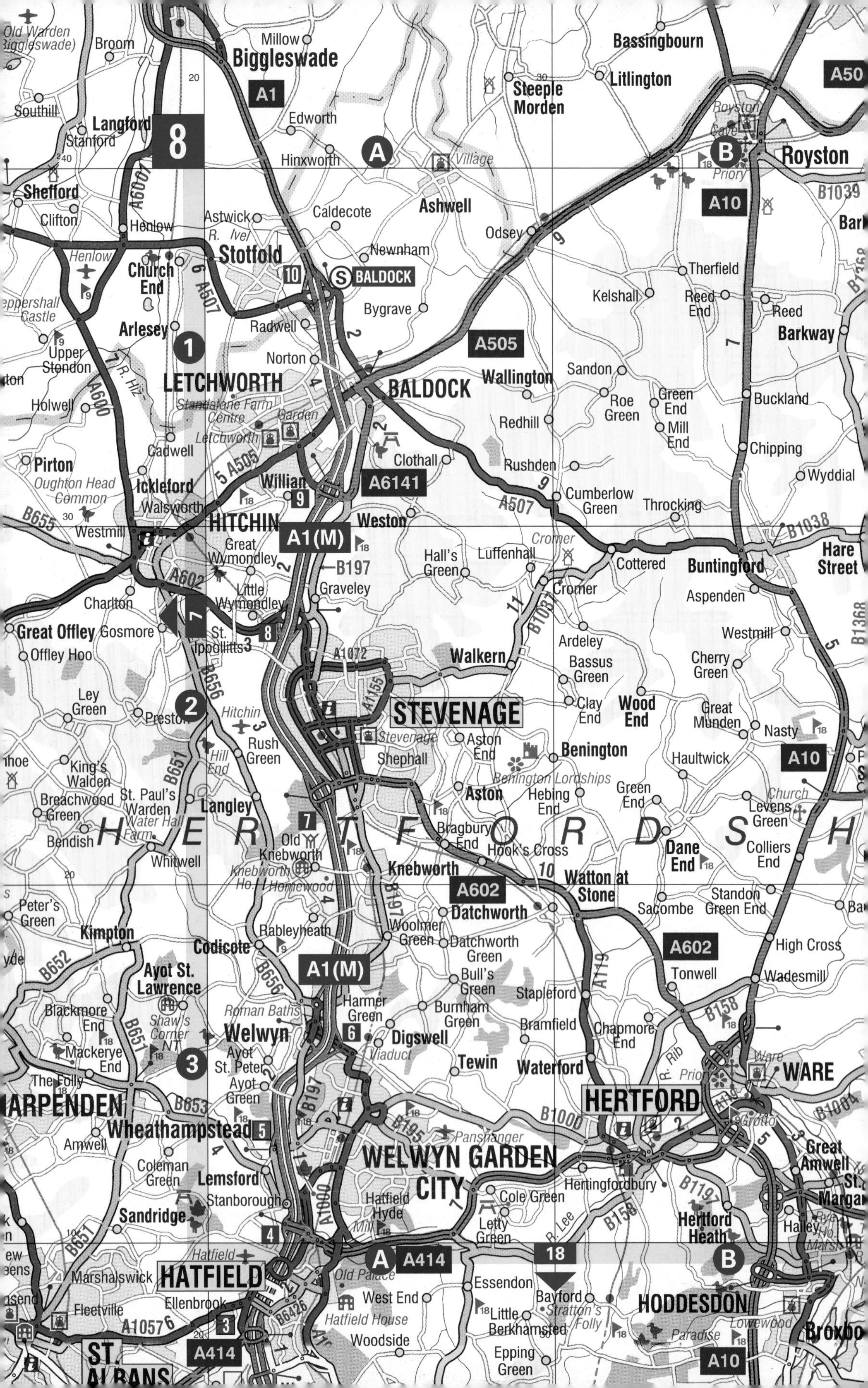

Biggleswade
Millow
Broom
Old Warden
Southill
Langford
Stanford
Shefford
Clifton
Henlow
Edworth
Hinxworth
Caldecote
Astwick
Stotfold
Church End
Arlesey
Radwell
Norton
Newnham
BALDOCK
Bygrave
Ashwell
Steeple Morden
Bassingbourn
Litlington
Royston
Odsey
Therfield
Kelshall
Reed End
Reed
Barkway
Sandon
Wallington
Roe Green
Green End
Mill End
Buckland
Chipping
Wyddial
Redhill
Rushden
Cumberlow Green
Throcking
LETCHWORTH
Upper Stondon
Holwell
Pirton
Cadwell
Ickleford
Walsworth
HITCHIN
Westmill
William
Clothall
Weston
Great Wymondley
Little Wymondley
Charlton
Great Offley
Gosmore
Offley Hoo
St. Ippollitts
Graveley
Hall's Green
Luffenhall
Cottered
Cromer
Buntingford
Hare Street
Aspenden
Westmill
Ardeley
Walkern
Bassus Green
Clay End
Wood End
Cherry Green
Great Munden
Nasty
STEVENAGE
Ley Green
Preston
Rush Green
Shephall
Aston End
Aston
Benington
Haultwick
King's Walden
Breachwood Green
St. Paul's Walden
Langley
Bendish
Whitwell
Hebing End
Green End
Levens Green
Bragbury End
Hook's Cross
Old Knebworth
Knebworth
Dane End
Colliers End
Watton at Stone
Standon Green End
Sacombe
Peter's Green
Kimpton
Codicote
Rableyheath
Woolmer Green
Datchworth
Datchworth Green
High Cross
Wadesmill
Tonwell
Ayot St. Lawrence
Blackmore End
Mackerye End
Harmer Green
Bull's Green
Burnham Green
Stapleford
Welwyn
Digswell
Bramfield
Chapmore End
Ayot St. Peter
Ayot Green
Tewin
Waterford
WARE
The Folly
HARPENDEN
Wheathampstead
HERTFORD
Great Amwell
Amwell
Coleman Green
Lemsford
Stanborough
WELWYN GARDEN CITY
Hatfield Hyde
Hertingfordbury
Cole Green
Letty Green
Sandridge
Hertford Heath
HATFIELD
Marshalswick
Essendon
West End
Bayford
HODDESDON
Ellenbrook
Fleetville
Little Berkhamsted
Woodside
Epping Green
ST. ALBANS
Broxbourne
HERTFORDSHIRE
A1
A1(M)
A10
A50
A505
A507
A600
A6001
A602
A6141
A1072
A1155
A1000
A119
A414
A1057
B197
B1039
B1038
B1368
B1037
B655
B656
B651
B652
B653
B158
B1000
B195
B1197
B1004
B6426
B1368

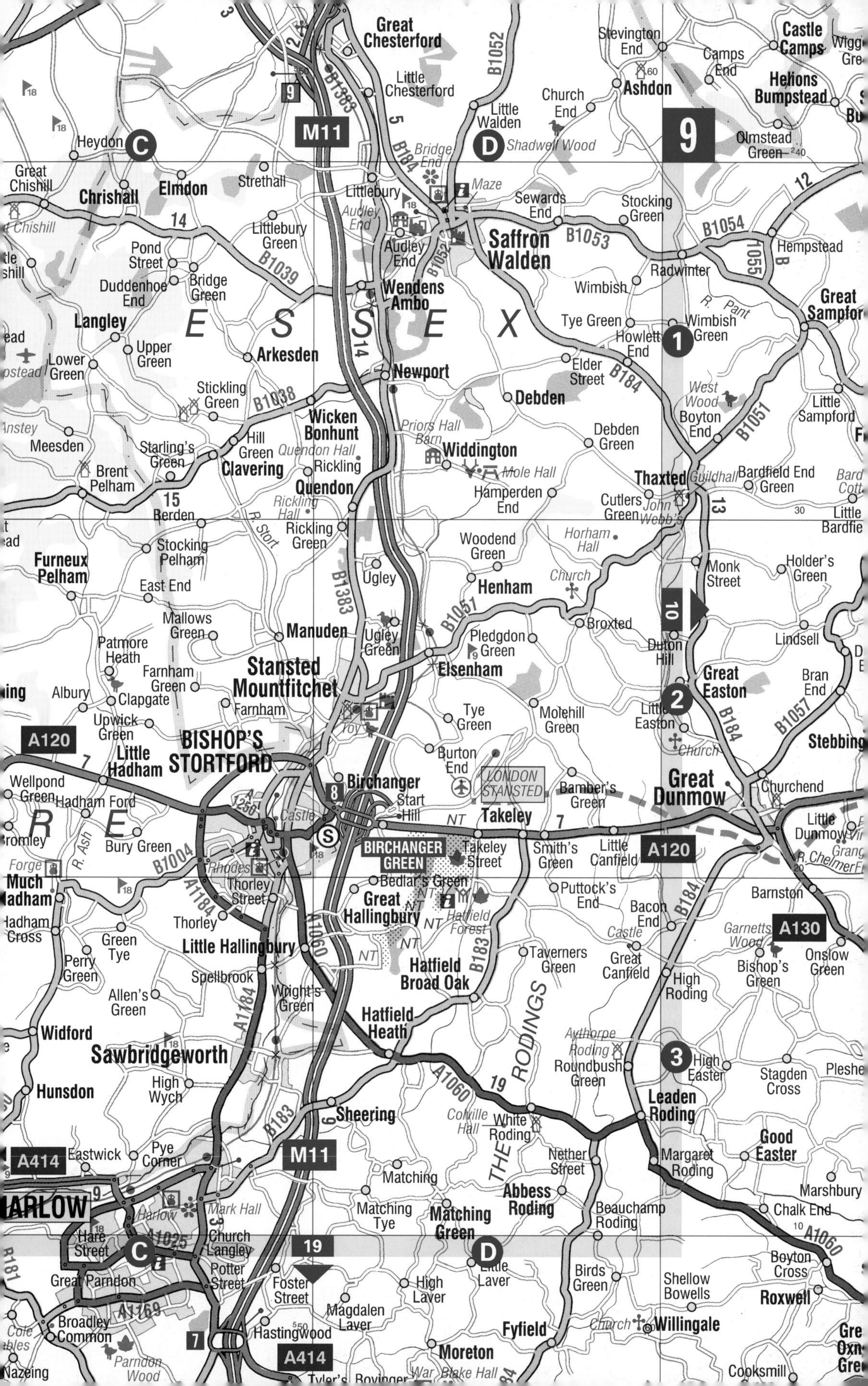

Great Chesterford
Little Chesterford
Stevington End
Ashdon
Castle Camps
Camps End
Helions Bumpstead
Church End
Little Walden
Shadwell Wood
Olmstead Green
Heydon
Great Chishill
Chrishall
Elmdon
Strethall
Littlebury
Audley End
Maze
Sewards End
Stocking Green
Saffron Walden
Hempstead
Radwinter
Littlebury Green
Pond Street
Duddenhoe End
Bridge Green
Wendens Ambo
Wimbish
Tye Green
Howlett End
Wimbish Green
Great Sampford
Langley
Upper Green
Lower Green
Arkesden
Newport
Elder Street
Debden
West Wood
Boyton End
Little Sampford
Stickling Green
Wicken Bonhunt
Priors Hall Barn
Widdington
Debden Green
Meesden
Hill Green
Starling's Green
Clavering
Quendon Hall
Rickling
Quendon
Brent Pelham
Mole Hall
Hamperden End
Thaxted
Guildhall
Bardfield End Green
Cutlers Green
John Webb's
Berden
Rickling Hall
Rickling Green
Horham Hall
Woodend Green
Furneux Pelham
Stocking Pelham
Ugley
Henham
Church
Monk Street
Holder's Green
East End
Mallows Green
Manuden
Ugley Green
Broxted
Pledgdon Green
Duton Hill
Lindsell
Patmore Heath
Albury
Farnham Green
Clapgate
Stansted Mountfitchet
Elsenham
Great Easton
Bran End
Farnham
Upwick Green
Tye Green
Molehill Green
Little Easton
Stebbing
Little Hadham
BISHOP'S STORTFORD
Burton End
LONDON STANSTED
Bamber's Green
Great Dunmow
Churchend
Wellpond Green
Hadham Ford
Birchanger
Start Hill
Takeley
Castle
Bury Green
BIRCHANGER GREEN
Takeley Street
Smith's Green
Little Canfield
Little Dunmow
Much Hadham
Rhodes
Thorley Street
Bedlar's Green
Puttock's End
Barnston
Hadham Cross
Thorley
Great Hallingbury
Hatfield Forest
Bacon End
Garnetts Wood
Green Tye
Little Hallingbury
Taverners Green
Great Canfield
Bishop's Green
Onslow Green
Perry Green
Spellbrook
Hatfield Broad Oak
High Roding
Allen's Green
Wright's Green
Widford
Hatfield Heath
Aythorpe Roding
Sawbridgeworth
High Easter
Roundbush Green
Stagden Cross
Pleshey
Hunsdon
High Wych
THE RODINGS
Leaden Roding
Sheering
Colville Hall
White Roding
Good Easter
Eastwick
Pye Corner
Nether Street
Margaret Roding
Matching
Marshbury
HARLOW
Mark Hall
Matching Tye
Matching Green
Abbess Roding
Beauchamp Roding
Chalk End
Hare Street
Church Langley
Great Parndon
Potter Street
Foster Street
High Laver
Little Laver
Birds Green
Boyton Cross
Shellow Bowells
Roxwell
Broadley Common
Magdalen Laver
Hastingwood
Fyfield
Willingale
Nazeing
Parndon Wood
Moreton
Blake Hall
Cooksmill
ESSEX
M11
A120
A130
A414
A1060
A1184
B184
B1383
B1052
B1053
B1054
B1039
B1038
B1051
B1057
B1004
B183

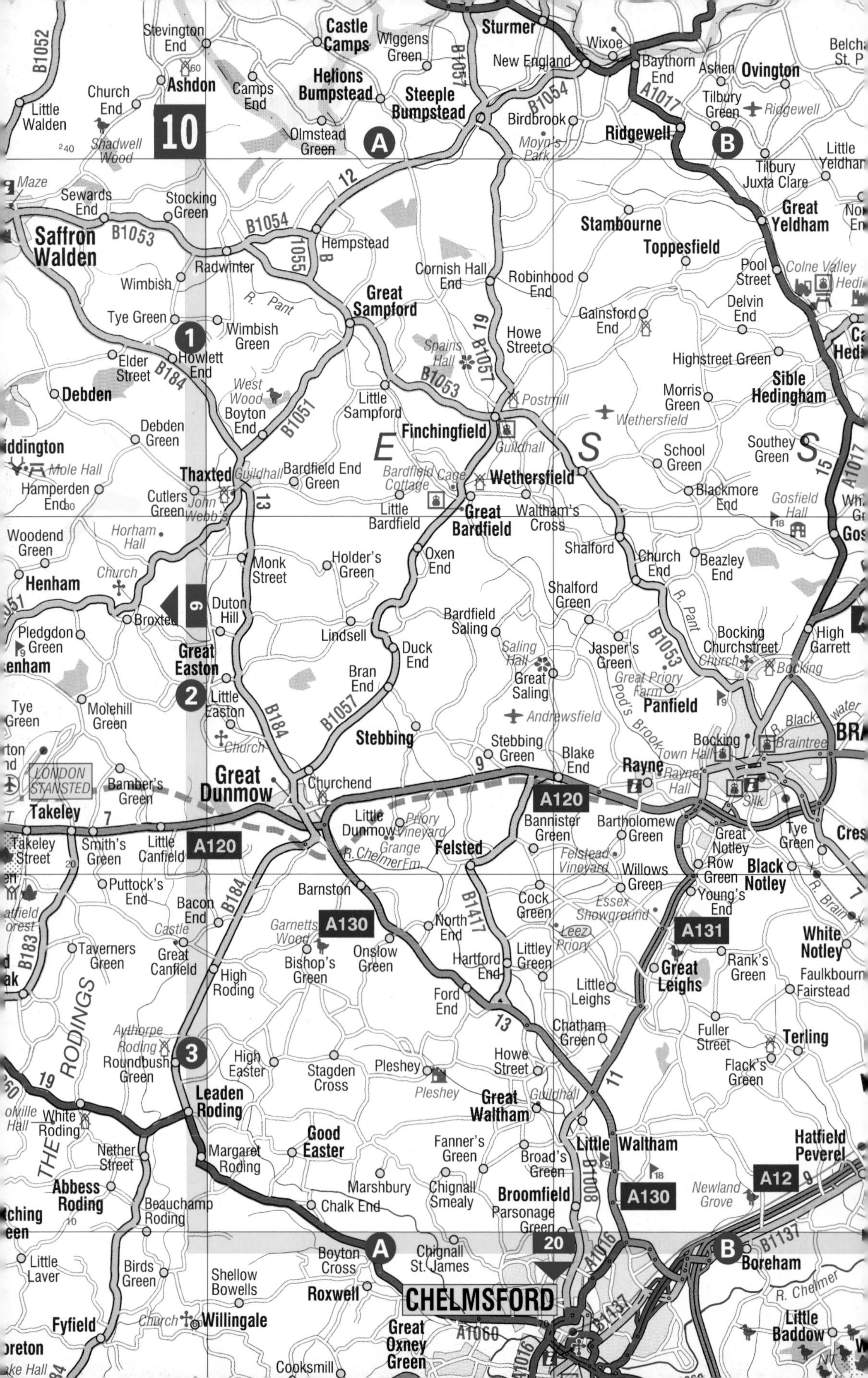

10
B1052
Little Walden
Church End
Stevington End
Ashdon
Shadwell Wood
Camps End
Castle Camps
Wiggens Green
Helions Bumpstead
Olmstead Green
Steeple Bumpstead
B1057
Sturmer
New England
Wixoe
Baythorn End
Ashen
Ovington
Belchamp St. P
B1054
Birdbrook
Moyn's Park
A1017
Ridgewell
Tilbury Green
Ridgewell
A
B
Little Yeldham
Tilbury Juxta Clare
Maze
Sewards End
Stocking Green
Saffron Walden
B1053
B1054
12
Hempstead
B1055
Radwinter
Wimbish
R. Pant
Cornish Hall End
Robinhood End
Stambourne
Toppesfield
Great Yeldham
Pool Street
Colne Valley
Hedingham
Delvin End
Tye Green
Wimbish Green
Great Sampford
Gainsford End
Howe Street
1
Howlett End
Elder Street
B184
Spains Hall
B1057
19
Highstreet Green
Sible Hedingham
Debden
West Wood
Boyton End
B1051
Little Sampford
B1053
Postmill
Morris Green
Wethersfield
Debden Green
Finchingfield
Guildhall
E
S
S
School Green
Southey Green
15
A1017
Saffron Walden
Mole Hall
Thaxted
Guildhall
Bardfield End Green
Bardfield Cage
Bardfield Cottage
Wethersfield
Hamperden End
Cutlers Green
John Webb's
13
Little Bardfield
Great Bardfield
Waltham's Cross
Blackmore End
Gosfield Hall
Gosfield
Woodend Green
Horham Hall
Church
Monk Street
Holder's Green
Oxen End
Shalford
Church End
Beazley End
Henham
6
Duton Hill
Shalford Green
R. Pant
Broxted
Pledgdon Green
Lindsell
Bardfield Saling
Duck End
Saling Hall
Jasper's Green
B1053
Bocking Churchstreet
High Garrett
Church
Bocking
Great Easton
Bran End
Great Saling
Great Priory Farm
Panfield
2
Little Easton
Tye Green
Molehill Green
B184
B1057
Andrewsfield
Pod's Brook
R. Blackwater
Church
Stebbing
Stebbing Green
Bocking
Town Hall
Braintree
LONDON STANSTED
Bamber's Green
Great Dunmow
Churchend
9
Blake End
Rayne
Rayne Hall
A120
Takeley
7
Little Dunmow
Priory Vineyard
Bannister Green
Bartholomew Green
Great Notley
Tye Green
Takeley Street
Smith's Green
Little Canfield
A120
Grange
R. Chelmer
Felsted
Felstead Vineyard
Willows Green
Row Green
Black Notley
Hatfield Forest
Puttock's End
Bacon End
B184
Barnston
Cock Green
Essex Showground
Young's End
R. Brain
B183
Castle
Garnetts Wood
A130
North End
B1417
Leez Priory
A131
White Notley
Taverners Green
Great Canfield
Bishop's Green
Onslow Green
Hartford End
Littley Green
Great Leighs
Rank's Green
Faulkbourne
Fairstead
THE RODINGS
High Roding
Ford End
Little Leighs
13
Aythorpe Roding
3
Roundbush Green
High Easter
Stagden Cross
Pleshey
Pleshey
Howe Street
Chatham Green
11
Fuller Street
Terling
Flack's Green
19
Leaden Roding
Great Waltham
Guildhall
White Roding
Colville Hall
Good Easter
Little Waltham
Hatfield Peverel
Nether Street
Margaret Roding
Fanner's Green
Broad's Green
B1008
Abbess Roding
Marshbury
Chignall Smealy
Broomfield
A130
A12
9
Newland Grove
Beauchamp Roding
Chalk End
Parsonage Green
Little Laver
A
Boyton Cross
Chignall St. James
20
A1016
B
Boreham
B1137
Birds Green
Shellow Bowells
Roxwell
CHELMSFORD
R. Chelmer
B1137
Fyfield
Church
Willingale
Great Oxney Green
A1060
A1016
Little Baddow
Cooksmill

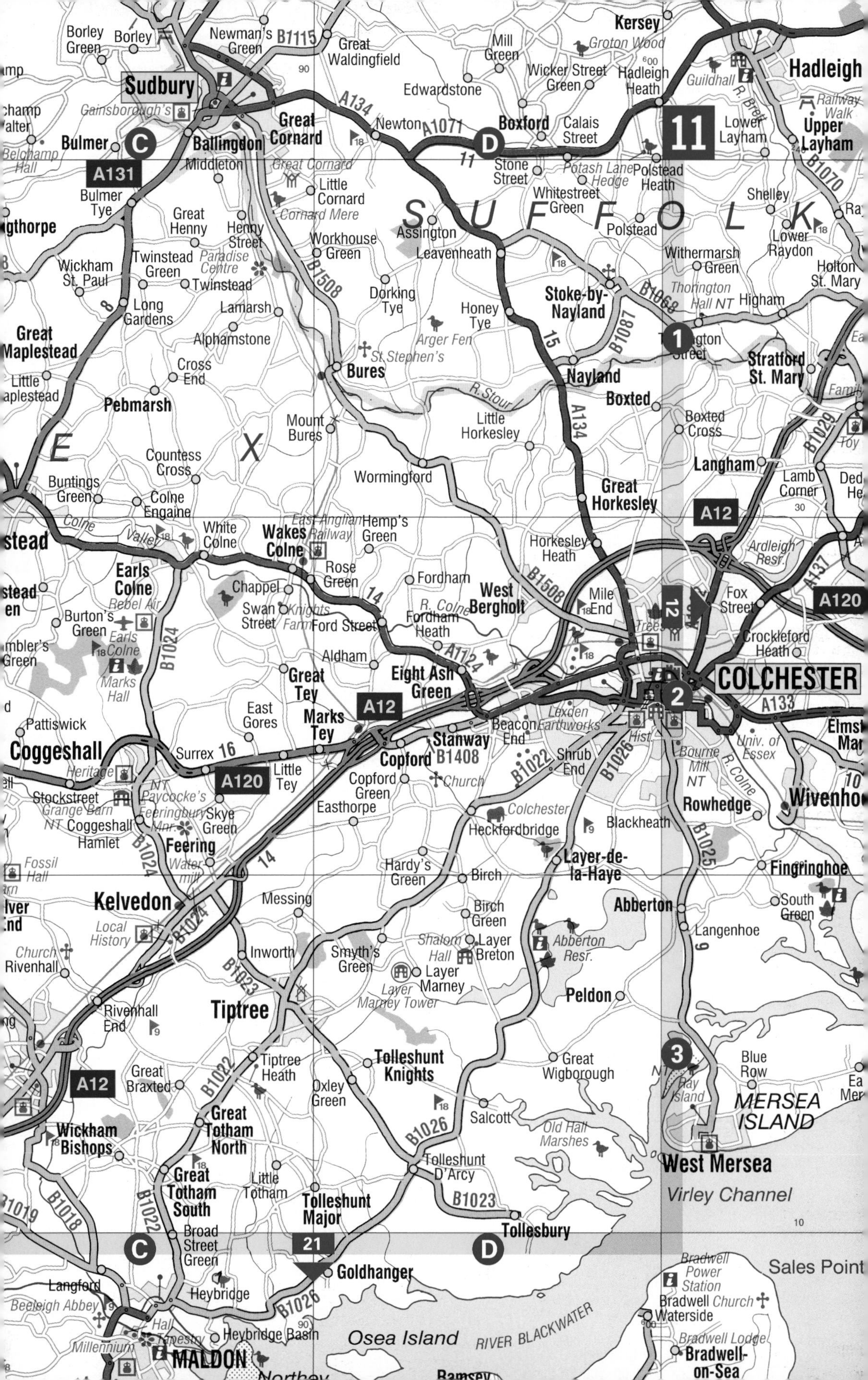

Borley Green
Borley
Newman's Green
B1115
Great Waldingfield
Kersey
Groton Wood
Mill Green
Wicker Street Green
Hadleigh Heath
Hadleigh
Guildhall
R. Brett
Railway Walk
Sudbury
Gainsborough's
Edwardstone
A134
Newton
A1071
Boxford
Calais Street
Lower Layham
Upper Layham
B1070
Bulmer
C
Ballingdon
Great Cornard
D
11
Stone Street
Potash Lane Hedge
Polstead Heath
A131
Middleton
Great Cornard
Little Cornard
Cornard Mere
Whitestreet Green
Shelley
Bulmer Tye
Great Henny
Henny Street
S U F F O L K
Assington
Polstead
Lower Raydon
Paradise Centre
Workhouse Green
Leavenheath
Withermarsh Green
Holton St. Mary
Wickham St. Paul
Twinstead Green
Twinstead
B1508
Dorking Tye
Stoke-by-Nayland
B1068
Thorington Hall NT
Higham
Long Gardens
Lamarsh
Honey Tye
B1087
Great Maplestead
Alphamstone
Arger Fen
15
1
St Stephen's
Cross End
Bures
Nayland
Stratford St. Mary
Little Maplestead
Pebmarsh
R. Stour
Boxted
Little Horkesley
Boxted Cross
B1029
Mount Bures
A134
E
X
Countess Cross
Langham
Wormingford
Lamb Corner
Buntings Green
Colne Engaine
Great Horkesley
Colne Valley
A12
White Colne
East Anglian Railway
Hemp's Green
Wakes Colne
Horkesley Heath
Ardleigh Resr.
Earls Colne
Rose Green
Fordham
B1508
Chappel
West Bergholt
Mile End
Fox Street
A120
A137
Swan Street
Knights Farm
R. Colne
Fordham Heath
12
Burton's Green
Rebel Air
Ford Street
Crockleford Heath
Earls Colne
14
Marks Hall
B1024
Aldham
A1124
Great Tey
Eight Ash Green
COLCHESTER
A12
2
East Gores
Marks Tey
Lexden Earthworks
A133
Pattiswick
Beacon End
Hist.
Univ. of Essex
Coggeshall
Surrex
16
Stanway
Copford
B1408
B1022
Shrub End
B1026
Bourne Mill NT
R. Colne
Heritage
A120
Little Tey
Stockstreet
NT Paycocke's
Grange Barn
NT Coggeshall
Copford Green
Church
Colchester
Rowhedge
Wivenhoe
Feeringbury Mnr.
Skye Green
Easthorpe
Heckfordbridge
Blackheath
Hamlet
Feering
B1025
Fossil Hall
B1024
Water mill
14
Hardy's Green
Birch
Layer-de-la-Haye
Fingringhoe
Kelvedon
Messing
Abberton
South Green
Local History
B1024
Birch Green
Langenhoe
Shalom Hall
Layer Breton
Abberton Resr.
Church
Rivenhall
Inworth
Smyth's Green
B1023
Layer Marney
Layer Marney Tower
Peldon
Tiptree
Rivenhall End
3
Tiptree Heath
Tolleshunt Knights
Great Wigborough
Blue Row
A12
Great Braxted
B1022
Oxley Green
NT Ray Island
MERSEA ISLAND
Salcott
Wickham Bishops
Great Totham North
B1026
Old Hall Marshes
Great Totham South
Little Totham
Tolleshunt D'Arcy
West Mersea
Virley Channel
B1019
B1018
B1022
Tolleshunt Major
B1023
Broad Street Green
Tollesbury
C
21
D
Goldhanger
Bradwell Power Station
Sales Point
Langford
Heybridge
Bradwell Church
Beeleigh Abbey
B1026
Waterside
RIVER BLACKWATER
Heybridge Basin
Osea Island
Bradwell Lodge
Millennium
MALDON
Bradwell-on-Sea

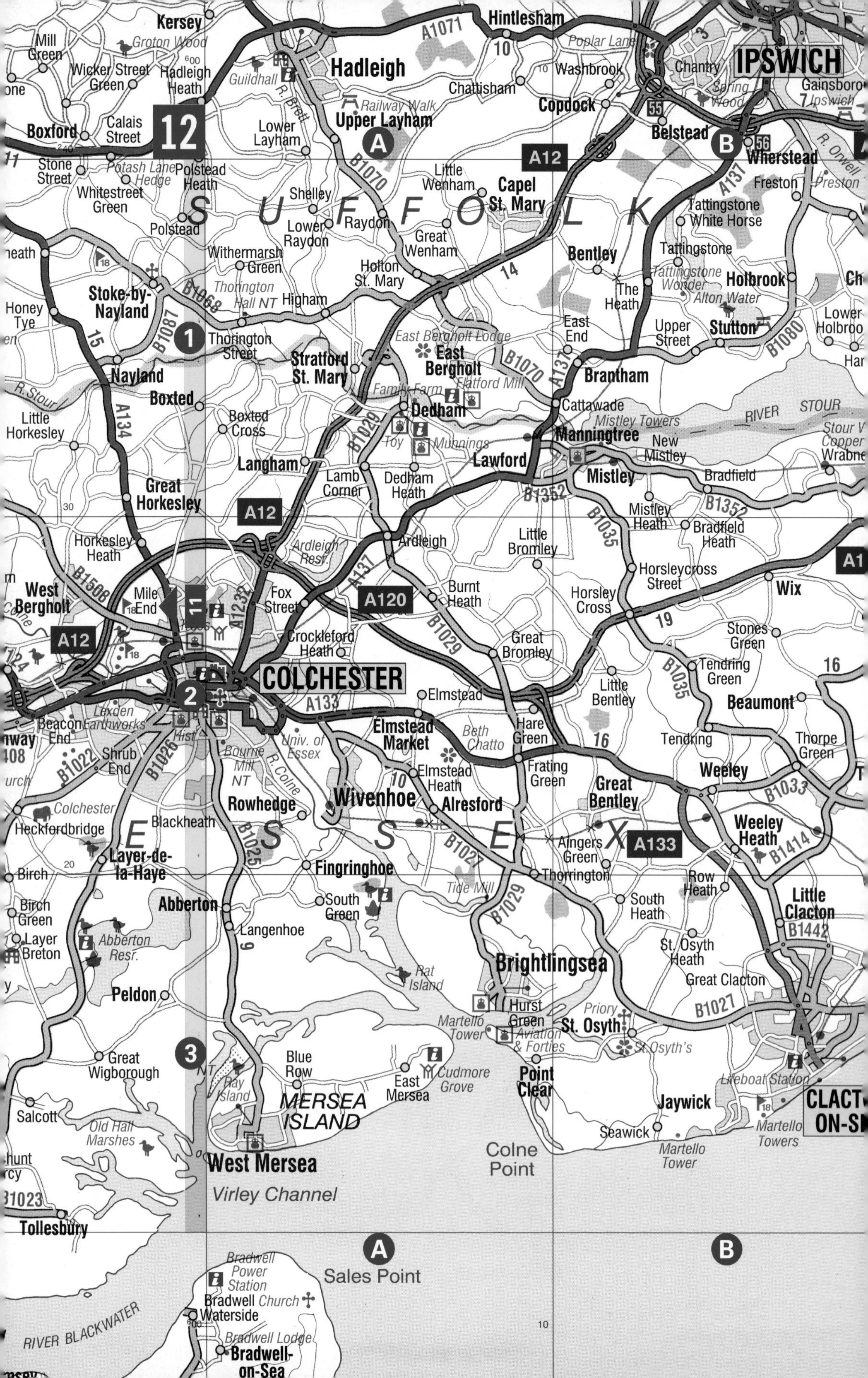
Kersey
Hintlesham
Mill Green
Groton Wood
A1071
Poplar Lane
IPSWICH
Wicker Street Green
Hadleigh Heath
Guildhall
R. Brett
Hadleigh
10
Washbrook
Chantry
Spring Wood
Gainsborough
Ipswich
Chattisham
Copdock
Railway Walk
Boxford
Calais Street
12
Lower Layham
Upper Layham
A
55
Belstead
B
56
Wherstead
A12
R. Orwell
Stone Street
Potash Lane Hedge
Polstead Heath
B1070
Little Wenham
Capel St. Mary
A137
Freston
Preston
Whitestreet Green
Shelley
S U F F O L K
Tattingstone White House
Polstead
Lower Raydon
Raydon
Great Wenham
Bentley
Tattingstone
Withermarsh Green
Holton St. Mary
14
Tattingstone Wonder
Holbrook
Stoke-by-Nayland
Thorington Hall NT
Higham
The Heath
Alton Water
B1068
Honey Tye
B1087
East End
Upper Street
Stutton
Lower Holbrook
15
1
Thorington Street
East Bergholt Lodge
B1080
Stratford St. Mary
East Bergholt
B1070
A137
Brantham
Nayland
Flatford Mill
Family Farm
R. Stour
Boxted
Cattawade
RIVER STOUR
Dedham
Mistley Towers
Little Horkesley
Boxted Cross
B1029
Manningtree
Stour Valley
Copper Wrabness
A134
Toy
Munnings
New Mistley
Langham
Lawford
Mistley
Bradfield
Lamb Corner
Dedham Heath
Great Horkesley
B1352
30
A12
Mistley Heath
B1352
Bradfield Heath
B1035
Ardleigh
Little Bromley
Horkesley Heath
Ardleigh Resr.
A1
Horsleycross Street
B1508
A137
West Bergholt
Mile End
11
A1232
Fox Street
A120
Burnt Heath
Horsley Cross
Wix
19
A12
Crockleford Heath
B1029
Great Bromley
Stones Green
Tendring Green
16
COLCHESTER
Little Bentley
B1035
2
Elmstead
A133
Beaumont
Lexden Earthworks
Beacon End
Univ. of Essex
Elmstead Market
Beth Chatto
Hare Green
Tendring
Thorpe Green
Hist.
Bourne Mill NT
R. Colne
16
B1022
Shrub End
B1026
Elmstead Heath
Frating Green
Great Bentley
Weeley
10
B1033
Colchester
Rowhedge
Wivenhoe
Alresford
Heckfordbridge
Blackheath
E S S E X
A133
Weeley Heath
B1025
B1027
Aingers Green
B1414
Layer-de-la-Haye
20
Birch
Fingringhoe
Thorrington
Row Heath
Little Clacton
Tide Mill
B1029
Birch Green
Abberton
South Green
South Heath
B1442
Layer Breton
Langenhoe
Abberton Resr.
9
St. Osyth Heath
Brightlingsea
Rat Island
Great Clacton
Peldon
Hurst Green
Priory
Martello Tower
St. Osyth
B1027
Aviation & Forties
St. Osyth's
3
Great Wigborough
Blue Row
East Mersea
Cudmore Grove
Point Clear
Lifeboat Station
Ray Island
NT
MERSEA ISLAND
Jaywick
CLACTON-ON-SEA
Salcott
Old Hall Marshes
Seawick
Martello Towers
Martello Tower
Colne Point
West Mersea
B1023
Virley Channel
Tollesbury
A
B
Bradwell Power Station
Sales Point
Bradwell Church
Bradwell Waterside
RIVER BLACKWATER
Bradwell Lodge
Bradwell-on-Sea
10

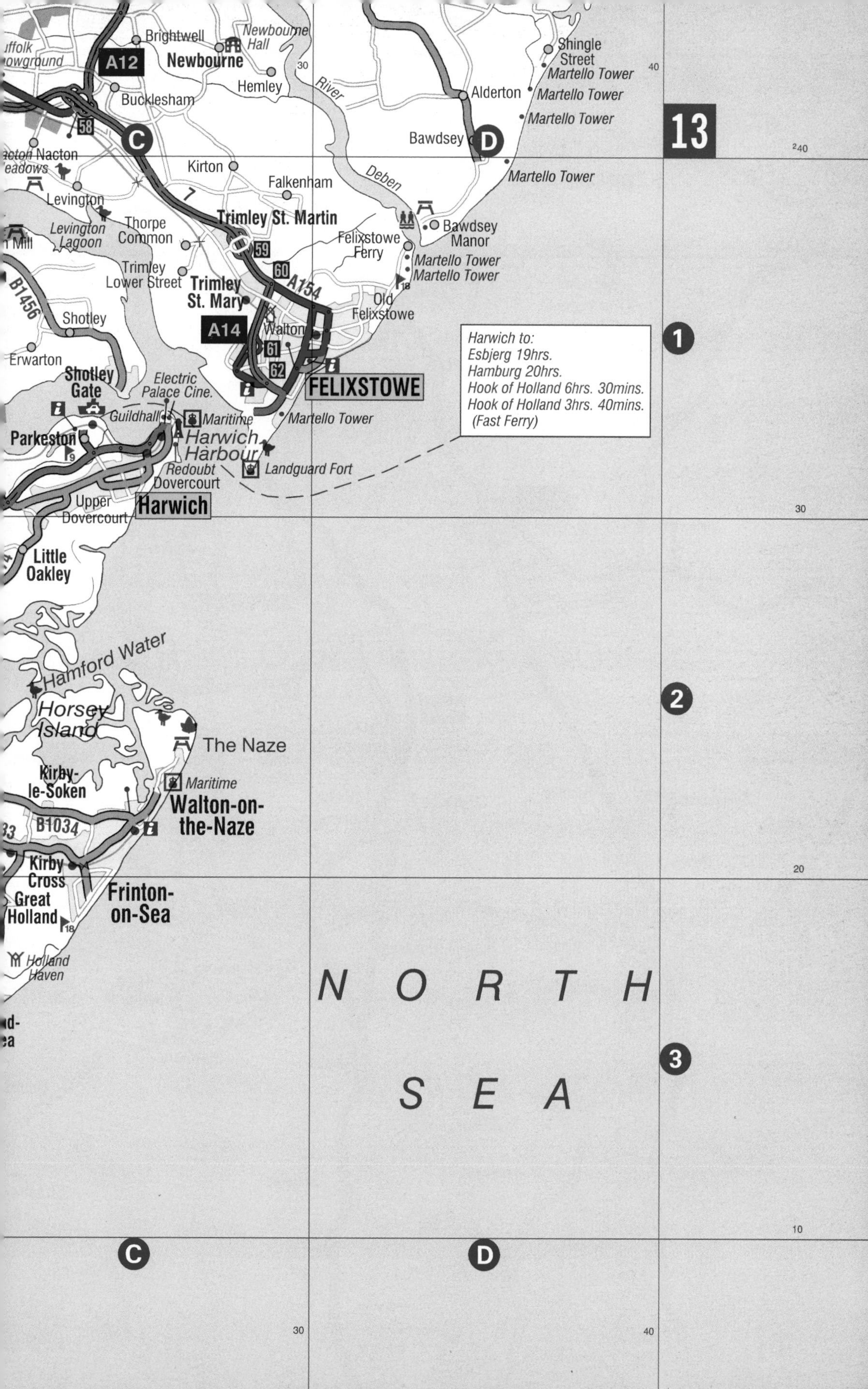

Brightwell
Newbourne Hall
A12
Newbourne
Hemley
Bucklesham
River
30
Shingle Street
Martello Tower
40
Alderton
Martello Tower
Martello Tower
13
²40
Suffolk Showground
Nacton
Meadows
58
C
Kirton
Falkenham
Deben
Bawdsey
D
Martello Tower
Levington
Thorpe
Common
Levington
Lagoon
Trimley St. Martin
Felixstowe
Ferry
Bawdsey Manor
1
Mill
Trimley
Lower Street
59
A154
Martello Tower
Martello Tower
B1456
Shotley
60
**Trimley
St. Mary**
Old
Felixstowe
18
Erwarton
A14
Walton
*Harwich to:
Esbjerg 19hrs.
Hamburg 20hrs.
Hook of Holland 6hrs. 30mins.
Hook of Holland 3hrs. 40mins.
(Fast Ferry)*
**Shotley
Gate**
*Electric
Palace Cine.*
61
62
FELIXSTOWE
Guildhall
Maritime
Martello Tower
Parkeston
9
*Harwich
Harbour*
Redoubt
Dovercourt
Landguard Fort
Upper
Dovercourt
Harwich
1
**Little
Oakley**
30
Hamford Water
*Horsey
Island*
The Naze
2
**Kirby-
le-Soken**
Maritime
B1034
**Walton-on-
the-Naze**
20
**Kirby
Cross**
**Great
Holland**
**Frinton-
on-Sea**
18
*Holland
Haven*
*d-
ea*
N O R T H
3
S E A
10
C
D
30
40

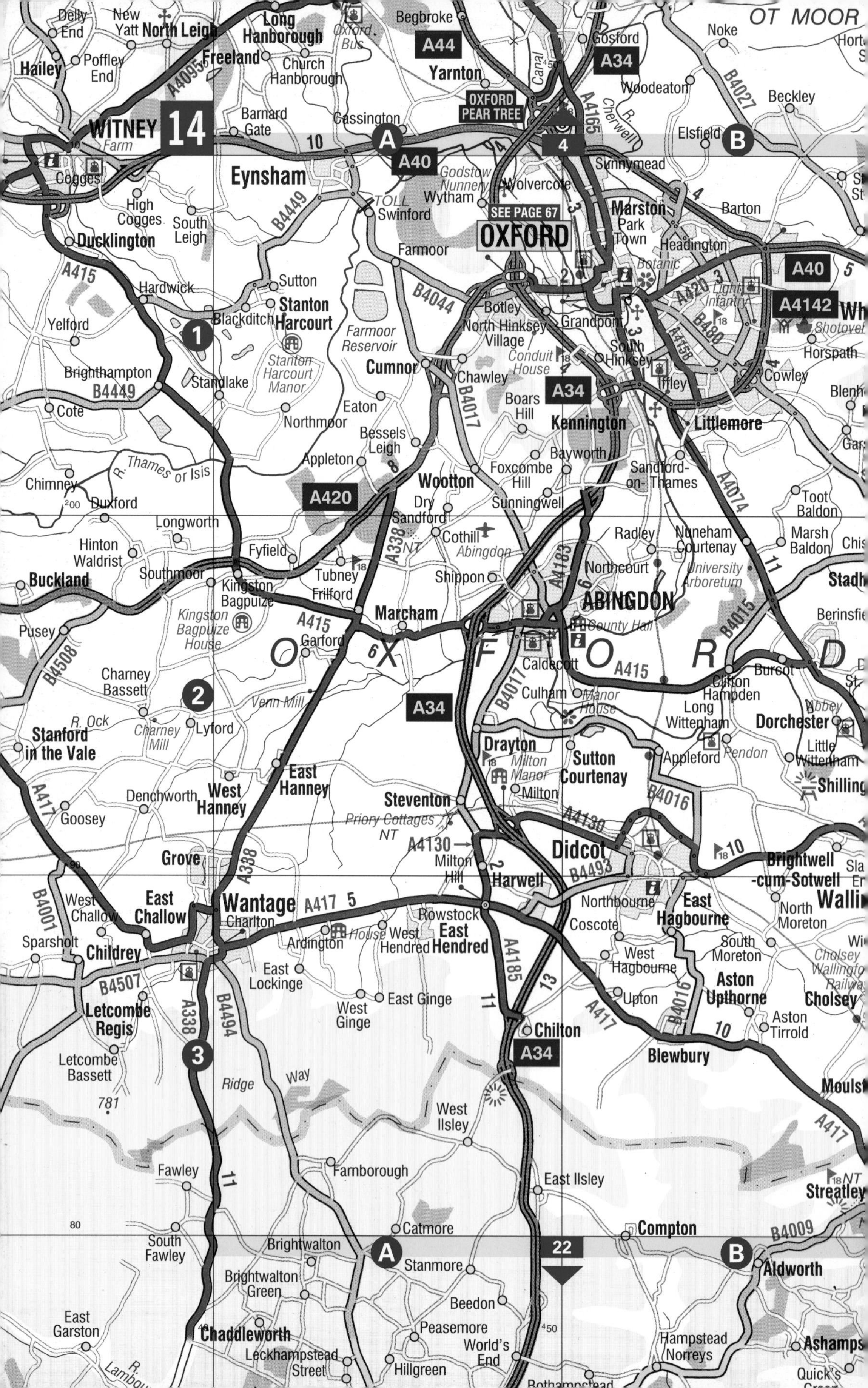

WITNEY
14
OXFORD
SEE PAGE 67
ABINGDON
Wantage
Didcot
Eynsham
Cumnor
Kennington
Littlemore
Marcham
Steventon
Harwell
Chilton
Blewbury
Compton
Aldworth
Chaddleworth
Grove
Drayton
Sutton Courtenay
Dorchester
Stanton Harcourt
Ducklington
Hailey
Freeland
Long Hanborough
Yarnton
Begbroke
Cassington
Kidlington
Botley
Cowley
Headington
Marston
Wootton
Radley
Culham
East Hendred
East Hagbourne
Aston Upthorne
Cholsey
Streatley
East Ilsley
West Ilsley
Farnborough
Catmore
Brightwalton
Stanmore
Beedon
Peasemore
Letcombe Regis
Childrey
East Challow
West Hanney
East Hanney
Stanford in the Vale
Buckland
Kingston Bagpuize
Fyfield
Standlake
Northmoor
Appleton
OXFORD PEAR TREE
OT MOOR
A34
A40
A44
A420
A415
A338
A417
A4130
A4185
A4142
B4017
B4016
B4494
B4507
B4001
B4508
B4449
B4044
B4009
22
4

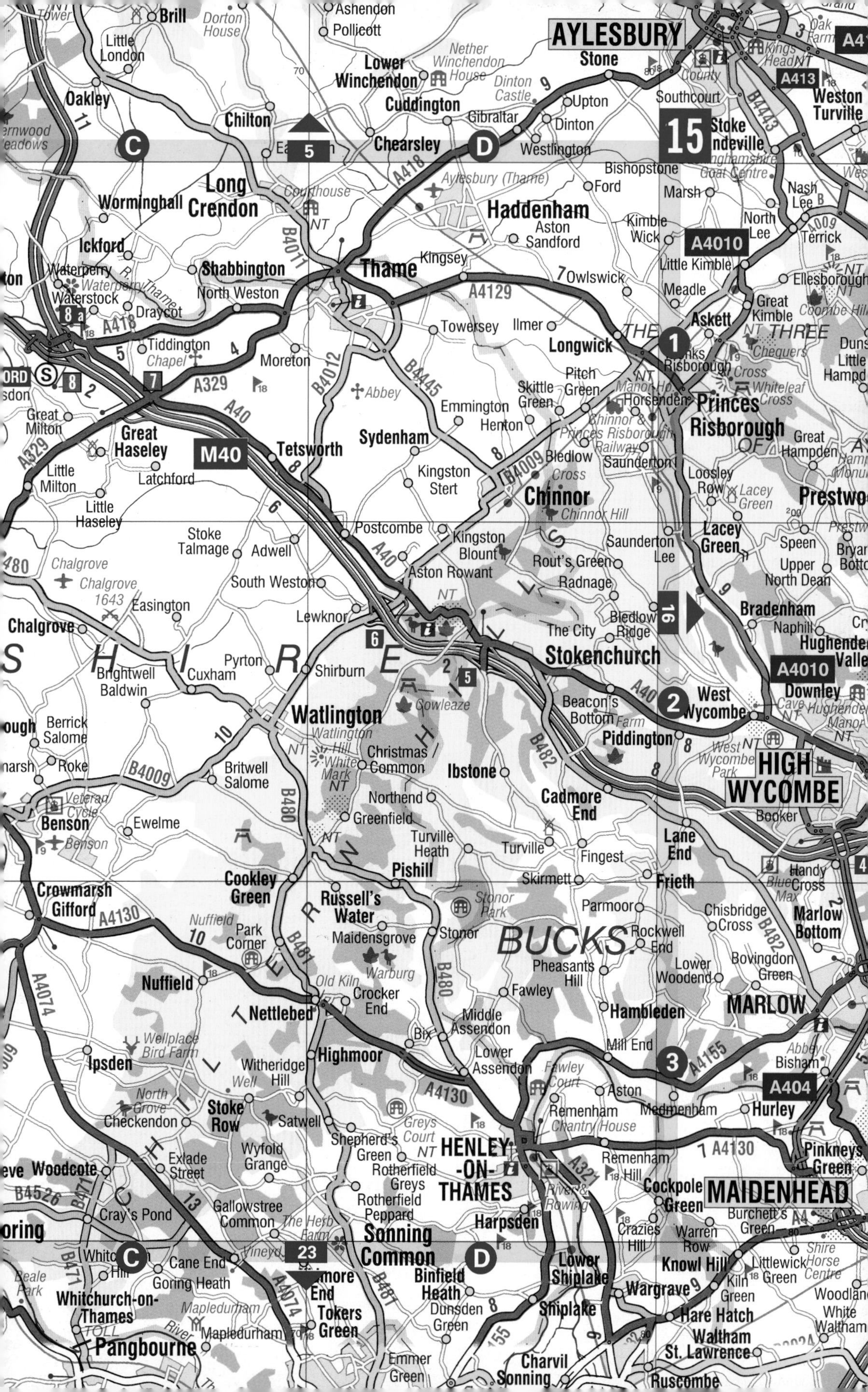

Brill
Dorton House
Ashendon
Pollicott
AYLESBURY
Stone
Little London
Nether Winchendon House
Lower Winchendon
Dinton Castle
Oakley
Cuddington
Upton
Gibraltar
Dinton
Chilton
Chearsley
Westlington
Southcourt
Weston Turville
15
Stoke Mandeville
A413
B4443
A418
Aylesbury (Thame)
Bishopstone
Ford
Marsh
Nash Lee
Long Crendon
Worminghall
Courthouse
NT
Haddenham
Aston Sandford
Kimble Wick
North Lee
Terrick
A4010
Ickford
B4011
Thame
Kingsey
Little Kimble
Shabbington
Waterperry
Waterstock
North Weston
Draycot
Owlswick
A4129
Meadle
Ellesborough
Great Kimble
Coombe Hill
Askett
A418
Tiddington
Chapel
Moreton
Towersey
Ilmer
Longwick
THE THREE
Chequers
Princes Risborough
Whiteleaf Cross
Horsenden
Chinnor & Princes Risborough Railway
Abbey
B4012
B4445
A329
Skittle Green
Pitch Green
Emmington
Henton
Great Milton
A40
Great Haseley
M40
Tetsworth
Sydenham
Bledlow
Cross
Saunderton
Great Hampden
Little Milton
Latchford
Kingston Stert
B4009
Chinnor
Chinnor Hill
Loosley Row
Lacey Green
Prestwood
Little Haseley
Stoke Talmage
Adwell
Postcombe
Kingston Blount
Saunderton Lee
Speen
Chalgrove
Chalgrove 1643
South Weston
Aston Rowant
Rout's Green
Radnage
Upper North Dean
Easington
Lewknor
Bledlow Ridge
16
Bradenham
Naphill
Chalgrove
The City
Hughenden Valley
Brightwell Baldwin
Cuxham
Pyrton
Shirburn
Stokenchurch
A4010
Downley
Watlington
Cowleaze
Beacon's Bottom
West Wycombe
Hughenden Manor
Berrick Salome
Roke
Watlington Hill
White Mark
Christmas Common
Piddington
West Wycombe Park
HIGH WYCOMBE
B4009
Britwell Salome
Ibstone
B482
Cadmore End
Booker
Benson
Veteran Cycle
Ewelme
Northend
Greenfield
B480
Lane End
Turville Heath
Turville
Fingest
Crowmarsh Gifford
Cookley Green
Pishill
Skirmett
Frieth
Handy Cross
A4130
Russell's Water
Stonor Park
Parmoor
Chisbridge Cross
Marlow Bottom
Nuffield
Park Corner
Maidensgrove
Stonor
BUCKS.
Rockwell End
Lower Woodend
Bovingdon Green
A4074
B481
Pheasants Hill
Fawley
Nuffield
Old Kiln
Warburg
Crocker End
Nettlebed
Hambleden
MARLOW
Middle Assendon
Bix
Wellplace Bird Farm
Ipsden
Highmoor
Mill End
Bisham
Witheridge Hill
Well
Lower Assendon
Fawley Court
A4155
North Grove
Checkendon
Stoke Row
Satwell
A4130
Aston
Remenham
Medmenham
Hurley
A404
Chantry House
Greys Court
Shepherd's Green
HENLEY-ON-THAMES
Exlade Street
Wyfold Grange
Rotherfield Greys
Remenham Hill
Pinkneys Green
Woodcote
A4130
B4526
B471
Rotherfield Peppard
A321
River & Rowing
Cockpole Green
MAIDENHEAD
Cray's Pond
Gallowstree Common
The Herb Farm
Sonning Common
Harpsden
Crazies Hill
Burchett's Green
Warren Row
Whitchurch Hill
Cane End
23
D
Vineyard
Lower Shiplake
Knowl Hill
Littlewick Green
Shire Horse Centre
Beale Park
Goring Heath
Binfield Heath
Tokers Green
Dunsden Green
Wargrave
Kiln Green
Whitchurch-on-Thames
Mapledurham
Shiplake
Hare Hatch
White Waltham
Pangbourne
River
Emmer Green
Charvil
Sonning
Waltham St. Lawrence
Ruscombe

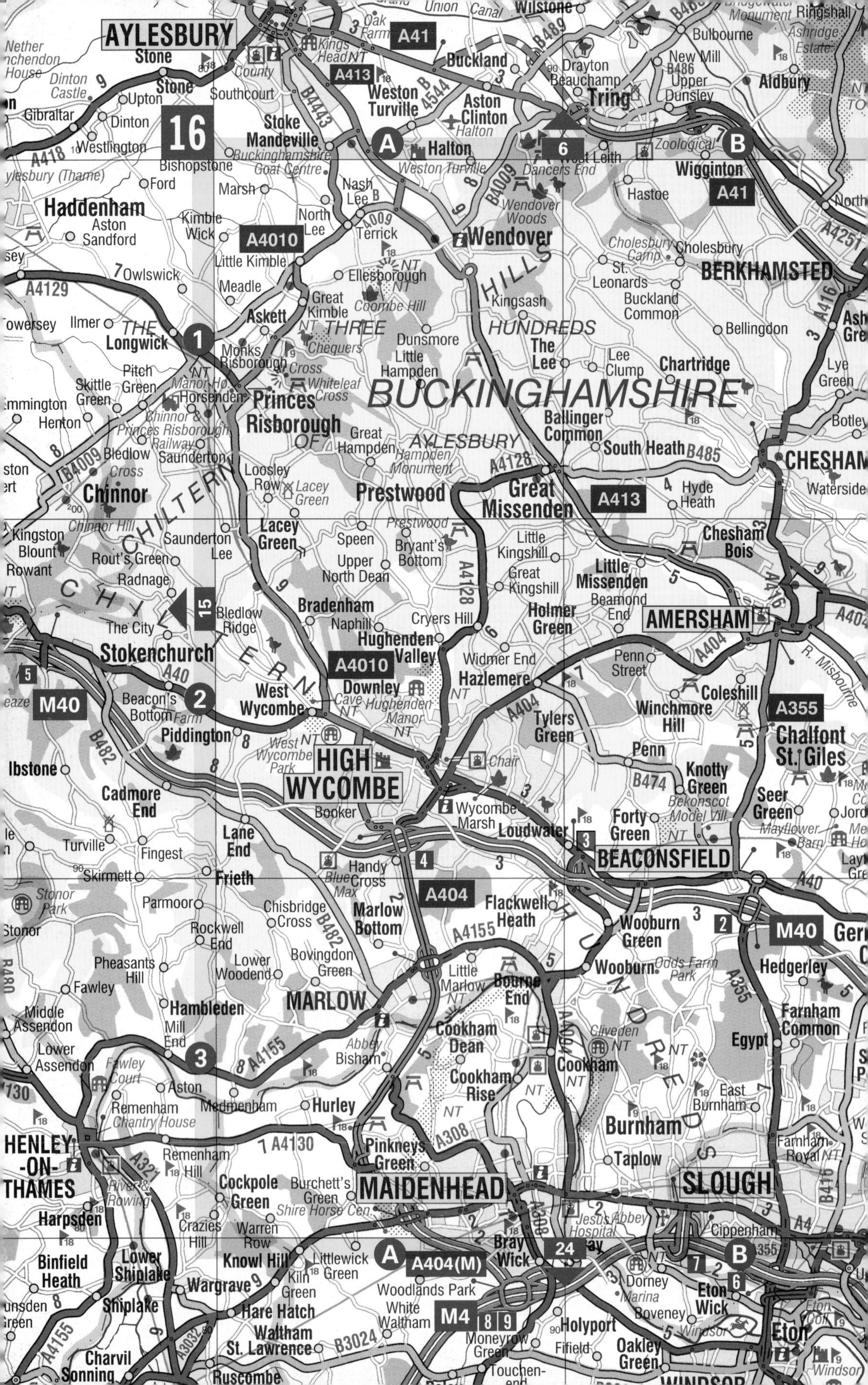

16
AYLESBURY
Grand Union Canal
Wilstone
Ringshall
Ashridge Estate
Bridgewater Monument
Nether Winchendon House
Stone
Oak Farm
A41
Bulbourne
New Mill
Dinton Castle
County
Kings Head NT
Buckland
Drayton Beauchamp
B489
B486
Upper Dunsley
Aldbury
Gibraltar
Upton
Stone
Southcourt
A413
Weston Turville
B4544
Aston Clinton
Tring
Dinton
B4443
Stoke Mandeville
Halton
6
Zoological
Wigginton
A418
Westlington
Buckinghamshire Goat Centre
A
B
West Leith
Dancers End
Aylesbury (Thame)
Bishopstone
Weston Turville
B4009
A41
Ford
Marsh
Nash Lee
Wendover Woods
Hastoe
Northchurch
Haddenham
Aston Sandford
Kimble Wick
North Lee
A4009
Terrick
A4010
Wendover
Cholesbury Camp
Cholesbury
A4251
BERKHAMSTED
Little Kimble
Ellesborough
St. Leonards
A4129
Owlswick
Meadle
HILLS
Buckland Common
A416
Towersey
Ilmer
Great Kimble
Coombe Hill
Kingsash
Bellingdon
THE
Askett
THREE
HUNDREDS
Longwick
1
Chequers
Dunsmore
Monks Risborough
Cross
Little Hampden
The Lee
Lee Clump
Chartridge
Lye Green
Skittle Green
Pitch Green
Manor Ho. NT
Whiteleaf Cross
BUCKINGHAMSHIRE
Emmington
Horsenden
Princes Risborough
Ballinger Common
Botley
Henton
Chinnor & Princes Risborough Railway
OF
Great Hampden
AYLESBURY
South Heath
B485
CHESHAM
B4009
Bledlow Cross
Saunderton
Hampden Monument
A4128
Chinnor
Loosley Row
Lacey Green
Prestwood
Great Missenden
A413
Hyde Heath
Waterside
CHILTERN
Chinnor Hill
Prestwood
Kingston Blount
Lacey Green
Speen
Bryant's Bottom
Little Kingshill
Chesham Bois
Saunderton Lee
Rout's Green
Upper North Dean
Rowant
Radnage
Great Kingshill
Little Missenden
CH
15
Bledlow Ridge
Bradenham
Beamond End
Holmer Green
AMERSHAM
The City
Naphill
Cryers Hill
Hughenden Valley
Stokenchurch
A4010
Widmer End
Penn Street
A404
R. Misbourne
A40
West Wycombe
Downley
Hughenden Manor NT
Hazlemere
Coleshill
M40
Beacon's Bottom
2
Cave NT
Tylers Green
Winchmore Hill
A355
Piddington
West Wycombe Park NT
Chalfont St. Giles
B482
HIGH WYCOMBE
Chair
Penn
Ibstone
Knotty Green
B474
Seer Green
Cadmore End
Booker
Wycombe Marsh
Bekonscot Model Vill.
Loudwater
Forty Green
Jordans
Turville
Lane End
Fingest
Mayflower Barn
BEACONSFIELD
Skirmett
Handy Cross
4
3
Blue Max
Frieth
A404
A40
Stonor Park
Parmoor
Flackwell Heath
Chisbridge Cross
Marlow Bottom
Stonor
Rockwell End
A4155
Wooburn Green
M40
Pheasants Hill
Lower Woodend
Bovingdon Green
Wooburn
Odds Farm Park
Hedgerley
Fawley
Little Marlow
Bourne End
A355
Middle Assendon
Hambleden
MARLOW
Farnham Common
Mill End
Cookham Dean
Cliveden NT
Egypt
Lower Assendon
3
A4155
Abbey
Bisham
Cookham
Fawley Court
Cookham Rise
East Burnham
Aston
Remenham
Medmenham
Hurley
Chantry House
Burnham
HENLEY-ON-THAMES
A4130
Pinkneys Green
A308
Farnham Royal
A321
Remenham Hill
Taplow
River & Rowing
Cockpole Green
Burchett's Green
MAIDENHEAD
SLOUGH
B416
Harpsden
Shire Horse Cen.
Crazies Hill
Warren Row
A308
Jesus Hospital
Abbey
Cippenham
A4
Binfield Heath
Lower Shiplake
Knowl Hill
Littlewick Green
A
A404(M)
Bray Wick
24
B
Kiln Green
Dorney
Wargrave
Woodlands Park
Marina
Eton Wick
Shiplake
Hare Hatch
White Waltham
M4
Holyport
Boveney
Eton
Eton Coll.
Waltham St. Lawrence
B3024
Moneyrow Green
Fifield
Oakley Green
Windsor
A4155
Charvil
Sonning
Ruscombe
Touchen-end
WINDSOR

HERTS.
17
Jockey End
Trowley Bottom
Great Gaddesden
Water End
Holtsmere End
Piccotts End
Potten End
Warners End
Bourne End
Chaulden
HEMEL HEMPSTEAD
Felden
Bovingdon
Rucklers Lane
Kings Langley
Bedmond
Chipperfield
Belsize
Bucks Hill
Hunton Bridge
Abbots Langley
Langleybury
Sarratt
Micklefield Green
Chenies
Chandler's Cross
Whippendell Wood
WATFORD
Croxley Green
RICKMANSWORTH
Batchworth
Moor Park
Eastbury
Maple Cross
West Hyde
Harefield
Denham
Denham Green
Tatling End
New Denham
Ickenham
Newyears Green
Bayhurst Wood
Ruislip Common
Lido
UXBRIDGE
Hillingdon
Cowley
Iver Heath
Shreding Green
Richings Park
West Drayton
Yiewsley
Sutton
Harmondsworth
Sipson
Harlington
Longford
Poyle
HARPENDEN
Hatching Green
Redbourn
Childwick Green
Wheathampstead
Amwell
Coleman Green
Lemsford
Sandridge
New Greens
Marshalswick
Townsend
Fleetville
Old Gorhambury
Roman Theatre
Verulamium Roman Town
ST. ALBANS
HATFIELD
Ellenbrook
Colney Heath
London Colney
Potters Crouch
Chiswell Green
Park Street
Frogmore
Bricket Wood
RADLETT
Colney Street
Mosquito Aircraft
Shenleybury
Shenley
Aldenham
Letchmore Heath
Patchetts Green
Elstree
BOREHAMWOOD
Green Street
Film Studios
BUSHEY
Oxhey
Bushey Heath
South Oxhey
Hatch End
NORTHWOOD
STANMORE
Harrow Weald
Wealdstone
HARROW
PINNER
Eastcote
RUISLIP
Rayners Lane
NORTHOLT
Harrow on the Hill
KENTON
Kingsbury
EDGWARE
Burnt Oak
Mill Hill
WEMBLEY
GREENFORD
Yeading
HAYES
SOUTHALL
HESTON
Osterley
Brentford
Hanwell
EALING
ACTON
Pitshanger
Kew
Syon House
Cranford
WILLESDEN
Kilburn
Neasden
Cricklewood
HENDON
Brent Cross
Shepherd's Bush
CHISWICK
HAMMERSMITH
BARNES
FULHAM
KENSINGTON
HAMPSTEAD
Welwyn
Hatfield Hyde
Old Palace
Hatfield House
West End
Woodside
Welham Green
Brookmans Park
Water End
South Mimms
POTTERS BAR
SOUTH MIMMS
Ridge
Bentley Heath
Monken Hadley
High Barnet
BARNET
Arkley
Totteridge
LONDON GATEWAY
Darlands Lake
FINCHLEY
Golders Green
M1
M10
M25
M4
A1(M)
A1
A41
A40
A312
A406
A414
A4

HARPENDEN
Wheathampstead
WELWYN GARDEN CITY
HERTFORD
Panshanger
Great Amwell
Amwell
Coleman Green
Lemsford
Stanborough
18
Hatfield Hyde
Cole Green
Hertingfordbury
Hertford Heath
Letty Green
8
Sandridge
Marshalswick
HATFIELD
A414
A10
Essendon
Old Palace
West End
Bayford
Stratton's Folly
HODDESDON
Fleetville
Ellenbrook
Hatfield House
Little Berkhamsted
Lowewood
Paradise
A1057
Woodside
ST. ALBANS
HERTFORDSHIRE
Broxbourne
Epping Green
Colney Heath
Welham Green
Wormley Wood
London Colney
Brookmans Park
Northaw Great Wood
Newgate Street
Hammond Street
Wormley
Turnford
Park Street
A1(M)
Water End
Cuffley
Frogmore
Castle
South Mimms
POTTERS BAR
Northaw Place
Northaw
Goff's Oak
Colney Street
Mosquito Aircraft
Shenleybury
CHESHUNT
Waltham Cross
SOUTH MIMMS
Ridge
Shenley
M25
Crews Hill
Capel Manor
RADLETT
Bentley Heath
Forty Hill
A1
Green Street
Botany Bay
Forty Hall
Enfield Wash
Letchmore Heath
BOREHAMWOOD
Monken Hadley
Patchetts Green
Hadley Wood
Trent Park
ENFIELD
Sewardstone
17
Elstree
Aldenham
High Barnet
Cockfosters
Film Studios
BARNET
Arkley
EAST BARNET
Winchmore Hill
Ponders End
Totteridge
SOUTHGATE
LONDON GATEWAY
Pickett's Lock Centre
M1
Whetstone
FRIERN BARNET
EDMONTON
A41
Darlands Lake
STANMORE
Burnt Oak
Mill Hill
FINCHLEY
A406
WOOD GREEN
Haringey
Weald
EDGWARE
Muswell Hill
Alex. Park
TOTTENHAM
WALTHAMSTOW
Wealdstone
HORNSEY
HARROW
Kingsbury
HENDON
Jewish
A503
Golders Green
KENTON
Brent Resr.
Beam Eng. Res.
Harrow on the Hill
Brent Cross
Highgate Cemy.
SEE PAGE 64
STOKE NEWINGTON
LEYTON
A4088
LONDON
Neasden
Stadium
Cricklewood
A102
A12
HAMPSTEAD
WEMBLEY
WILLESDEN
CAMDEN TOWN
ISLINGTON
HACKNEY
Kilburn
FINSBURY
BETHNAL GREEN
A501
SHOREDITCH
MARYLEBONE
STEPNEY
Holborn
EALING
A40
PADDINGTON
WEST END
CITY
A13
POPLAR
Hanwell
ACTON
Shepherd's Bush
Hyde Park
Pitshanger
KENSINGTON
A4
26
M4
WESTMINSTER
BERMONDSEY
CHISWICK
CHELSEA
LAMBETH
Brentford
HAMMERSMITH
DEPTFORD
GREENWICH
Kew Br.
Kew
BARNES
A2
CAMBERWELL
Syon House
North Sheen
A316
FULHAM
Palace
BATTERSEA
BRIXTON
A202

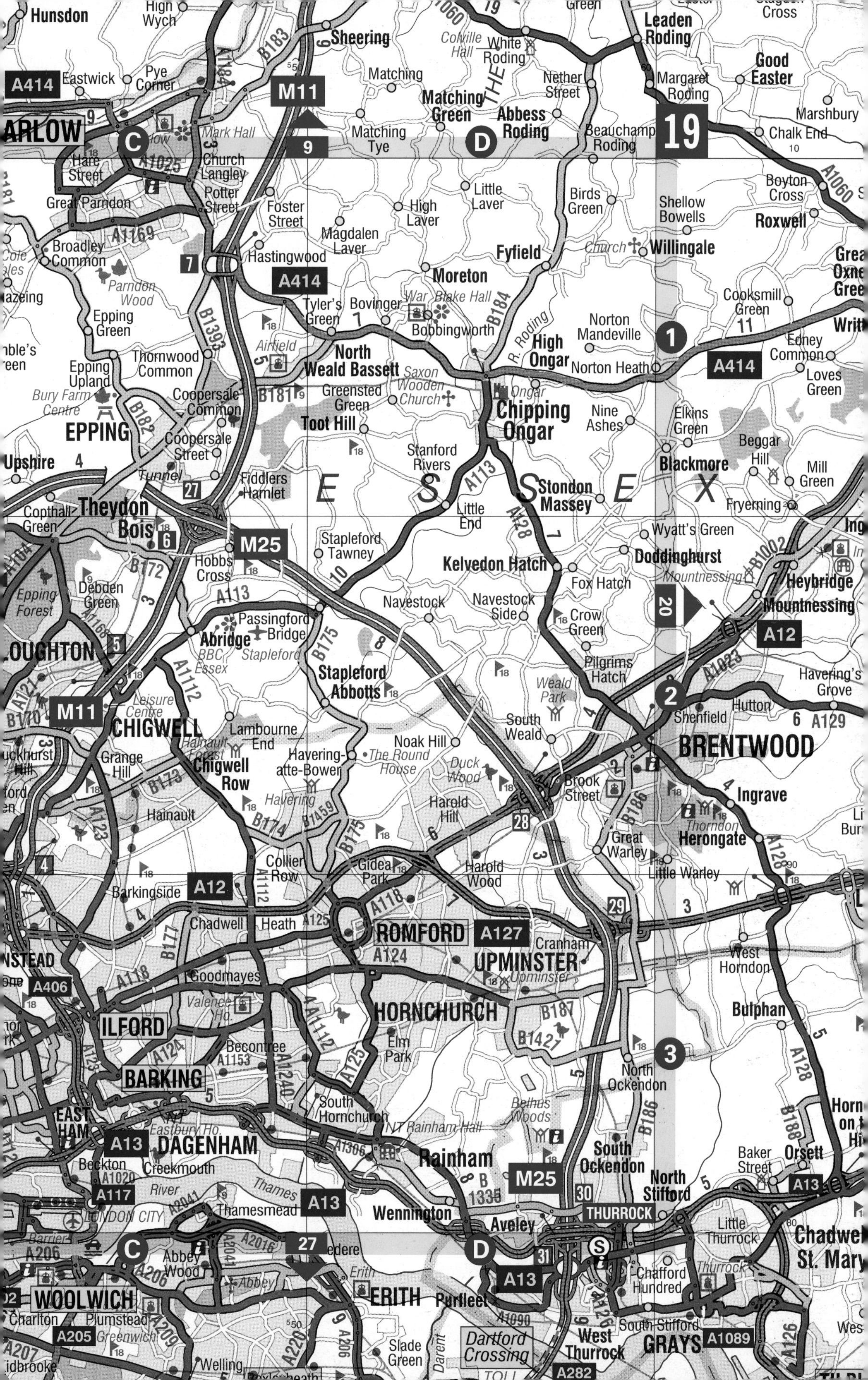

Hunsdon
Sheering
Leaden Roding
Good Easter
Matching
White Roding
Margaret Roding
Marshbury
Matching Green
Abbess Roding
Beauchamp Roding
Chalk End
HARLOW
Matching Tye
19
Church Langley
Great Parndon
Foster Street
High Laver
Little Laver
Birds Green
Shellow Bowells
Boyton Cross
Roxwell
Broadley Common
Magdalen Laver
Hastingwood
Fyfield
Willingale
Moreton
Epping Green
Tyler's Green
Bovinger
Bobbingworth
Cooksmill Green
Norton Mandeville
High Ongar
Norton Heath
Edney Common
Epping Upland
Thornwood Common
North Weald Bassett
Loves Green
Coopersale Common
Greensted Green
Chipping Ongar
Nine Ashes
Elkins Green
EPPING
Toot Hill
Stanford Rivers
Beggar Hill
Upshire
Coopersale Street
Blackmore
Mill Green
Fiddlers Hamlet
Stondon Massey
Theydon Bois
Little End
Fryerning
Copthall Green
E S S E X
Wyatt's Green
Stapleford Tawney
Doddinghurst
Hobbs Cross
Kelvedon Hatch
Fox Hatch
Heybridge
Debden Green
Navestock
Navestock Side
Mountnessing
Passingford Bridge
Abridge
Crow Green
LOUGHTON
Stapleford Abbotts
Pilgrims Hatch
Havering's Grove
Shenfield
Hutton
CHIGWELL
Lambourne End
South Weald
BRENTWOOD
Grange Hill
Chigwell Row
Havering-atte-Bower
Noak Hill
Brook Street
Ingrave
Hainault
Harold Hill
Great Warley
Herongate
Collier Row
Gidea Park
Harold Wood
Little Warley
Barkingside
Chadwell Heath
ROMFORD
UPMINSTER
Cranham
West Horndon
Goodmayes
ILFORD
HORNCHURCH
Bulphan
Elm Park
North Ockendon
BARKING
Becontree
South Hornchurch
EAST HAM
DAGENHAM
Rainham
South Ockendon
Beckton
Creekmouth
Baker Street
Orsett
North Stifford
Thamesmead
Wennington
Aveley
THURROCK
Little Thurrock
Chadwell St. Mary
Abbey Wood
ERITH
Purfleet
Chafford Hundred
WOOLWICH
Charlton
Plumstead
Slade Green
Dartford Crossing
West Thurrock
South Stifford
GRAYS
Welling
M11
M25
A414
A12
A13
A127
A1089
A282

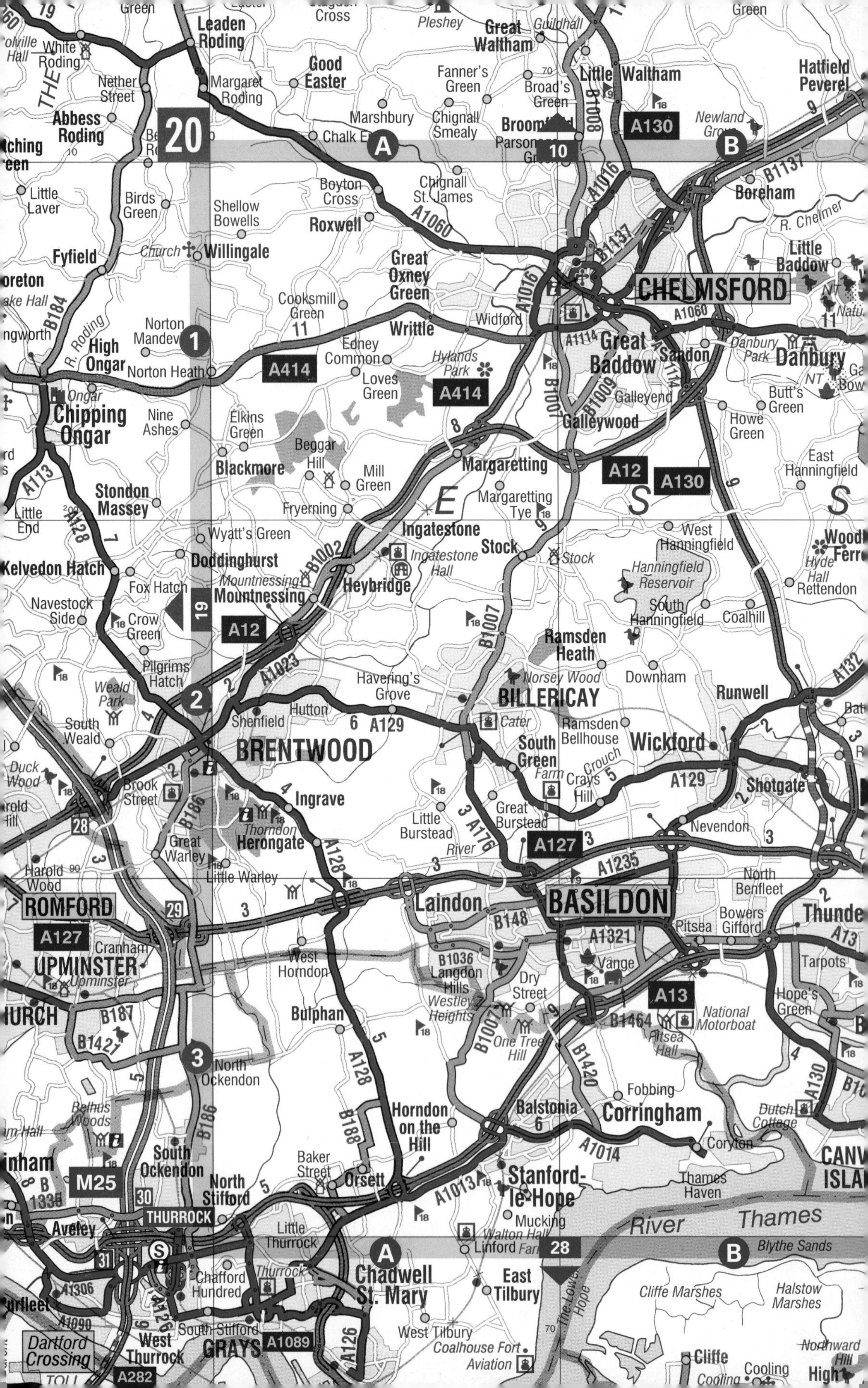
20
Leaden Roding
White Roding
Good Easter
Pleshey
Great Waltham
Little Waltham
Hatfield Peverel
Margaret Roding
Abbess Roding
Marshbury
Chignall Smealy
Broomfield
A130
Chalk End
A
10
B
Boreham
Little Laver
Birds Green
Shellow Bowells
Boyton Cross
Chignall St. James
Roxwell
A1060
Willingale
Fyfield
Great Oxney Green
CHELMSFORD
Little Baddow
Cooksmill Green
Writtle
Widford
A1016
A1137
High Ongar
Norton Heath
A414
Edney Common
Loves Green
Hylands Park
Great Baddow
Sandon
Danbury
Chipping Ongar
Nine Ashes
Elkins Green
Galleyend
Galleywood
Butt's Green
Howe Green
Blackmore
Beggar Hill
Mill Green
Margaretting
A12
East Hanningfield
Stondon Massey
Fryerning
Margaretting Tye
Ingatestone
Stock
West Hanningfield
Kelvedon Hatch
Wyatt's Green
Doddinghurst
Mountnessing
Heybridge
Ingatestone Hall
Hanningfield Reservoir
Rettendon
Navestock Side
Fox Hatch
Crow Green
19
B1007
South Hanningfield
Coalhill
Ramsden Heath
Pilgrims Hatch
Weald Park
A1023
Havering's Grove
Norsey Wood
Downham
BILLERICAY
Runwell
South Weald
Shenfield
Hutton
A129
Cater
Ramsden Bellhouse
BRENTWOOD
South Green
Wickford
Duck Wood
Brook Street
Crays Hill
Shotgate
Ingrave
Great Burstead
Nevendon
Thorndon
Herongate
Little Burstead
A176
A127
Great Warley
Harold Wood
Little Warley
A1235
North Benfleet
ROMFORD
Laindon
BASILDON
Bowers Gifford
Pitsea
B148
Cranham
A1321
UPMINSTER
West Horndon
B1036
Langdon Hills
Vange
Tarpots
Dry Street
A13
Hope's Green
Westley Heights
B187
Bulphan
B1464
National Motorboat
B1427
One Tree Hill
Pitsea Hall
North Ockendon
B1420
Fobbing
Bethus Woods
Horndon on the Hill
Balstonia
Corringham
Dutch Cottage
B186
B188
A128
A1014
Coryton
South Ockendon
Baker Street
Orsett
Stanford-le-Hope
M25
North Stifford
A1013
Thames Haven
THURROCK
Mucking
River Thames
Aveley
Little Thurrock
Walton Hall
Linford
28
Blythe Sands
Chafford Hundred
Thurrock
Chadwell St. Mary
East Tilbury
Cliffe Marshes
Halstow Marshes
A1306
A1090
South Stifford
West Tilbury
Coalhouse Fort
Dartford Crossing
West Thurrock
GRAYS
A1089
A126
Aviation
Cliffe
Cooling
Northward Hill
A282

Braxted Oxley Green B1026 Salcott Old Hall Marshes MERSEA ISLAND

Wickham Bishops Great Totham North Tolleshunt D'Arcy B1023 West Mersea Channel

Great Totham South Little Totham Toleshunt **11** Tollesbury **D** Sales Point

Broad Street Green B1022 Goldhanger B1026 Bradwell Power Station Bradwell Church Waterside

Langford Heybridge Osea Island RIVER BLACKWATER Bradwell Lodge Bradwell-on-Sea

Beeleigh Abbey Hall Tapestry Heybridge Basin Ramsey Island **1** B1021

Millennium **MALDON** Northey Island St. Lawrence Church Tillingham

A414 Leper Maldon 991 NT Dengie Marshes

Woodham Mortimer Hazeleigh B1018 Steeple Dengie Dengie Marshes

Rudley Green Vineyard Mundon Ramsey Asheldham

Purleigh B1010 Maylandsea Mayland 200

Howegreen Cold Norton 14 Latchingdon B1018 Southminster

E Stow Maries B1010 B1018 **X** Mangapps Farm B1021

B1012 Hall Wood B1010 Ostend Stoneyhills Holliwell Point

South Woodham Ferrers North Fambridge Burnham-on-Crouch **Burnham-on-Crouch**

Hullbridge South Fambridge Lion Creek River Crouch **2** Foulness Point

Jakapeni Rare Breeds **Hockley** **Ashingdon** Canewdon Paglesham Churchend Wallasea Island DANGER AREA Courtsend

B1013 Paglesham Eastend Roach Churchend

Hawkwell Stroud Green Ballards Gore Great Stambridge River **FOULNESS ISLAND**

A1015 **RAYLEIGH** The Old House Church Potton Island Maplin Sands 90

27 Aircraft Eastwood LONDON SOUTHEND **Rochford** Barling

adleigh 7 Prittlewell Priory Barling Little Wakering **3**

8 Prittlewell A1159 Bournes Green North Shoebury DANGER AREA **Great Wakering**

Leigh-on-Sea A13 Southchurch Southchurch Hall **N O R T H**

Heritage Beecroft Galy Westcliff-on-Sea **4** Sea Life Thorpe Bay **Shoeburyness**

Two Tree Island **SOUTHEND-ON-SEA** B1016 **SHOEBURY NESS** **S E A**

wlands Pier 80

Leigh Beck **C** **29** **D**

Allhallows-on-Sea 90 600

Allhallows **Grain**

Lower Stoke **SHEERNESS**

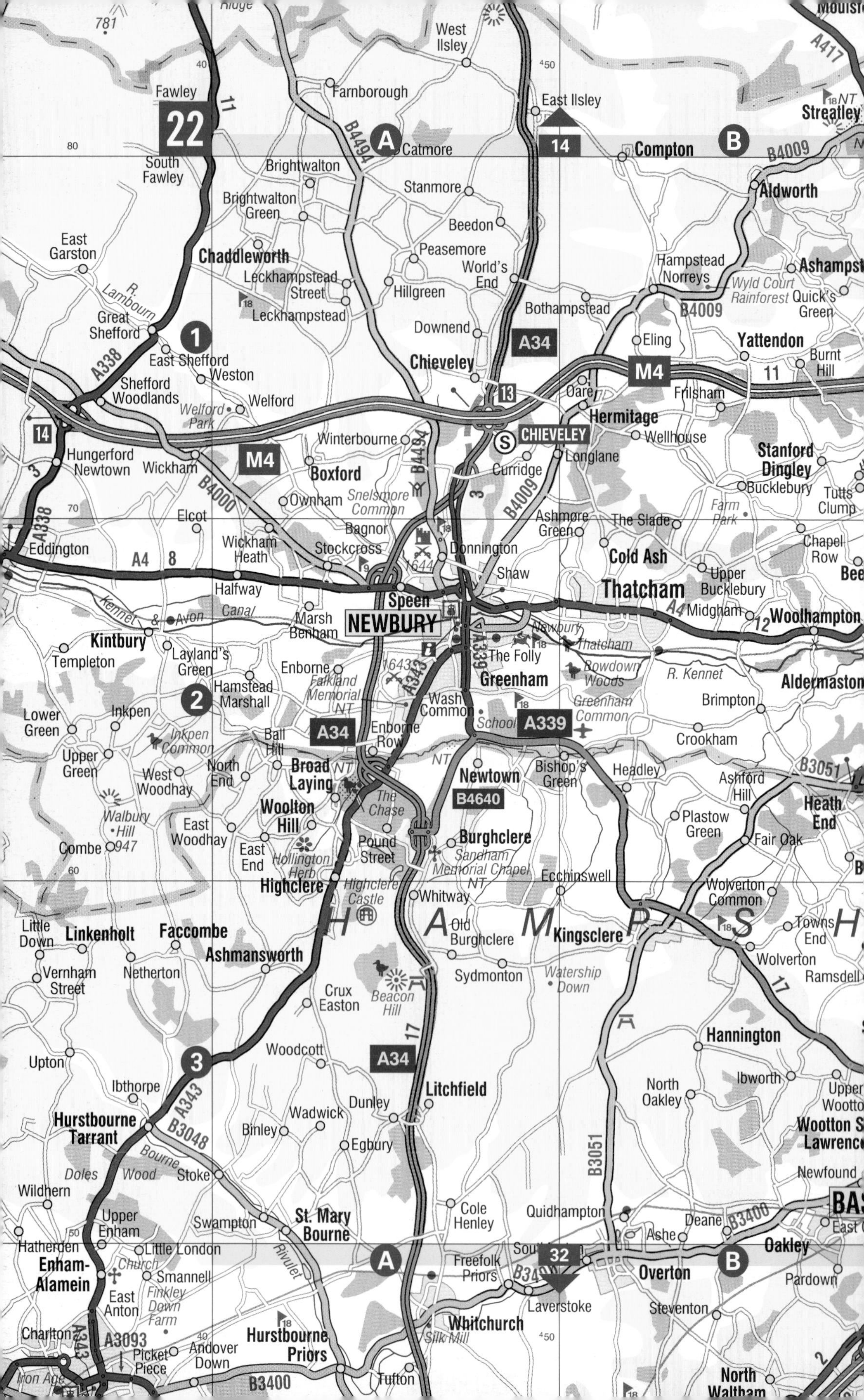

781
West Ilsley
Farnborough
East Ilsley
Fawley
22
11
B4494
A
Catmore
14
Compton
B
B4009
Streatley
A417
South Fawley
Brightwalton
Stanmore
Aldworth
Brightwalton Green
Beedon
East Garston
Chaddleworth
Peasemore
World's End
Hampstead Norreys
Ashampstead
R. Lambourn
Leckhampstead Street
Hillgreen
Wyld Court Rainforest
Quick's Green
Great Shefford
Leckhampstead
Bothampstead
B4009
1
Downend
Eling
Yattendon
Burnt Hill
A338
East Shefford
Weston
A34
Chieveley
M4
11
Shefford Woodlands
Welford
13
Oare
Frilsham
Welford Park
Hermitage
14
Winterbourne
CHIEVELEY
Wellhouse
Hungerford Newtown
Wickham
M4
Boxford
B4494
Curridge
Longlane
Stanford Dingley
B4000
Ownham
Snelsmore Common
B4009
Bucklebury
Tutts Clump
A338
Elcot
Bagnor
Ashmore Green
The Slade
Farm Park
Wickham Heath
Stockcross
Donnington
Chapel Row
Eddington
A4
8
Cold Ash
1644
Shaw
Halfway
Speen
Thatcham
Upper Bucklebury
Kennet & Avon Canal
Marsh Benham
NEWBURY
A4
Midgham
12
Woolhampton
Kintbury
A339
Newbury Thatcham
Templeton
Layland's Green
Enborne
1643
The Folly
Greenham
Bowdown Woods
R. Kennet
Aldermaston
Falkland Memorial NT
A343
Hamstead Marshall
2
Wash Common
Greenham Common
Brimpton
Lower Green
Inkpen
School
A339
Crookham
Inkpen Common
Ball Hill
A34
Enborne Row
Upper Green
West Woodhay
North End
Broad Laying
NT
Newtown
Bishop's Green
Headley
Ashford Hill
B3051
Heath End
The Chase
B4640
Plastow Green
Walbury Hill
Woolton Hill
East Woodhay
Burghclere
Fair Oak
Combe
947
East End
Hollington Herb
Pound Street
Sandham Memorial Chapel NT
Ecchinswell
Highclere
Highclere Castle
Whitway
Wolverton Common
H A M P S H
Little Down
Linkenholt
Faccombe
Old Burghclere
Kingsclere
Towns End
Ashmansworth
Vernham Street
Netherton
Sydmonton
Watership Down
Wolverton
Ramsdell
17
Crux Easton
Beacon Hill
17
Hannington
Woodcott
A34
Upton
3
Ibthorpe
Litchfield
North Oakley
Ibworth
Upper Wootton
Dunley
A343
Wadwick
Hurstbourne Tarrant
B3048
Binley
Egbury
Wootton St Lawrence
Bourne
Doles Wood
Stoke
B3051
Newfound
Wildhern
Cole Henley
Quidhampton
Upper Enham
Swampton
St. Mary Bourne
Deane
B3400
Ashe
East
Hatherden
Little London
Enham-Alamein
Church
Smannell
A
Freefolk Priors
32
Overton
B
Oakley
Rivulet
East Anton
Finkley Down Farm
B3400
Laverstoke
Pardown
Whitchurch
Steventon
Charlton
A3093
A343
Hurstbourne Priors
Silk Mill
Picket Piece
Andover Down
B3400
Tufton
North Waltham
Iron Age

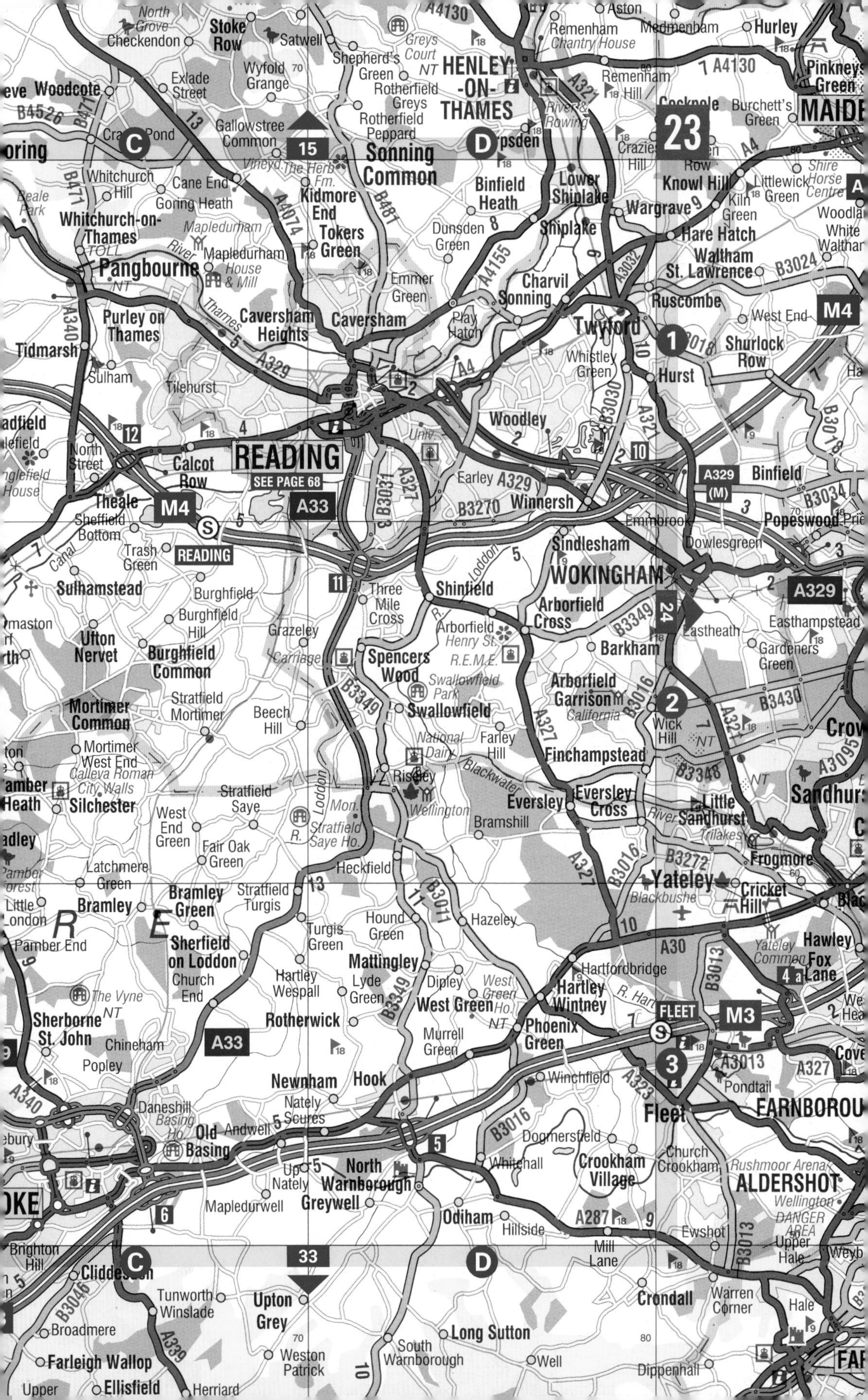
23
READING
SEE PAGE 68
HENLEY-ON-THAMES
Sonning Common
Caversham
Caversham Heights
Pangbourne
Whitchurch-on-Thames
Purley on Thames
Tidmarsh
Tilehurst
Calcot Row
Theale
Sulhamstead
Burghfield
Burghfield Common
Mortimer Common
Silchester
Bramley
Sherfield on Loddon
Sherborne St. John
Chineham
Popley
Old Basing
Cliddesden
Upton Grey
Greywell
North Warnborough
Odiham
Hook
Newnham
Rotherwick
Mattingley
Hartley Wintney
Phoenix Green
Fleet
Church Crookham
Crookham Village
ALDERSHOT
FARNBOROUGH
Yateley
Sandhurst
Finchampstead
Eversley
Eversley Cross
Arborfield Garrison
Arborfield Cross
Arborfield
Barkham
WOKINGHAM
Sindlesham
Winnersh
Woodley
Earley
Shinfield
Spencers Wood
Swallowfield
Riseley
Three Mile Cross
Grazeley
Twyford
Hurst
Ruscombe
Wargrave
Shiplake
Lower Shiplake
Charvil
Sonning
Binfield
Binfield Heath
Knowl Hill
Hare Hatch
Waltham St. Lawrence
Shurlock Row
Popeswood
Easthampstead
Crowthorne
Little Sandhurst
Frogmore
Cricket Hill
Hawley
Fox Lane
Crondall
Ewshot
Long Sutton
South Warnborough
Ellisfield
Farleigh Wallop
Herriard
Kidmore End
Tokers Green
Mapledurham
Goring Heath
Woodcote
Checkendon
Stoke Row
Remenham
Hurley
Medmenham
Aston
Hartfordbridge
Winchfield
Dogmersfield
Crookham Village
Mill Lane
Hillside
Murrell Green
West Green
Dipley
Hazeley
Heckfield
Stratfield Turgis
Stratfield Saye
Stratfield Mortimer
Beech Hill
Mortimer West End
Pamber Heath
Bramley Green
Little London
Pamber End
Daneshill
Basing
Mapledurwell
Nately Scures
Up Nately
Tunworth
Winslade
Broadmere
Weston Patrick
Well
Dippenhall
Warren Corner
Hale
Upper Hale
M4
M3
A33
A329
A327
A321
A4
A30
A340
A4074
A4155
A4130
B3016
B3349
B3011
B3013
B3030
B3024
B3034
B3430
B3348
B3272
B3270
B3031
B3046
A339
A287
A323
A3013
A3095
A3032
B481
B471
B4526
15
33
C
D

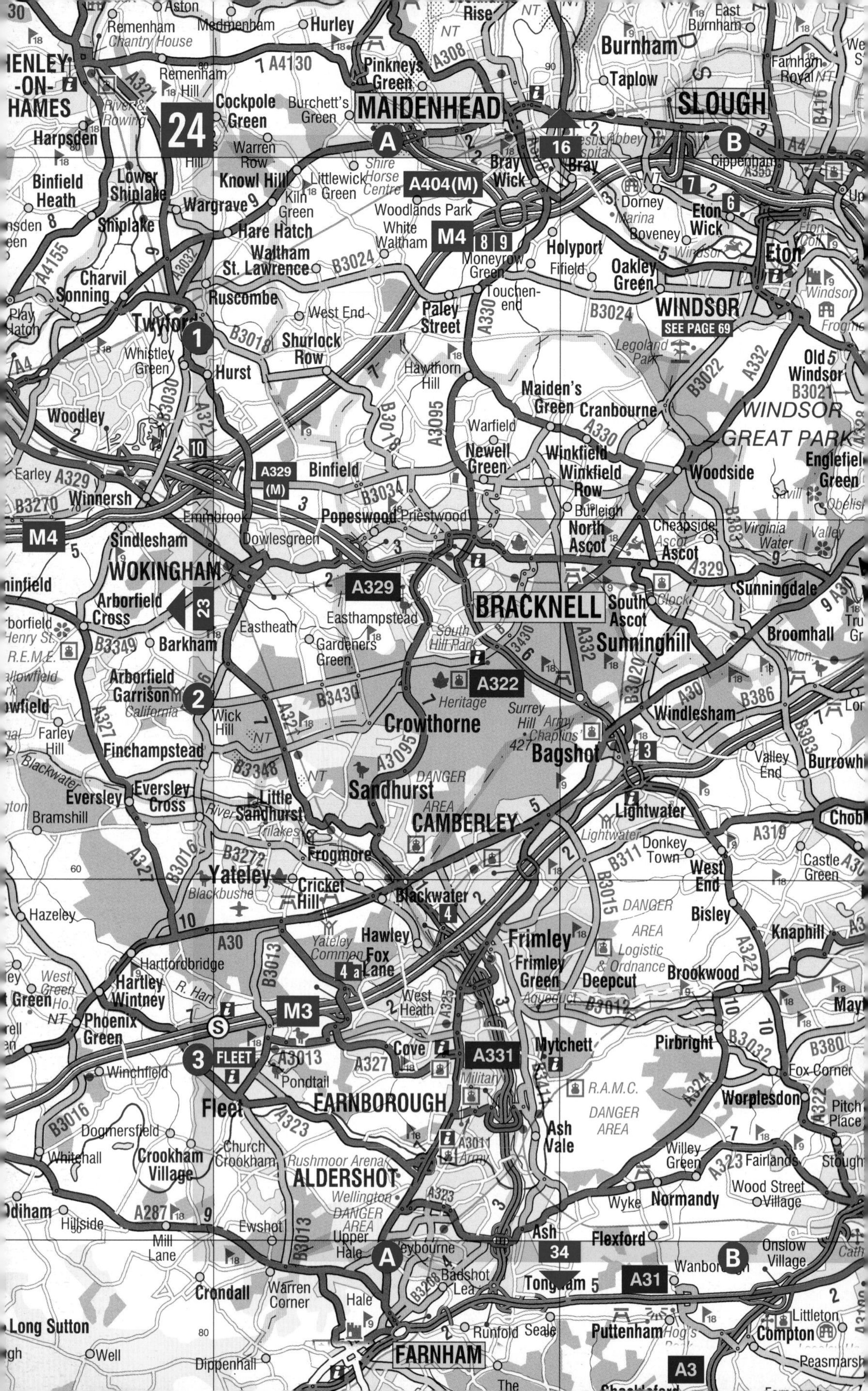

Aston
Remenham
Chantry House
Medmenham
Hurley
Rise
NT
East Burnham
Burnham
HENLEY-ON-THAMES
A4130
Pinkneys Green
A308
Taplow
Farnham Royal
Remenham Hill
River & Rowing
24
Cockpole Green
Burchett's Green
MAIDENHEAD
SLOUGH
B416
Harpsden
Warren Row
A
16
B
Jesus Abbey Hospital
Cippenham
A4
A355
Binfield Heath
Lower Shiplake
Knowl Hill
Littlewick Green
Shire Horse Centre
A404(M)
Bray Wick
Bray
Dorney
7
6
Eton Wick
Marina
Up
Shiplake
Wargrave
Kiln Green
Woodlands Park
Hare Hatch
White Waltham
M4
8 9
Holyport
Boveney
Windsor
Eton
Eton Coll.
A4155
A3032
Charvil
Waltham St. Lawrence
B3024
Moneyrow Green
Fifield
Oakley Green
Windsor
Sonning
Ruscombe
Touchen-end
Paley Street
WINDSOR
SEE PAGE 69
Frogmore
Twyford
1
West End
A330
B3024
Legoland Park
Play Hatch
Whistley Green
B3018
Shurlock Row
B3022
A332
Old Windsor
A4
Hurst
Hawthorn Hill
Maiden's Green
Cranbourne
B3021
WINDSOR GREAT PARK
B3030
A321
Woodley
A3095
B3018
Warfield
10
Newell Green
Winkfield
A330
Englefield Green
Earley
A329
A329 (M)
Binfield
Winkfield Row
Woodside
Winnersh
B3270
B3034
Priestwood
Burleigh
Savill
Obelisk
Popeswood
Emmbrook
M4
Sindlesham
Dowlesgreen
North Ascot
Cheapside
Ascot
Virginia Water
Valley
Ascot
WOKINGHAM
A329
A329
B383
Sunningdale
A30
Arborfield Cross
23
Arborfield
Easthampstead
BRACKNELL
South Ascot
Clock
Henry St.
Eastheath
South Hill Park
B3430
A332
Sunninghill
Broomhall
R.E.M.E.
B3349
Barkham
Gardeners Green
Arborfield Garrison
2
A322
B3020
A30
Heritage
B386
California
Wick Hill
B3430
A321
Crowthorne
Surrey Hill
Army Chaplins'
Windlesham
Farley Hill
A327
Finchampstead
NT
427
Bagshot
3
B383
Valley End
Burrowhill
Blackwater
B3348
A3095
DANGER
Sandhurst
Eversley
Eversley Cross
Little Sandhurst
AREA
5
Lightwater
Chobham
Bramshill
River
Trilakes
CAMBERLEY
Lightwater
A319
A327
B3016
B3272
Frogmore
B311
Donkey Town
Castle Green
Yateley
Blackbushe
Cricket Hill
Blackwater
B3015
West End
Hazeley
A30
10
Yateley Common
Hawley
4
DANGER AREA
Bisley
Knaphill
Hartfordbridge
Fox Lane
4a
Frimley
Logistic & Ordnance
West Green
Hartley Wintney
B3013
A325
Frimley Green
Deepcut
Brookwood
A322
R. Hart
West Heath
Aqueduct
B3012
May
M3
Phoenix Green
S
Pirbright
10
Winchfield
3
FLEET
A3013
Cove
A331
Mytchett
B3032
B380
A327
Military
A3011
Fox Corner
Pondtail
R.A.M.C.
Worplesdon
A322
Pitch Place
B3016
FARNBOROUGH
DANGER AREA
Fleet
A323
A324
Dogmersfield
Ash Vale
Whitehall
Church Crookham
Crookham Village
Rushmoor Arena
Army
Willey Green
A323
Fairlands
Stoughton
ALDERSHOT
Wellington
Wood Street Village
Odiham
Hillside
A287
DANGER AREA
A323
Wyke
Normandy
Ewshot
Upper Hale
Mill Lane
Ash
Flexford
Onslow Village
B3013
Aldershot
Heybourne
34
Badshot Lea
B
Crondall
Warren Corner
B3208
Tongham
A31
Wanborough
Hale
Seale
Littleton
Long Sutton
Runfold
Puttenham
Hog's Back
Compton
Well
Dippenhall
FARNHAM
Peasmarsh
A3
The

UXBRIDGE
WEMBLEY
WILLESDEN
Kilburn
Iver Heath
Hillingdon
GREENFORD
Cowley
Yeading
EALING
ACTON
25
HAYES
SOUTHALL
West Drayton
Yiewsley
Richings Park
Shredding Green
Sutton
Pottery Collection
HESTON
Pitshanger
CHISWICK
KENSINGTON
Harmondsworth
Sipson
Harlington
Brentford
Osterley
HAMMERSMITH
BARNES
FULHAM
Kew
North Sheen
Heston
Longford
LONDON HEATHROW
Cranford
Poyle
Syon House
ISLEWORTH
PUTNEY
HOUNSLOW
Rugby Grd.
RICHMOND
Roehampton
Hatton
Stanwell Moor
Stanwell
East Bedfont
Marble Hill Ho.
Ham House
Richmond Park
Ham
TWICKENHAM
WANDSWORTH
ASHFORD
FELTHAM
Feltham hill
Hanworth
Kempton Park
Hampton
TEDDINGTON
WIMBLEDON
Egham Hythe
STAINES
Queen Mary Resr.
SUNBURY
Hampton Wick
Thorpe
Laleham
Littleton
Upper Halliford
West Molesey
East Molesey
Hampton Court
KINGSTON UPON THAMES
26
NEW MALDEN
MORDEN
Shepperton
CHERTSEY
WALTON-ON-THAMES
Thames Ditton
SURBITON
Tolworth
Lyne
WEYBRIDGE
Sandown Park
Long Ditton
Worcester Park
Addlestone
ESHER
Hook
Chessington
CARSHALTON
Ottershaw
Row Town
New Haw
Brooklands
Hersham
Whiteley Village
Claygate
Claremont
Chessington World of Adventures
Bourne Hall
Cheam
SUTTON
Woodham
Fairmile
Malden Rushett
EWELL
Sheerwater
West Byfleet
Byfleet
Cobham
Oxshott
EPSOM
Painshill Park
Stoke D'Abernon
Pachesham
Ashtead
BANSTEAD
Pyrford
Wisley
R.H.S.
Downside
WOKING
Ripley
Martyr's Green
Semaphore Tower
Epsom Downs
Burgh Heath
Old Woking
Send Marsh
Ockham
Effingham Common
LEATHERHEAD
Tadworth
Send
Little Bookham
Fetcham
Headley
Walton on the Hill
Kingswood
Burntcommon
East Horsley
Great Bookham
Mickleham
Lower Kingswood
Effingham
Norbury Park
West Clandon
East Clandon
West Horsley
Polesden Lacey
Westhumble
Box Hill
Margery
Clandon Park
Hatchlands Park
Sheepleas
Ranmore Common
Chapel
Salomons
Buckland
Merrow
NORTH DOWNS
SURREY
Betchworth
SEE PAGE 66
35
Silent Pool
Westcott
Brockham
REIGATE
GUILDFORD
Gomshall
DORKING
Strood Green
Gadbrook
Chilworth
Wotton
Doversgreen
Albury
Shere
Abinger Hammer
Stonebridge
Crossways Farm
North Holmwood
Leigh
Red Cross
Blackheath
Brook
Sutton
Friday Street
Dawesgreen
Blackbrook
Sidlowbridge
M25
M4
M3
A3
A24
A30
A4
A40
A312
A316
A308
A243
A240
A217
A205
A309
A406
17
1
2
3
C
D

26
WEMBLEY
WILLESDEN
Kilburn
TOWN
FINSBURY
BETHNAL GREEN
MARYLEBONE
A501
SHOREDITCH
Holborn
STEPNEY
ACTON
EALING
A406
A40
WEST END
CITY
A13
POPLAR
Hanwell
Shepherd's Bush
PADDINGTON
A
Hyde Park
18
B
KENSINGTON
WESTMINSTER
Pitshanger
A4
BERMONDSEY
M4
CHISWICK
CHELSEA
LAMBETH
Brentford
HAMMERSMITH
DEPTFORD
A2
Kew
BARNES
FULHAM
CAMBERWELL
North Sheen
A316
Palace
BATTERSEA
BRIXTON
A202
Syon House
ISLEWORTH
PUTNEY
A3
A20
Rugby Grd.
A205
CLAPHAM
LEWISHAM
RICHMOND
Roehampton
WANDSWORTH
Horniman
Marble Hill Ho.
Ham House
Richmond Park
Upper Tooting
A214
A23
Dulwich
Crystal Palace
Ham
West Norwood
WIMBLEDON
Sydenham
TEDDINGTON
A24
STREATHAM
Crystal Palace
Penge
Hampton Wick
A308
KINGSTON UPON THAMES
MERTON
South Norwood
MITCHAM
Thornton Heath
BECKENHAM
Hampton Court
25
MORDEN
NEW MALDEN
A297
A23
SURBITON
A3
Tolworth
Long Ditton
Addiscombe
A232
A309
A240
Worcester Park
CARSHALTON
Carew Beddington
CROYDON
ESHER
Hook
A24
A232
Addington
Claygate
Chessington
Bourne Hall
Horton
Cheam
SUTTON
WALLINGTON
Chessington World of Adventures
Little Holland Ho.
Palace
Selsdon
A243
Malden Rushett
EWELL
PURLEY
Selsdon Wood
Sanderstead
Oxshott
EPSOM
A240
Farleigh
A22
Woodmansterne
Hamsey Green
Ashtead
BANSTEAD
Chelsham
Whyteleafe
Kenley
9
A24
COULSDON
Old Coulsdon
Epsom Downs
Burgh Heath
Chipstead
Pinnacle
LEATHERHEAD
Tadworth
Hooley
A23
East Surrey
WARLINGHAM
M25
Walton on the Hill
Kingswood
Chaldon
Woldingham
Mugswell
7
3
Headley
A217
CATERHAM
Great Bookham
A24
Lower Kingswood
Mickleham
Norbury Park
Margery
Gatton
Westhumble
Box Hill
Merstham
Warwick Wold
Godstone
Oxted
8
Brewer Street
Chapel
Salomons
Buckland
REDHILL
Tandridge
Betchworth
Nutfield
Bletchingley
36
Brockham
A
Priory
Bletchingley Castle
B
M23
Strood Green
Gadbrook
REIGATE
South Nutfield
South Godstone
DORKING
Doversgreen
Stonebridge
North Holmwood
Leigh
Dawesgreen
Redhill
Crowhurst Lane End
Sidlowbridge
Salfords
A22
Blackbrook
Outwood
Blindley Heath
S U R R E Y

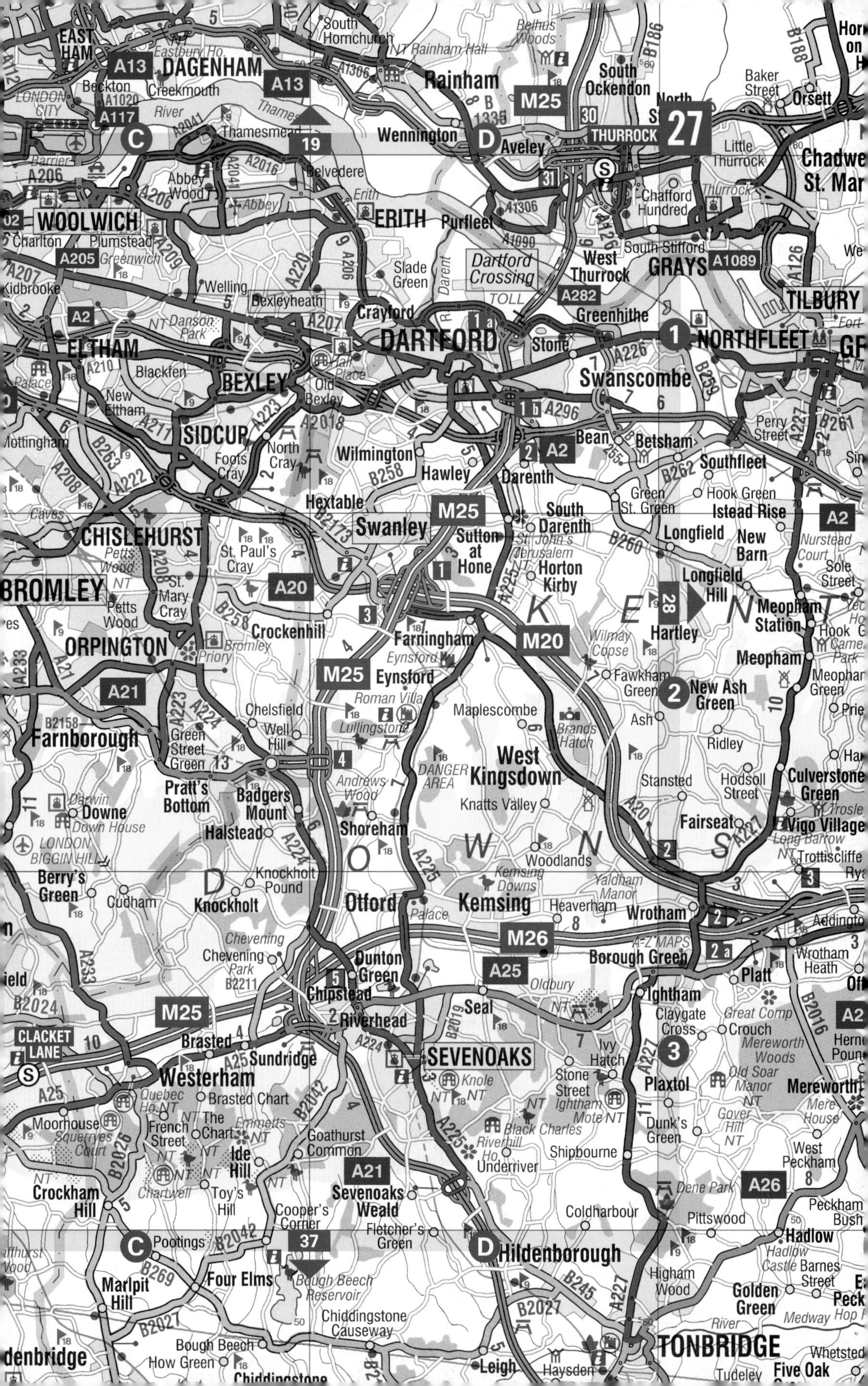

EAST HAM
DAGENHAM
South Hornchurch
NT Rainham Hall
Belhus Woods
Rainham
South Ockendon
Baker Street
Orsett
Beckton
Creekmouth
A13
M25
LONDON CITY
River Thames
Thamesmead
Wennington
Aveley
THURROCK
27
Little Thurrock
Chadwell St. Mary
19
Belvedere
Abbey Wood
Chafford Hundred
WOOLWICH
ERITH
Purfleet
Charlton
Plumstead
Greenwich
Slade Green
Dartford Crossing
TOLL
West Thurrock
South Stifford
GRAYS
A1089
TILBURY
Kidbrooke
Welling
Bexleyheath
Crayford
Greenhithe
ELTHAM
DARTFORD
Stone
NORTHFLEET
Blackfen
BEXLEY
Old Bexley
Hall Place
Swanscombe
New Eltham
Perry Street
SIDCUP
North Cray
Foots Cray
Wilmington
Hawley
Darenth
Bean
Betsham
Southfleet
Green St. Green
Hook Green
Istead Rise
Hextable
Swanley
M25
South Darenth
Sutton at Hone
St. John's Jerusalem
CHISLEHURST
St. Paul's Cray
Petts Wood
St. Mary Cray
Longfield
New Barn
Nurstead Court
Sole Street
Horton Kirby
Longfield Hill
BROMLEY
A20
Crockenhill
Farningham
M20
Hartley
Meopham Station
ORPINGTON
Priory
Eynsford
Wilmay Copse
Meopham
KENT
28
Fawkham Green
New Ash Green
Meopham Green
A21
Roman Villa
Lullingstone
Chelsfield
Well Hill
Maplescombe
Brands Hatch
Ash
Ridley
Farnborough
Green Street Green
Pratt's Bottom
Badgers Mount
DANGER AREA
West Kingsdown
Andrews Wood
Stansted
Hodsoll Street
Culverstone Green
Downe
Down House
Darwin
Knatts Valley
Halstead
Shoreham
Fairseat
Vigo Village
LONDON BIGGIN HILL
Trosley
Long Barrow
Woodlands
DOWNS
Trottiscliffe
Berry's Green
Cudham
Knockholt
Knockholt Pound
Otford
Kemsing
Kemsing Downs
Yaldham Manor
Heaverham
Wrotham
Addington
Palace
M26
A-Z MAPS
Chevening
Chevening Park
Dunton Green
Borough Green
Wrotham Heath
Chipstead
A25
Oldbury
Platt
M25
Riverhead
Seal
Ightham
Claygate Cross
Great Comp
Crouch
CLACKET LANE
Brasted
Sundridge
SEVENOAKS
Ivy Hatch
Mereworth Woods
Westerham
Knole
Stone Street
Ightham Mote
Plaxtol
Mereworth
Quebec Ho
Brasted Chart
Old Soar Manor
Moorhouse
Squerryes Court
French Street
The Chart
Emmetts
Goathurst Common
Black Charles
Riverhill Ho
Dunk's Green
Gover Hill
Mere House
Ide Hill
Underriver
Shipbourne
West Peckham
Chartwell
Toy's Hill
A21
A26
Crockham Hill
Sevenoaks Weald
Cooper's Corner
Dene Park
Coldharbour
Peckham Bush
Pittswood
Hadlow
Pootings
37
Fletcher's Green
Hildenborough
Hadlow Castle
Barnes Street
Four Elms
Bough Beech Reservoir
Marlpit Hill
Higham Wood
Golden Green
Chiddingstone Causeway
River Medway
Bough Beech
How Green
Edenbridge
Leigh
Haysden
TONBRIDGE
Tudeley
Five Oak
Chiddingstone

28
M25
South Ockendon
North Stifford
Baker Street
Orsett
Horndon on the Hill
A13
Balstonia
Corringham
Fobbing
Coryton
Stanford-le-Hope
Thames Haven
Mucking
20
River Thames
Aveley
THURROCK
Little Thurrock
Chadwell St. Mary
Linford
Walton Hall Farm
East Tilbury
Blythe Sands
Cliffe Marshes
Halstow Marshes
Chafford Hundred
West Thurrock
South Stifford
GRAYS
A1089
West Tilbury
Coalhouse Fort Aviation
Dartford Crossing
TOLL
A282
Greenhithe
TILBURY
Fort
Cliffe
Cooling
High Halstow
Stone
NORTHFLEET
GRAVESEND
Swanscombe
Milton Chantry
DANGER AREA
Church Street
Cooling Street
DARTFORD
Chalk
Lower Higham
Cliffe Woods
Bean
Betsham
Southfleet
Perry Street
Singlewell
Higham
Shorne
Shorne Ridgeway
Chattenden
Wainscott
Lower Upnor
Upper Upnor
A2
Darenth
Green St. Green
Hook Green
Istead Rise
Thong
Frindsbury
M25
Sutton at Hone
South Darenth
St. John's Jerusalem
Horton Kirby
Longfield
New Barn
Nurstead Court
Sole Street
Owletts NT
Cobham Hall
STROOD
Brompton
Longfield Hill
Meopham Station
College
Cobham
Henley Street
Borstal
ROCHESTER
SEE PAGE 66
M20
27
Hartley
Wilmay Copse
Hook Green
Yeoman's Ho. NT
Camer Park
Luddesdown
Cuxton
M2
MEDWAY TOWNS
CHATHAM
Fawkham Green
Meopham
Meopham Green
North Halling
Maplescombe
Brands Hatch
Ash
New Ash Green
Priestwood
Upper Halling
Halling
Wouldham
Rochester
Hempstead
West Kingsdown
Ridley
Harvel
Holly Hill Wood
A228
Walderslade
Stansted
Hodsoll Street
Culverstone Green
Burham
Blue Bell Hill
Knatts Valley
Fairseat
Trosley
Vigo Village
Long Barrow NT
Snodland
Birling
Ham Hill
Kit's Coty Houses
Eccles
Westfield Wood
Woodlands
Kemsing Downs
Trottiscliffe
Ryarsh
New Hythe
Lunsford
Priory
Aylesford
A229
Yaldham Manor
Kemsing
Heaverham
Wrotham
Addington
Leybourne
Larkfield
Boxley
M26
A-Z MAPS
Borough Green
Wrotham Heath
West Malling
Ditton
East Malling
Allington
Sandling
A25
Oldbury
Ightham
Platt
Offham
Tower
B2246
Seal
Great Comp
A228
MAIDSTONE
Claygate Cross
Crouch
Mereworth Woods
Herne Pound
Kings Hill
Barming Pl.
Barming Heath
Ivy Hatch
Stone Street
Knole NT
Ightham Mote NT
Plaxtol
Old Soar Manor NT
Mereworth
Kent Street
Wateringbury
East Barming
Mote House
Shepway
Black Charles
Riverhill Ho.
Dunk's Green
Gover Hill NT
Mere House
Mereworth
Teston
West Farleigh
East Farleigh
Underriver
Shipbourne
West Peckham
A228
Nettlestead
Loose
Wool Ho. NT
Boughton Green
Dene Park
A26
Nettlestead Green
Coxheath
Coldharbour
Pittswood
Hadlow
Peckham Bush
Yalding
Linton
Boughton Monchelsea
Hildenborough
Hadlow Castle
Barnes Street
Hale Street
38
Hunton
Boughton Monchelsea Place
Higham Wood
Golden Green
East Peckham
Hop Farm
Yalding
Laddingford
Benover
Reed Court Farm
Chainhurst
Beult R.
A229
River Medway
Beltring
TONBRIDGE
Whetsted
Queen Street
Collier Street
Leigh
Haysden
Tudeley
Five Oak
Milebush

SHOEBURY NESS
29
21
C
D
Allhallows-on-Sea
Allhallows
Grain
Lower Stoke
Wallend
Isle of Grain
SHEERNESS
Minster
Marine Town
Mile Town
Halfway Houses
Queenborough
Rushenden
Chetney Marshes
Eastchurch
Warden
Warden Point
Leysdown-on-Sea
Brambledown
ISLE OF SHEPPEY
Elmley Island
Elmley Marshes
Isle of Harty
The Swale
RIVER MEDWAY
Thamesport
Upchurch
Lower Halstow
Iwade
Kemsley
Milton Regis
SITTINGBOURNE
Conyer
Teynham
FAVERSHAM
Newington
Bobbing
Borden
Bapchild
Oare
Ospringe
Graveney
Goodnestone
Preston
M2
Newnham
Doddington
Sheldwich
Selling
Hollingbourne
Harrietsham
Lenham
Leeds
Broomfield
Langley Heath
Kingswood
Sutton Valence
Ulcombe
Lenham Heath
Charing
Challock
Godmersham
Charing Heath
Egerton
Westwell
Boughton Lees
Boughton Aluph
M20
39
MAIDSTONE
MEDWAY
A249
A2
A20
A251
A252
A28
A299

Ⓐ

Ⓑ

600

10

80

SHEERNESS

Coastal Park

Gatehouse
Minster

East End

Warden Point

B2008

Eastchurch

Warden

B2231

Brambledown

**Leysdown-
on-Sea**

Herne Ba

70

ISLE *OF* *SHEPPEY*

Leysdown Coastal
Park

HERNE BAY

mley
and
and

Elmley
Marshes

Isle of Harty

Shell
Ness

Hampton

Tankerton

Swalecliffe

The
Swale

The Swale

The

Swale

Whitstable Bay

Seasalter

WHITSTABLE

Chestfield

5 **Greenhill**

ne & Kemsley
lway

South Swale
Nature Reserve

South Swale

South
Street

**West
End**

Herne
Comm

Sailing Barge

Conyer

Oare
Marshes

A290

Herr

A291

A2

BOURNE

Uplees

Teynham
Street

Graveney

Denstroude

Clowes
Wood

Brambles
Wildlife
Park

Calcott

Broad
Oak

Teynham

Luddenham

Oare

Heritage
Centre

A299

Yorkletts

Honey Hill

Bird Garden

Sturry

sham

Lynsted

Lewson Street

FAVERSHAM

Goodnestone
Homestall
Farm

Dargate

Hernhill

Blean
Wood

Blean

**Tyler
Hill**

University
of Kent

Fo
Tow

60

ttwood

Ospringe

Preston

Mount Ephraim

Church Wood

**Rough
Common**

A290

CANTERH

M2

Newnham

dington

Painter's
Forstal

Prospect
Tower

Doddington
Place

Eastling

Belmont

6

A251

North
Street

2

7

18

A2

Boughton under Blean

Dunkirk

7

SEE P.

A2050

Cath

Litt

Howletts
Zoo Park

A257

South Street

Oversland

Harbledown

Sheldwich

Sheldwich
Lees

Selling

Chartham
Hatch

Thanington
Without

A2050

Hogben's
Hill

18

Perry
Wood

**Old Wives
Lees**

Perrywood

Shottenden

Bagham

**Shalmsford
Street**

Chartham

Nackington

Bridge

Throwley
Forstal

Leaveland

Badlesmere

Chilham

Watermill

Garlinge
Green

Lower
Hardres

3

12

A252

Park
Wood

*Chilham
Castle*

14

Bishopsbourne

Stalisfield
Green

Petham

Denge
Wood

B2068

Kings

Molash

King's
Wood

Godmersham

Waltham

*Wye
(Crundale Downs)*

Earley
Wood

Stocker's
Head

A252

Challock

Paddock

Challock

The
Lees

A251

50

40

Derri

Archbishop's
Palace

Bilt

**Boughton
Aluph**

Crundale

S
Street

Yockletts
Bank

Bossingham

Elha
Vin

Westwell
Leacon

Ⓐ

North Leigh

**Stelling
Minnis**

ng
th

A28

Stour

Wye Crown Hassell
Street

Ⓑ

Little
Chart

Ram
Lane

Westwell

**Boughton
Lees**

Goat
Lees

Wye

Bodsham

1

29

2

5

5

K

E

7

5

18

A290

18

N

O

R

T

H

D

O

W

N

S

MARGATE
Westgate on Sea
Westbrook · Cliftonville · Kingsgate
Lifeboat House · Foreness Point
Tudor Ho. · B205

NORTH FORELAND
St. Peter's · Bleak House
Dreamland · Westwood · Dickens' House
Reculver Towers · Minnis Bay · Quex House
Regulbium Roman Fort · **BROADSTAIRS**
Birchington · Northwood
Hillborough · **A299** · **A28** · Westwood

ISLE OF THANET · R.A.F. · **RAMSGATE**
Acol · Manston · Northwood
Boyden Gate · Monkton · Manston
Sarre · St. Nicholas at Wade · Chislet
A253 · **A253** · Cliffs End · NT · Motor
Monkton · Rural Life
Minster · Ebbsfleet · Pegwell Bay
West Stourmouth · R. Stour · NT
East Stourmouth · **A256** · Richborough Port
Westmarsh · Paramour Street · Richborough Castle
Preston · Ware · Elmstone · Goldstone Amphitheatre
Stourmarsh · Hoaden · Great Stonar
Nash · Cooper Street · White
Wickhambreaux · Wingham Bird Park · **Sandwich** · Sandwich Bay
Ickham · **Ash** · Marshborough · Guildhall · TOLL
Wingham · Vineyard · **Woodnesborough**
Staple · Hammill · **Worth**
Goodnestone Park · **Eastry** · Ham · The Small Downs
Goodnestone · Heronden · Sandown
Chillenden · Knowlton · Finglesham · Local History · Victoriana
Nonington · Betteshanger · Time-Ball Tower
Easole Street · Northbourne · Sholden · **DEAL** · The Downs
Frogham · Northbourne Ct. · Deal
Tilmanstone · Elvington · **Great Mongeham** · Walmer
Womenswold · **Ripple** · Walmer
Barfrestone · East Kent Light Rly · East Studdal · **41** · DANGER
Woolage Green · **Eythorne** · Sutton · **Kingsdown** · NT
Shepherdswell or Sibertswold · Ashley · **Ringwould**
Coldred · West Langdon · NT
Wootton · **Martin** · **Martin Mill** · East Langdon
A256

South Channel

A256 · A257 · A258
B2048 · B2050 · B2046

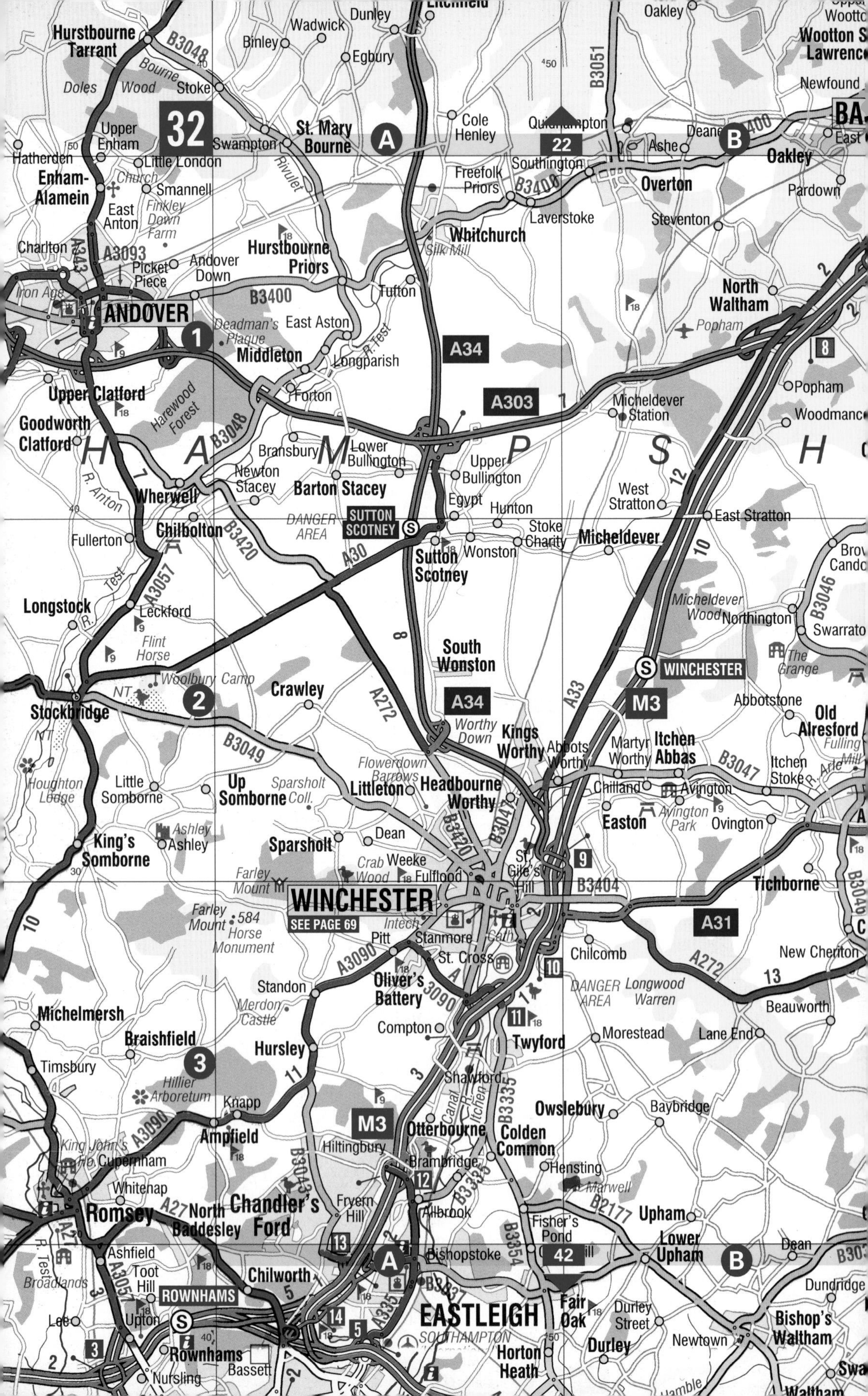
32
Litchfield
Dunley
Wadwick
Binley
Egbury
Hurstbourne Tarrant
B3048
Bourne
Doles Wood
Farm
Stoke
Oakley
Wootton St Lawrence
Newfound
B3051
450
Upper Enham
Swampton
St. Mary Bourne
A
Cole Henley
Quidhampton
22
Ashe
Deane
B
B3400
Oakley
Hatherden
Little London
Enham-Alamein
Church
Smannell
Rivulet
Freefolk Priors
Southington
B3400
Overton
Pardown
East Anton
Finkley Down Farm
Laverstoke
Steventon
Charlton
A343
A3093
Hurstbourne Priors
Whitchurch
Silk Mill
Picket Piece
Andover Down
Tufton
North Waltham
Iron Age
ANDOVER
B3400
Deadman's Plaque
East Aston
Popham
1
Middleton
R. Test
Longparish
A34
8
Popham
Upper Clatford
Forton
A303
Micheldever Station
Woodmancote
Harewood Forest
Goodworth Clatford
B3048
Bransbury
Lower Bullington
Upper Bullington
H
A
M
P
S
H
R. Anton
Newton Stacey
Barton Stacey
Egypt
Hunton
West Stratton
12
Wherwell
East Stratton
Chilbolton
DANGER AREA
SUTTON SCOTNEY
Stoke Charity
Micheldever
Fullerton
B3420
A30
Sutton Scotney
Wonston
10
Brown Candover
Test
A3057
Micheldever Wood
Northington
B3046
Longstock
Leckford
Swarraton
R.
Flint Horse
South Wonston
The Grange
WINCHESTER
Woolbury Camp
NT
Stockbridge
2
Crawley
A272
A34
A33
M3
Abbotstone
Old Alresford
Worthy Down
Kings Worthy
Abbots Worthy
Martyr Worthy
Itchen Abbas
B3049
Fulling Mill
Flowerdown Barrows
B3047
Itchen Stoke
R. Arle
Houghton Lodge
Little Somborne
Up Somborne
Sparsholt Coll.
Littleton
Headbourne Worthy
Chilland
Avington
B3420
B3047
Easton
Avington Park
Ovington
King's Somborne
Ashley
Ashley
Dean
Sparsholt
Crab Wood
Weeke
Fulflood
St. Giles's Hill
9
B3404
Farley Mount
WINCHESTER
SEE PAGE 69
Tichborne
A31
Farley Mount
584 Horse Monument
Intech
Pitt
Stanmore
Cath.
St. Cross
A3090
Chilcomb
New Cheriton
A272
Oliver's Battery
10
DANGER AREA
Longwood Warren
13
Standon
Merdon Castle
Michelmersh
Compton
11
Beauworth
Braishfield
Morestead
Lane End
Timsbury
3
Hursley
Twyford
Hillier Arboretum
Shawford
Canal
R. Itchen
B3335
Owslebury
Baybridge
Knapp
A3090
Ampfield
M3
Otterbourne
Colden Common
King John's Ho.
Cupernham
Hiltingbury
B3043
Brambridge
12
Hensting
Marwell
Whitenap
Fryern Hill
Allbrook
B3335
B2177
Romsey
A27
North Baddesley
Chandler's Ford
Upham
Fisher's Pond
B3354
Lower Upham
A27
13
A
Bishopstoke
42
Dean
B
Ashfield
R. Test
Broadlands
A3057
Toot Hill
Chilworth
B3037
Dundridge
ROWNHAMS
5
Fair Oak
Durley Street
Bishop's Waltham
Lee
Upton
14
EASTLEIGH
A335
SOUTHAMPTON
Horton Heath
Durley
Newtown
3
Rownhams
Bassett
5
Nursling
Waltham

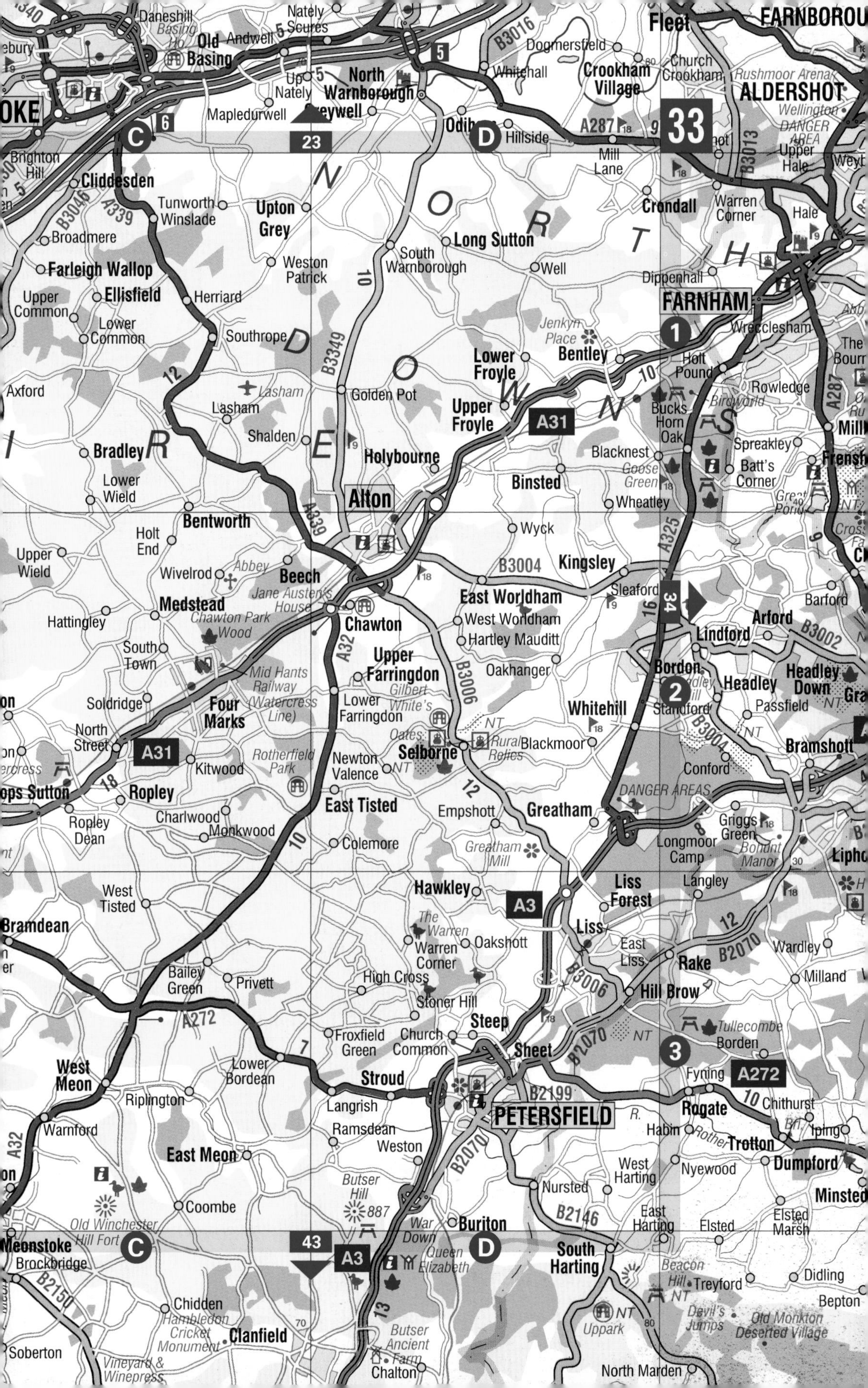

34
Fleet
FARNBOROUGH
Worplesdon
Dogmersfield
Crookham Village
Church Crookham
Rushmoor Arena
ALDERSHOT
Ash Vale
DANGER AREA
Whitehall
Willey Green
Fairlands
Normandy
Wood Street Village
Wyke
Flexford
Ash
24
Odiham
Hillside
Ewshot
Upper Hale
Weybourne
Mill Lane
Crondall
Warren Corner
Hale
Badshot Lea
Tongham
Wanborough
Onslow Village
Long Sutton
Well
Dippenhall
FARNHAM
Runfold
Seale
Puttenham
Hog's Back
Compton
Littleton
Loseley Ho.
Peasmarsh
Crooksbury Hill
The Sands
Shackleford
Farncombe
Jenkyn Place
Bentley
Wrecclesham
Waverley
Charleshill
Hurtmore
Lower Froyle
Holt Pound
The Bourne
Peper Harow
Eashing
Upper Froyle
Rowledge
Tilford
Bucks Horn Oak
Birdworld
Old Kiln Rural Life
Elstead
Millbridge
Milford
Busbridge Lakes
Blacknest
Spreakley
Little Pond
Thursley
Tuesley
Goose Green
Batt's Corner
Frensham
Frensham Common
Wheelerstreet
Hydestile
Binsted
Great Pond
Rushmoor
Wheatley
Feathercombe
Witley
Wyck
Crosswater Farm
Bowlhead Green
Wormley
Kingsley
Churt
Hambledon
East Worldham
Sleaford
Barford
Beacon Hill
Brook
Sandhills
West Worldham
Arford
Lindford
Devil's Punch Bowl
Woodland Walk
Combe Common
Hartley Mauditt
Hindhead
Gibbet Hill
Oakhanger
Bordon
Headley Mill
Headley
Headley Down
Grayshott
Grayswood
Chiddingfold
Old Thorn
Whitehill
Standford
Passfield
Killinghurst
Ramster
Rural Relics
Blackmoor
Bramshott
Haslemere
Ramsnest Common
Conford
Shottermill
DANGER AREAS
Greatham
Griggs Green
Hammer
Camelsdale
Haste Hill
Ansteadbrook
Fisherstreet
Longmoor Camp
Bohunt Manor
Liphook
Linchmere
Kingsley Green
Black Down
The Lake
Greatham Mill
Liss Forest
Langley
Shulbrede Priory
Roundhurst Common
Hollycombe Steam Collection
Northchapel
Liss
Ironworks
Fernhurst
Lurgashall Winery
Oakshott
East Liss
Rake
Wardley
Dial Green
Milland
Woodmansgreen
Lurgashall
Hill Brow
Steep
Redford
Henley
Bexleyhill
Lickfold
Tullecombe
Borden
Sheet
Fyning
Cowdray Park
Rogate
Chithurst
Woolbeding
Lodsworth
Petworth Park
Petworth House
PETERSFIELD
Habin
Iping
Cowdray Ruins
Easebourne
River
Manor of Dean
Upperton
Trotton
Stedham
Dumpford
Nyewood
West Harting
MIDHURST
Tillington
Nursted
Minsted
Cowdray
Selham
West Lavington
South Ambersham
Coultershaw Bridge
Buriton
East Harting
Elsted
Elsted Marsh
Cocking Causeway
South Harting
44
Beacon Hill
Treyford
Didling
Heyshott
Hoyle
Upper Norwood
Bepton
Burton Pond
Uppark
Devil's Jumps
Old Monkton Deserted Village
Cocking
Graffham
Duncton
North Marden
East Lavington
Barlavington
A31
A3
A287
A325
A323
A286
A283
A272
A3100
B3001
B3002
B3004
B3006
B3013
B2070
B2131
B2146
B2199
NT

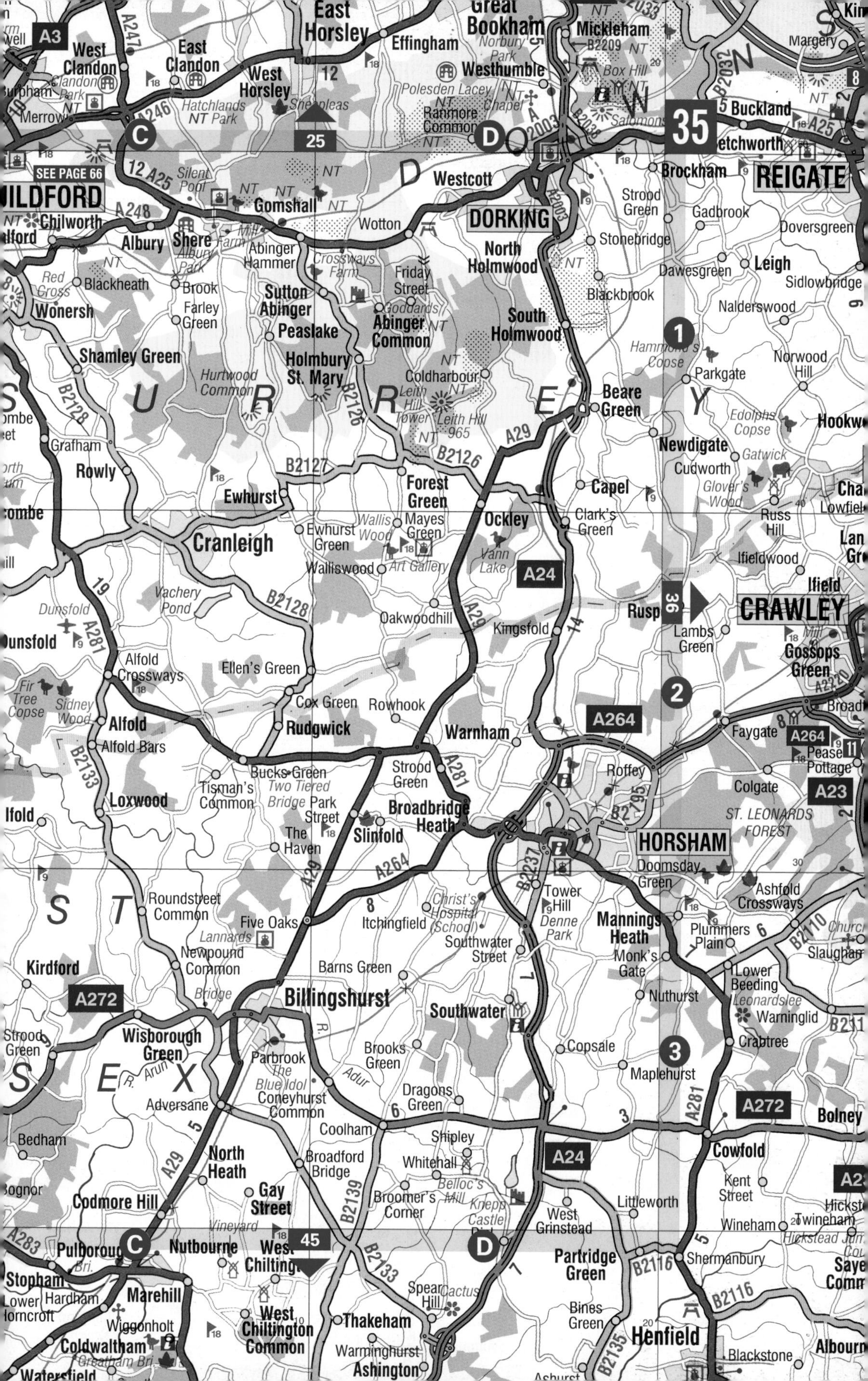
A3
West Clandon
Clandon Park
East Clandon
A247
West Horsley
East Horsley
Effingham
Great Bookham
Norbury Park
Mickleham
B2209
Box Hill
Westhumble
Polesden Lacey
Merrow
Burpham
A246
Hatchlands NT Park
Sheepleas
Ranmore Common
B2033
Margery
Buckland
A25
B2032
35
Betchworth
Salomons
C
25
D
SEE PAGE 66
GUILDFORD
Silent Pool
Gomshall
Westcott
Brockham
REIGATE
A248
Chilworth
Albury
Shere
Albury Park
Abinger Hammer
Wotton
DORKING
A2003
Strood Green
Gadbrook
Doversgreen
Stonebridge
Crossways Farm
Friday Street
North Holmwood
Leigh
Dawesgreen
Sidlowbridge
Red Cross
Blackheath
Brook
Sutton Abinger
Blackbrook
Wonersh
Farley Green
Goddards
Abinger Common
South Holmwood
Nalderswood
Peaslake
Shamley Green
Hurtwood Common
Holmbury St. Mary
Coldharbour
Hammond's Copse
Norwood Hill
Parkgate
B2128
B2126
Leith Hill Tower
Leith Hill 965
Beare Green
Edolph's Copse
Hookwood
A29
Newdigate
Grafham
Rowly
B2127
Gatwick
Cudworth
Forest Green
Capel
Glover's Wood
Ewhurst
Ockley
Clark's Green
Russ Hill
Lowfield
Cranleigh
Ewhurst Green
Wallis Wood
Mayes Green
Vann Lake
Ifieldwood
Walliswood
Art Gallery
A24
Ifield
Vachery Pond
B2128
Rusp
36
CRAWLEY
Dunsfold
Oakwoodhill
Kingsfold
Lambs Green
Dunsfold
A281
Gossops Green
Alfold Crossways
Ellen's Green
Fir Tree Copse
Sidney Wood
Cox Green
Rowhook
A264
Alfold
Rudgwick
Warnham
Faygate
A264
Alfold Bars
Strood Green
Roffey
Pease Pottage
B2133
Bucks Green
Tisman's Common
Two Tiered Bridge
Park Street
Colgate
A23
Loxwood
Broadbridge Heath
Ifold
Slinfold
ST. LEONARDS FOREST
The Haven
HORSHAM
B2195
Doomsday Green
A264
B2237
Roundstreet Common
Tower Hill
Ashfold Crossways
Itchingfield
Christ's Hospital (School)
Denne Park
Mannings Heath
Five Oaks
Plummers Plain
B2110
Lannards
Southwater Street
Monk's Gate
Slaugham
Newpound Common
Kirdford
Barns Green
Lower Beeding
Leonardslee
A272
Nuthurst
Billingshurst
Southwater
Warninglid
Bridge
Strood Green
Wisborough Green
Crabtree
Copsale
Brooks Green
Parbrook
The Blue Idol
Maplehurst
R. Arun
Adur
Adversane
Coneyhurst Common
Dragons Green
A272
Bolney
Bedham
Coolham
Shipley
Cowfold
Whitehall
A24
Broadford Bridge
North Heath
Belloc's Mill
Knepp Castle
Kent Street
Gay Street
Broomer's Corner
Littleworth
Codmore Hill
West Grinstead
Twineham
Hickstead
B2139
Wineham
Vineyard
Pulborough
Nutbourne
West Chiltington
45
Partridge Green
Hickstead Jun.
A283
B2116
Shermanbury
Stopham
B2133
Lower Hardham
Marehill
Spear Hill
Cactus
Horncroft
B2116
Wiggonholt
Thakeham
Bines Green
West Chiltington Common
Henfield
Coldwaltham
Greatham Bri.
Warminghurst
B2135
Blackstone
Albourne
Ashington
Waterstield
Ashurst

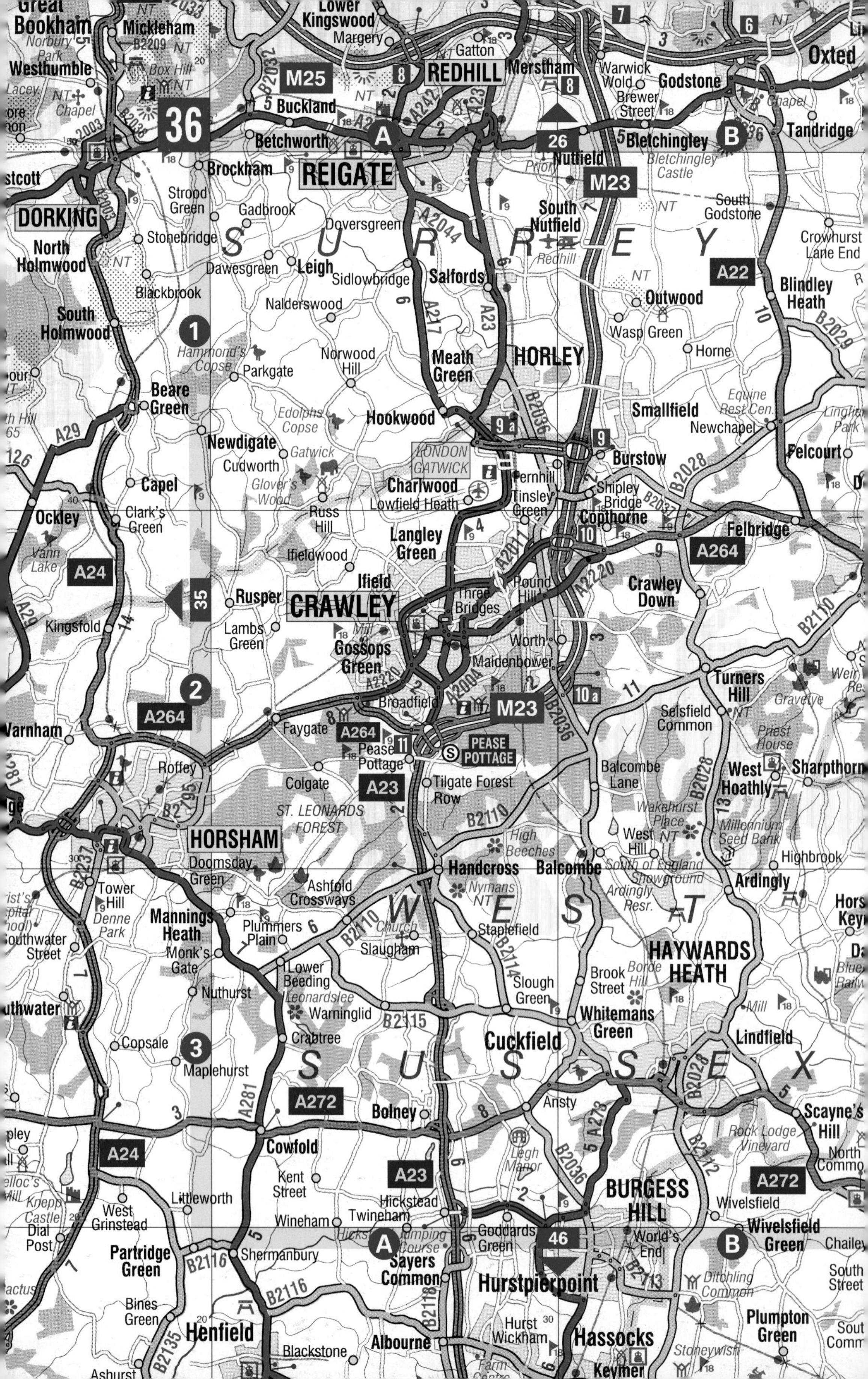

Great Bookham
Mickleham
Lower Kingswood
Margery
Gatton
Merstham
Warwick Wold
Godstone
Oxted
Norbury Park
B2209
Box Hill
Westhumble
M25
8
REDHILL
Brewer Street
Chapel
Tandridge
Buckland
36
Betchworth
A
26
Bletchingley
B
Nuthfield
Brockham
REIGATE
Priory
Bletchingley Castle
M23
DORKING
Strood Green
Gadbrook
South Nutfield
South Godstone
North Holmwood
Stonebridge
Doversgreen
A2044
Crowhurst Lane End
S U R R E Y
Dawesgreen
Leigh
Sidlowbridge
Salfords
Redhill
A22
Blackbrook
Nalderswood
Outwood
Blindley Heath
South Holmwood
A217
A23
Wasp Green
B2029
1
Hammond's Copse
Parkgate
Norwood Hill
Meath Green
HORLEY
Horne
Beare Green
Equine Rest Cen.
Edolphs Copse
Hookwood
Smallfield
Newchapel
A29
Newdigate
B2036
9a
9
Gatwick
LONDON GATWICK
Burstow
Pelcourt
Cudworth
Fernhill
B2028
Capel
Glover's Wood
Charlwood
Shipley Bridge
Tinsley Green
Lowfield Heath
Russ Hill
Clark's Green
Ockley
Copthorne
10
Felbridge
Langley Green
Vann Lake
Ifieldwood
A264
A24
A2011
Crawley Down
Ifield
Pound Hill
A2220
Rusper
CRAWLEY
35
Three Bridges
Kingsfold
Lambs Green
B2110
Gossops Green
Worth
Maidenbower
Turners Hill
2
A2004
10a
Gravetye
Broadfield
M23
Selsfield Common
Warnham
A264
Faygate
Pease Pottage
11
PEASE POTTAGE
Priest House
Roffey
Colgate
A23
Tilgate Forest Row
Balcombe Lane
West Hoathly
Sharpthorne
ST. LEONARDS FOREST
Wakehurst Place
Millennium Seed Bank
HORSHAM
High Beeches
West Hill
Highbrook
Doomsday Green
Handcross
Balcombe
South of England Showground
B2237
Tower Hill
Ashfold Crossways
Nymans
Ardingly
Ardingly Resr.
Denne Park
Mannings Heath
W E S T
Plummers Plain
Church
Staplefield
Southwater Street
Slaugham
Monk's Gate
Lower Beeding
B2114
HAYWARDS HEATH
Brook Street
Slough Green
Borde Hill
Nuthurst
Leonardslee
Warninglid
B2115
Southwater
Whitemans Green
Cuckfield
Mill
Crabtree
Lindfield
Copsale
3
Maplehurst
S U S S E X
A281
A272
Ansty
Bolney
Scayne's Hill
A24
Cowfold
Legh Manor
Rock Lodge Vineyard
B2036
North Common
A273
Kent Street
A23
BURGESS HILL
A272
Knepp Castle
Littleworth
Hickstead
Wivelsfield
West Grinstead
Wineham
Twineham
Jumping Course
Dial Post
Goddards Green
46
World's End
Wivelsfield Green
Chailey
Partridge Green
Shermanbury
A
Sayers Common
B
B2116
Hurstpierpoint
B2113
Ditchling Common
South Street
B2116
Plumpton Green
Bines Green
B2118
Henfield
Hurst Wickham
Hassocks
Stoneywish
B2135
Blackstone
Albourne
Keymer
Ashurst

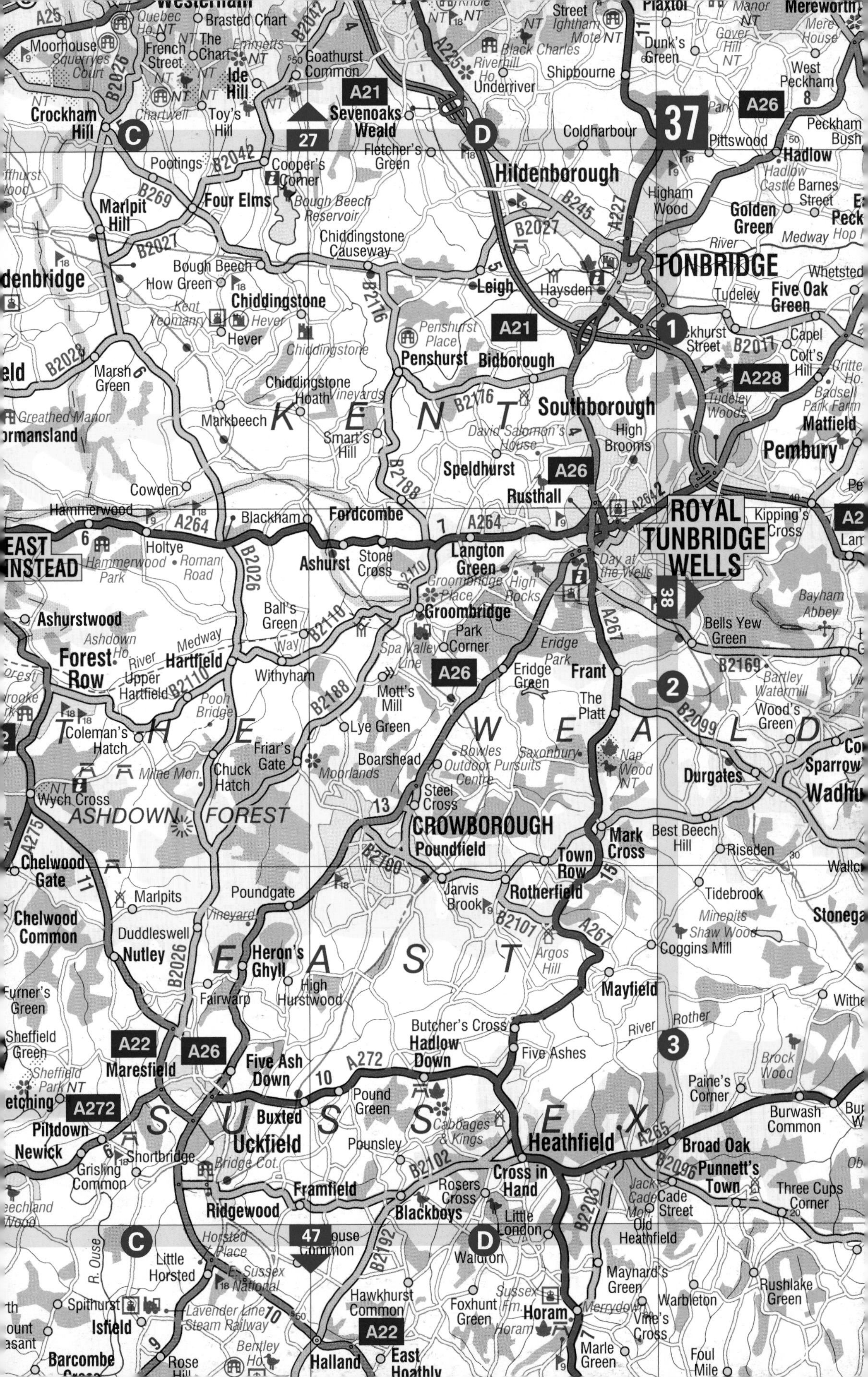

Westerham
Brasted Chart
Moorhouse
French Street
The Chart
Ide Hill
Goathurst Common
Sevenoaks Weald
Underriver
Shipbourne
Plaxtol
Dunk's Green
Mereworth
West Peckham
Crockham Hill
Toy's Hill
27
A21
A26
37
Coldharbour
Pittswood
Hadlow
Peckham Bush
Pootings
Cooper's Corner
Fletcher's Green
Hildenborough
Four Elms
Marlpit Hill
Bough Beech Reservoir
Chiddingstone Causeway
Higham Wood
Golden Green
Barnes Street
TONBRIDGE
Edenbridge
Bough Beech
How Green
Chiddingstone
Leigh
Haysden
Tudeley
Five Oak Green
Hever
Penshurst Place
Penshurst
Bidborough
Capel
Colt's Hill
A228
Marsh Green
Chiddingstone Hoath
Markbeech
K E N T
Southborough
High Brooms
Matfield
Pembury
Smart's Hill
Speldhurst
Rusthall
Cowden
Hammerwood
Blackham
Fordcombe
ROYAL TUNBRIDGE WELLS
Kipping's Cross
EAST GRINSTEAD
Holtye
Ashurst
Stone Cross
Langton Green
Groombridge
38
Ashurstwood
Forest Row
Hartfield
Withyham
Ball's Green
Park Corner
Bells Yew Green
Bayham Abbey
Eridge Green
Frant
The Platt
Mott's Mill
Lye Green
Coleman's Hatch
Friar's Gate
Boarshead
Durgates
Wadhurst
Sparrow's Green
Wood's Green
Chuck Hatch
Wych Cross
ASHDOWN FOREST
Steel Cross
CROWBOROUGH
Poundfield
Mark Cross
Best Beech Hill
Riseden
Chelwood Gate
Town Row
Jarvis Brook
Rotherfield
Tidebrook
Stonegate
Marlpits
Poundgate
Chelwood Common
Duddleswell
Nutley
Heron's Ghyll
Coggins Mill
E A S T
Argos Hill
Mayfield
Fairwarp
High Hurstwood
Butcher's Cross
Hadlow Down
Five Ashes
A22
Maresfield
Five Ash Down
Paine's Corner
Burwash Common
Buxted
Pound Green
Uckfield
Piltdown
Newick
Shortbridge
Pounsley
Heathfield
Broad Oak
Punnett's Town
S U S S E X
Framfield
Cross in Hand
Rosers Cross
Blackboys
Ridgewood
Three Cups Corner
Cade Street
Old Heathfield
47
Little London
Waldron
Little Horsted
Maynard's Green
Rushlake Green
Warbleton
Spithurst
Isfield
Hawkhurst Common
Foxhunt Green
Horam
Vine's Cross
Barcombe
Halland
East Hoathly
Marle Green
Foul Mile

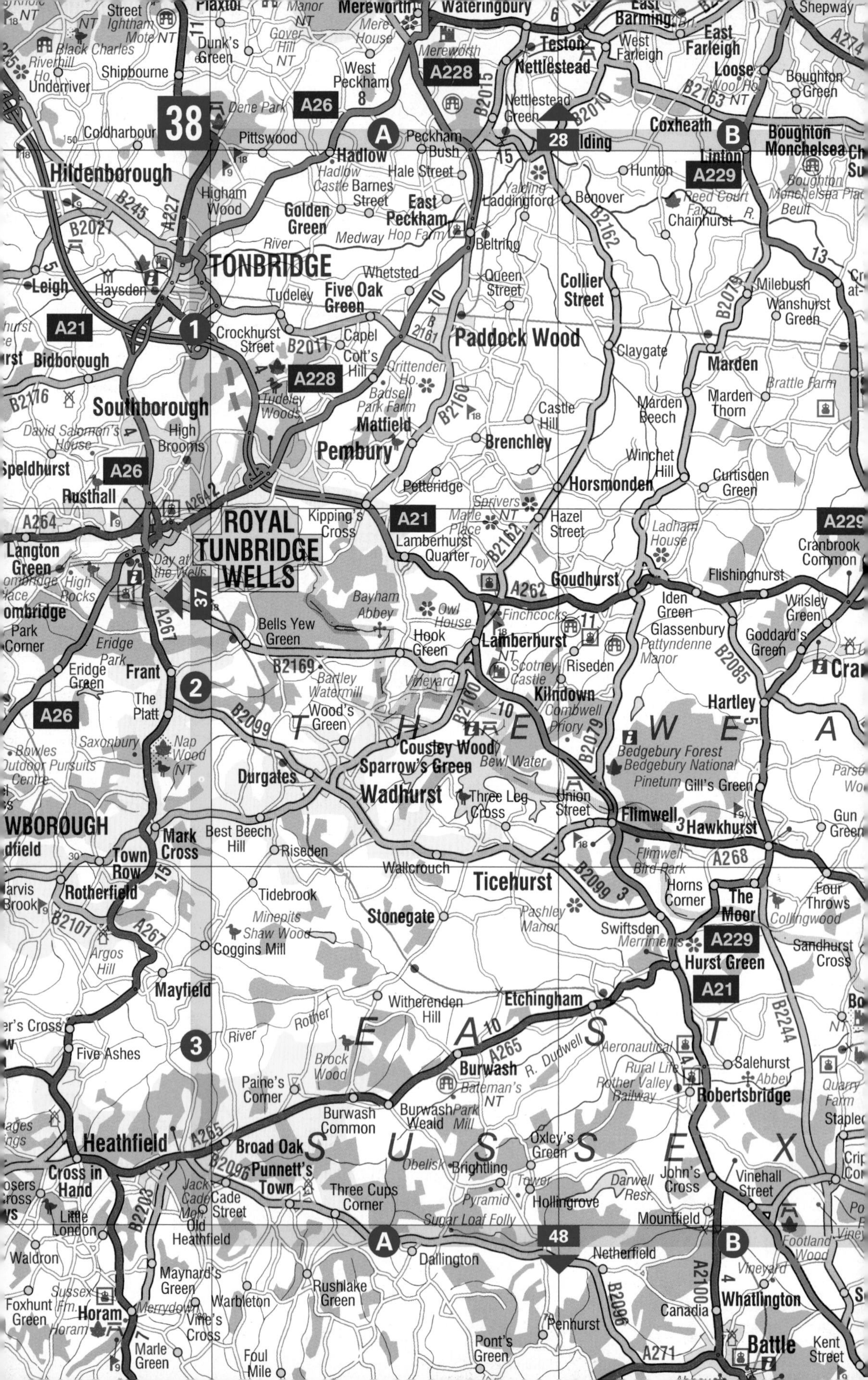

38
Hildenborough
TONBRIDGE
Hadlow
Golden Green
East Peckham
Five Oak Green
Paddock Wood
Collier Street
Marden
Southborough
Pembury
Matfield
Brenchley
Horsmonden
ROYAL TUNBRIDGE WELLS
Lamberhurst
Goudhurst
Frant
Wadhurst
Ticehurst
Flimwell
Hawkhurst
Mayfield
Rotherfield
Heathfield
Burwash
Etchingham
Hurst Green
Robertsbridge
Battle
Whatlington
Horam
Dallington
Broad Oak
Punnett's Town
Cross in Hand
Stonegate
Mark Cross
Town Row
Crowborough
Langton Green
Rusthall
Speldhurst
Bidborough
Leigh
Tudeley
Capel
Crockhurst Street
Kilndown
Cousley Wood
Sparrow's Green
Durgates
Three Leg Cross
Bewl Water
Bedgebury Forest
Linton
Coxheath
Loose
Teston
Nettlestead
Wateringbury
Mereworth
East Farleigh
West Farleigh
Boughton Monchelsea
Yalding
Laddingford
Beltring
Hunton
T H E W E A L D
E A S T S U S S E X
A21
A26
A228
A229
A262
A264
A265
A267
A268
A271
A2100
B2015
B2010
B2162
B2079
B2160
B2161
B2017
B2169
B2099
B2100
B2085
B2096
B2203
B2101
B2244
B2163
B2027
B2176
28
48
37

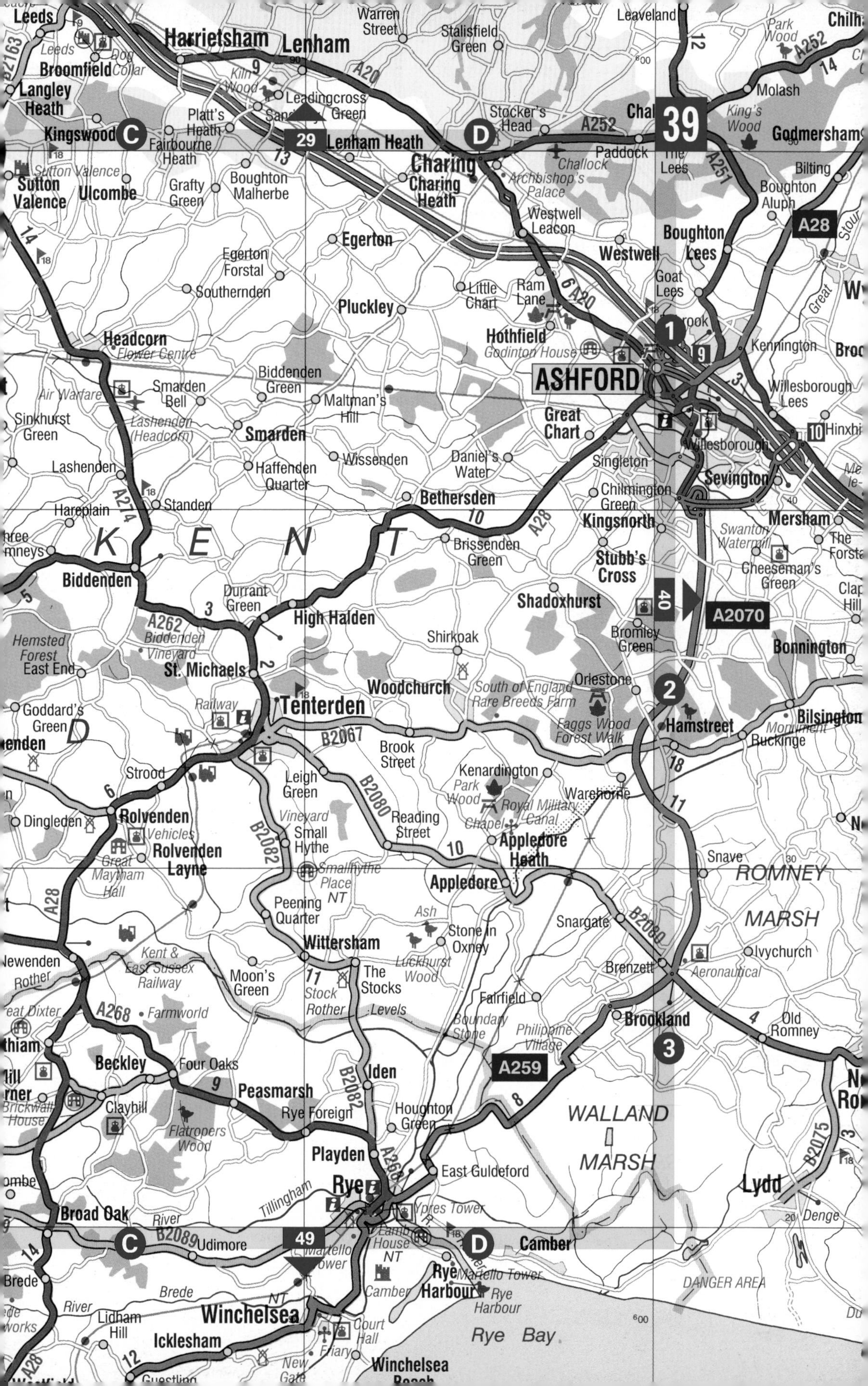
39
Leeds
Harrietsham
Lenham
Warren Street
Stalisfield Green
Leaveland
Park Wood
A252
Molash
King's Wood
Godmersham
Broomfield
Dog Collar
Kiln Wood
Leadingcross Green
Langley Heath
Platt's Heath
Sandway
Stocker's Head
A252
Chal
Kingswood
C
Fairbourne Heath
29
Lenham Heath
D
Challock
Paddock
The Lees
A251
Sutton Valence
Ulcombe
Grafty Green
Boughton Malherbe
Charing
Charing Heath
Archbishop's Palace
Bilting
Boughton Aluph
Westwell Leacon
A28
Egerton
Westwell
Boughton Lees
Egerton Forstal
Southernden
Pluckley
Little Chart
Ram Lane
Goat Lees
Great Stour
Hothfield
Godinton House
Kennington
Headcorn
Flower Centre
ASHFORD
Willesborough Lees
Biddenden Green
Smarden Bell
Air Warfare
Maltman's Hill
Lashenden (Headcorn)
Great Chart
Hinxhill
Sinkhurst Green
Smarden
Willesborough
Singleton
Lashenden
Haffenden Quarter
Wissenden
Daniel's Water
Sevington
Chilmington Green
A274
Standen
Bethersden
Mersham
Hareplain
Kingsnorth
Swanton Watermill
K E N T
Brissenden Green
A28
Stubb's Cross
Cheeseman's Green
Biddenden
Durrant Green
40
Shadoxhurst
A2070
High Halden
Bromley Green
A262
Biddenden Vineyard
Shirkoak
Bonnington
Hemsted Forest
East End
St. Michaels
Orlestone
Woodchurch
South of England Rare Breeds Farm
Goddard's Green
Railway
Tenterden
Faggs Wood Forest Walk
Hamstreet
Bilsington
B2067
Monument
Buckinge
Brook Street
Strood
Leigh Green
Kenardington
Park Wood
Warehorne
Royal Military Canal
Dingleden
Rolvenden
Vineyard
B2080
Reading Street
Chapel
Vehicles
Small Hythe
Appledore Heath
Rolvenden Layne
Great Maytham Hall
B2082
Smallhythe Place NT
Appledore
Snave
ROMNEY
A28
Peening Quarter
Ash
Snargate
MARSH
Stone in Oxney
B2080
Kent & East Sussex Railway
Wittersham
Ivychurch
Newenden
Moon's Green
The Stocks
Luckhurst Wood
Brenzett
Aeronautical
Rother
Stock
Rother
Levels
Fairfield
A268
Farmworld
Boundary Stone
Brookland
Old Romney
Philippine Village
A259
Beckley
Four Oaks
Iden
Peasmarsh
B2082
Houghton Green
Clayhill
Rye Foreign
WALLAND
Flatropers Wood
MARSH
B2075
Playden
A268
East Guldeford
Lydd
Rye
Tillingham
Broad Oak
Ypres Tower
River
Denge
Lamb House
C
B2089
Udimore
49
Martello Tower
D
Camber
NT
Rye Harbour
Martello Tower
Rye Harbour
Brede
Camber
DANGER AREA
River
Brede
NT
Lidham Hill
Winchelsea
Court Hall
Rye Bay
Icklesham
Friary
New Gate
Winchelsea Beach

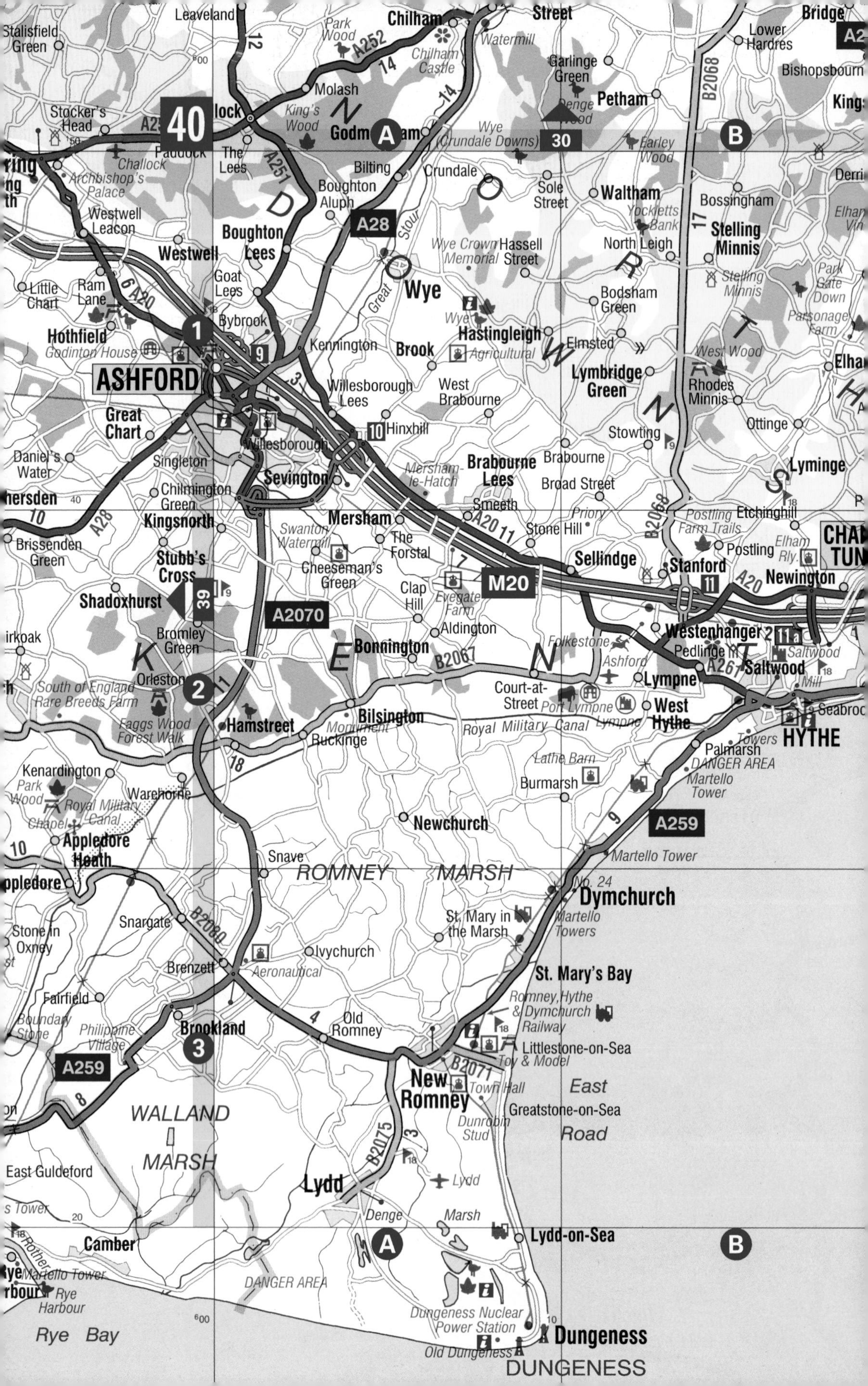

40
Leaveland
Chilham
Street
Bridge
Stalisfield Green
Park Wood
A252
Chilham Castle
Watermill
Lower Hardres
Garlinge Green
B2068
Bishopsbourne
Molash
Petham
Stocker's Head
King's Wood
Denge Wood
Godmersham
Wye (Crundale Downs)
30
Earley Wood
A
B
Challock
Paddock
The Lees
A251
Bilting
Crundale
Archbishop's Palace
Boughton Aluph
Sole Street
Waltham
Bossingham
A28
Yockletts Bank
Stelling Minnis
Westwell Leacon
Boughton Lees
Westwell
Wye Crown Memorial
Hassell Street
North Leigh
Great Stour
Goat Lees
Wye
Bodsham Green
Little Chart
Ram Lane
A20
Bybrook
Hastingleigh
Elmsted
Parsonage Farm
Hothfield
Godinton House
Kennington
Brook
Agricultural
West Wood
ASHFORD
Willesborough Lees
West Brabourne
Lymbridge Green
Rhodes Minnis
Great Chart
Hinxhill
Stowting
Ottinge
Willesborough
Daniel's Water
Singleton
Sevington
Mersham-le-Hatch
Brabourne Lees
Brabourne
Lyminge
Chilmington Green
Broad Street
Smeeth
Priory
Postling Farm Trails
Etchinghill
Kingsnorth
Swanton Watermill
Mersham
The Forstal
Stone Hill
Postling
Elham Rly.
Brissenden Green
Stubb's Cross
Cheeseman's Green
Sellindge
Stanford
Newington
Shadoxhurst
39
A2070
Clap Hill
Evegate Farm
M20
Aldington
Westenhanger
Bromley Green
Bonnington
Folkestone
Pedlinge
Saltwood
Ashford
A261
Orleston
B2067
Court-at-Street
Lympne
South of England Rare Breeds Farm
Port Lympne
West Hythe
Seabrook
Faggs Wood Forest Walk
Hamstreet
Bilsington
Monument
Ruckinge
Royal Military Canal
HYTHE
Towers
Palmarsh
DANGER AREA
Kenardington
Lathe Barn
Martello Tower
Park Wood
Warehorne
Burmarsh
Royal Military Canal
Chapel
Newchurch
A259
Appledore Heath
Snave
Martello Tower
ROMNEY MARSH
No. 24
Dymchurch
Appledore
Snargate
B2080
St. Mary in the Marsh
Martello Towers
Stone in Oxney
Ivychurch
Brenzett
Aeronautical
St. Mary's Bay
Fairfield
Romney, Hythe & Dymchurch Railway
Boundary Stone
Philippine Village
Brookland
Old Romney
Littlestone-on-Sea
Toy & Model
A259
B2071
New Romney
Town Hall
East
Greatstone-on-Sea
WALLAND MARSH
Dunrobin Stud
Road
B2075
East Guldeford
Lydd
Lydd
Denge
Marsh
Camber
Lydd-on-Sea
Rother
Martello Tower
Rye Harbour
DANGER AREA
Rye Bay
Dungeness Nuclear Power Station
Dungeness
Old Dungeness
DUNGENESS
NORTH DOWNS
KENT

41
The Downs
DEAL
Deal
Walmer
Victoriana
Time-Ball Tower
Local History
Sholden
Northbourne
Northbourne Ct.
Finglesham
Betteshanger
Great Mongeham
Ripple
Heronden
Chillenden
Knowlton
Nonington
Easole Street
Frogham
Tilmanstone
Elvington
Womenswold
Barfrestone
East Kent Light Rlwy
Eythorne
Woolage Green
Shepherdswell or Sibertswold
Coldred
Lydden
Wootton
Lydden
Temple Ewell
St. John's Commandery
Ewell Minnis
Kearsney
River
Crabble Corn Mill
Buckland
Swingfield Street
Butterfly Centre
Alkham
St. Radigund's Abbey
Drellingore
West Hougham
Church Hougham
Maxton
Hawkinge
Capel-le-Ferne
East Studdal
Sutton
Ashley
West Langdon
Martin
Martin Mill
East Langdon
Ringwould
Kingsdown
DANGER AREA
Dover Patrol Monument
St.Margaret's at Cliffe
Guston
Whitfield
West Cliffe
The Bay
St. Margaret's Bay
The Pines
SOUTH FORELAND
SEE PAGE 63
DOVER
Western Docks
Samphire Hoe
East Wear Bay
Martello Towers
FOLKESTONE
SEE PAGE 68
A2
A20
A256
A258
A260
B2011
B2046
31
Dover to:
Calais 1hr. 10mins.
Calais 50mins. (Fast Ferry)
Dunkirk 2hrs.
Ostend 2hrs. (Fast Ferry)
Zeebrugge 4hrs. 30mins.
CHANNEL TUNNEL
Folkestone to
Calais 35mins.
STRAIT OF DOVER
ENGLISH CHANNEL

42
Romsey
Chandler's Ford
Eastleigh
Southampton
SEE PAGE 69
Totton
Hythe
Fareham
Hamble-le-Rice
Hedge End
West End
Bishop's Waltham
Wickham
Stubbington
Lee-on-the-Solent
Beaulieu
Fawley
Cowes
East Cowes
Newport
Yarmouth
Freshwater
Isle of Wight
The Solent
New Forest
Hampshire
M3
M27
M271
A3054
A326
Southampton Water
Needs Ore Point
Osborne Bay
Gurnard Bay
Thorness Bay
Newtown Bay
Cowes Roads

PETERSFIELD
43
33
44
Rogate
Chithurst
Iping
Trotton
Dumpford
Minsted
Elsted Marsh
Habin
Nyewood
West Harting
Nursted
South Harting
Buriton
War Down
Queen Elizabeth
Butser Hill
887
Langrish
Ramsdean
Weston
Riplington
Warnford
East Meon
Coombe
Old Winchester Hill Fort
Meonstoke
Brockbridge
Chidden
Hambledon Cricket Monument
Clanfield
Soberton
Vineyard & Winepress
Hambledon
Catherington
Blendworth
HORNDEAN
FOREST OF BERE
Anthill Common
Hoe Gate
Worlds End
Denmead
Lovedean
Anmore
Cowplain
Soake
Furzeley Corner
WATERLOOVILLE
Southwick
Stakes
Purbrook
Fort Widley
Ports Down
Wymering
Drayton
Cosham
Port Solent
Farlington
Hilsea
North End
Landport
Fratton
Portsea
H.M.S. Victory
Whale Island
Milton
Pumping
Rvl. Marines
Eastney
Southsea
PORTSMOUTH
SEE PAGE 68
Spitbank Fort
Horse Sand Fort
SPITHEAD
No Man's Land Fort
Wireless
Nettlestone Point
Seaview
Flamingo Park
St. Helen's Fort
Bembridge Point
Maritime
Bembridge
FORELAND
Lane End
Lifeboat
Whitecliff Bay
ISLE OF WIGHT
PORTSEA ISLAND
Langstone Harbour
Langstone
Stoke
Northney
North Hayling
Tye
Fleet
SOUTH HAYLING
West Town
HAYLING ISLAND
Hayling Bay
Sandy Point
East Head
HAVANT
Leigh Park
Bedhampton
Warblington
Durrants
New Brighton
Emsworth
Church
Hermitage
Butser Ancient Farm
Chalton
Finchdean
Deanlane End
Rowland's Castle
The King's Stone
Forestside
Stansted Park
Lordington
Aldsworth
Westbourne
Woodmancote
Breach
Hambrook
Southbourne
Nutbourne
Chidham
Thorney Island
West Thorney
West Itchenor
Rookwood
West Wittering
East Wittering
Bracklesham
Earnley
Almodington
Highleigh
Somerley
Rejectamenta
Earnley Gdns.
Shipton Green
Birdham
Bosham
Broadbridge
Fishbourne
Apuldram
Apuldram Roses
D-Day
CHICHESTER
West Ashling
East Ashling
Funtington
Sennicotts
Woodend
West Stoke
Kingley Vale
King's Graves Barrows
Stoughton
Walderton
West Dean
Chilgrove
East Marden
Up Marden
West Marden
Compton
Bevis' Thumb
North Marden
Uppark
Devil's Jumps
Old Monkton Deserted Village
Beacon Hill
Treyford
Didling
Bepton
SOUTH DOWNS
WEST SUSSEX
Norton
Farm Centre
Donnington
A3
A3(M)
A27
A259
A32
A286
A2030
A288
A3023
M27
M275
B2070
B2146
B2149
B2148
B2147
B2150
B2177
B2178
B2179
B2198
B2199
B2141
B2201
B2145
B3340
B3395
B3330
Portsmouth to:
Bilbao 35hrs.
Caen 6hrs.
Cherbourg 5hrs.
Cherbourg 2hrs. 45mins. (Fast Ferry, Seasonal)
Guernsey 6hrs. 30mins.
Jersey 10hrs.
Le Havre 5hrs. 30mins. (Fast Ferry)
St. Malo 8hrs. 45mins. (Seasonal)

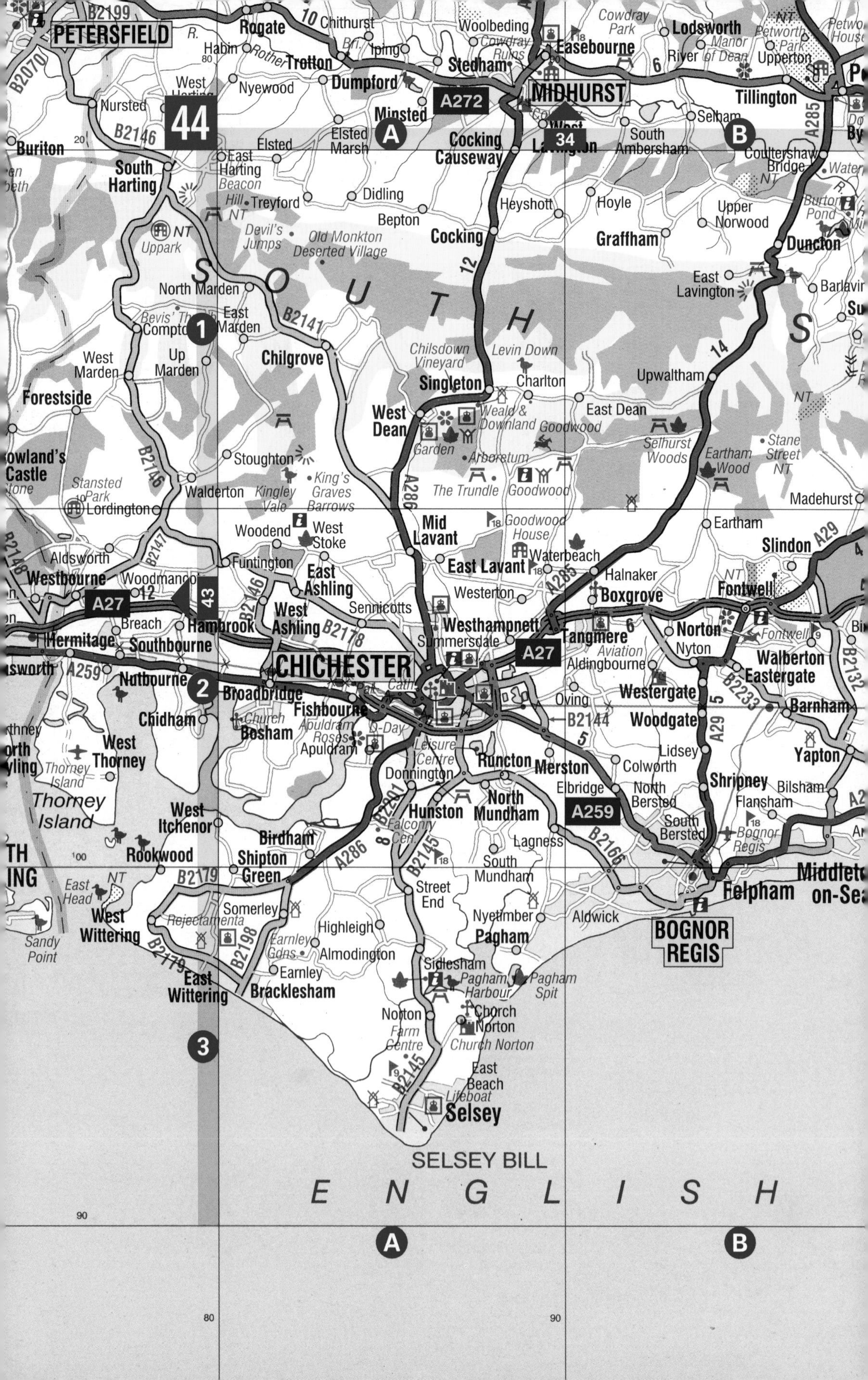

44
PETERSFIELD
Rogate
Chithurst
Woolbeding
Cowdray Park
Lodsworth
Petworth Park
Habin
Rother
Trotton
Iping
Cowdray Ruins
Easebourne
Manor of Dean
River
Upperton
Stedham
West Harting
Nyewood
Dumpford
Minsted
A272
MIDHURST
Tillington
Nursted
Elsted Marsh
Cocking Causeway
West Lavington
34
South Ambersham
Selham
Buriton
B2146
Elsted
East Harting
Coultershaw Bridge
South Harting
Harting Beacon
Hill
Treyford
Didling
Heyshott
Hoyle
Upper Norwood
Burton Pond
Uppark
NT
Devil's Jumps
Old Monkton Deserted Village
Bepton
Cocking
Graffham
Duncton
S O U T H
North Marden
East Lavington
Barlavington
Bevis' Thumb
Compton
East Marden
B2141
West Marden
Up Marden
Chilgrove
Chilsdown Vineyard
Levin Down
Upwaltham
Singleton
Charlton
Forestside
West Dean
Weald & Downland
East Dean
Goodwood
Garden
Arboretum
Selhurst Woods
Eartham Wood
Stane Street
Rowland's Castle
Stansted Park
Stoughton
King's Graves Barrows
Kingley Vale
Walderton
The Trundle
Lordington
Madehurst
A286
Mid Lavant
Goodwood House
Eartham
Woodend
West Stoke
Slindon
A29
Aldsworth
Funtington
East Lavant
Waterbeach
Halnaker
Westbourne
Woodmancote
East Ashling
A285
Boxgrove
Fontwell
B2147
B2148
A27
43
Westerton
Sennicotts
Breach
Hambrook
West Ashling
Westhampnett
Tangmere
Norton
Hermitage
Southbourne
B2178
Summersdale
Aviation
Nyton
Walberton
Eastergate
CHICHESTER
Aldingbourne
A259
Nutbourne
Broadbridge
Fishbourne
Westergate
Oving
B2233
Barnham
Chidham
Bosham
Apuldram Roses
D-Day
Apuldram
B2144
Woodgate
West Thorney
Thorney Island
Leisure Centre
Runcton
Merston
Colworth
Lidsey
Yapton
Donnington
Elbridge
North Bersted
Shripney
Bilsham
West Itchenor
Hunston
North Mundham
Flansham
Birdham
B2201
Falconry Cen.
Lagness
South Bersted
Bognor Regis
Rookwood
Shipton Green
South Mundham
B2166
Middleton-on-Sea
B2179
Street End
Felpham
East Head
West Wittering
Somerley
Nyetimber
Aldwick
Rejectamenta
B2145
BOGNOR REGIS
Sandy Point
Highleigh
Pagham
Earnley Gdns.
Almodington
B2198
Earnley
Sidlesham
East Wittering
Bracklesham
Pagham Harbour
Pagham Spit
Church Norton
Norton
Farm Centre
3
East Beach
Lifeboat
Selsey
SELSEY BILL
E N G L I S H
A
B

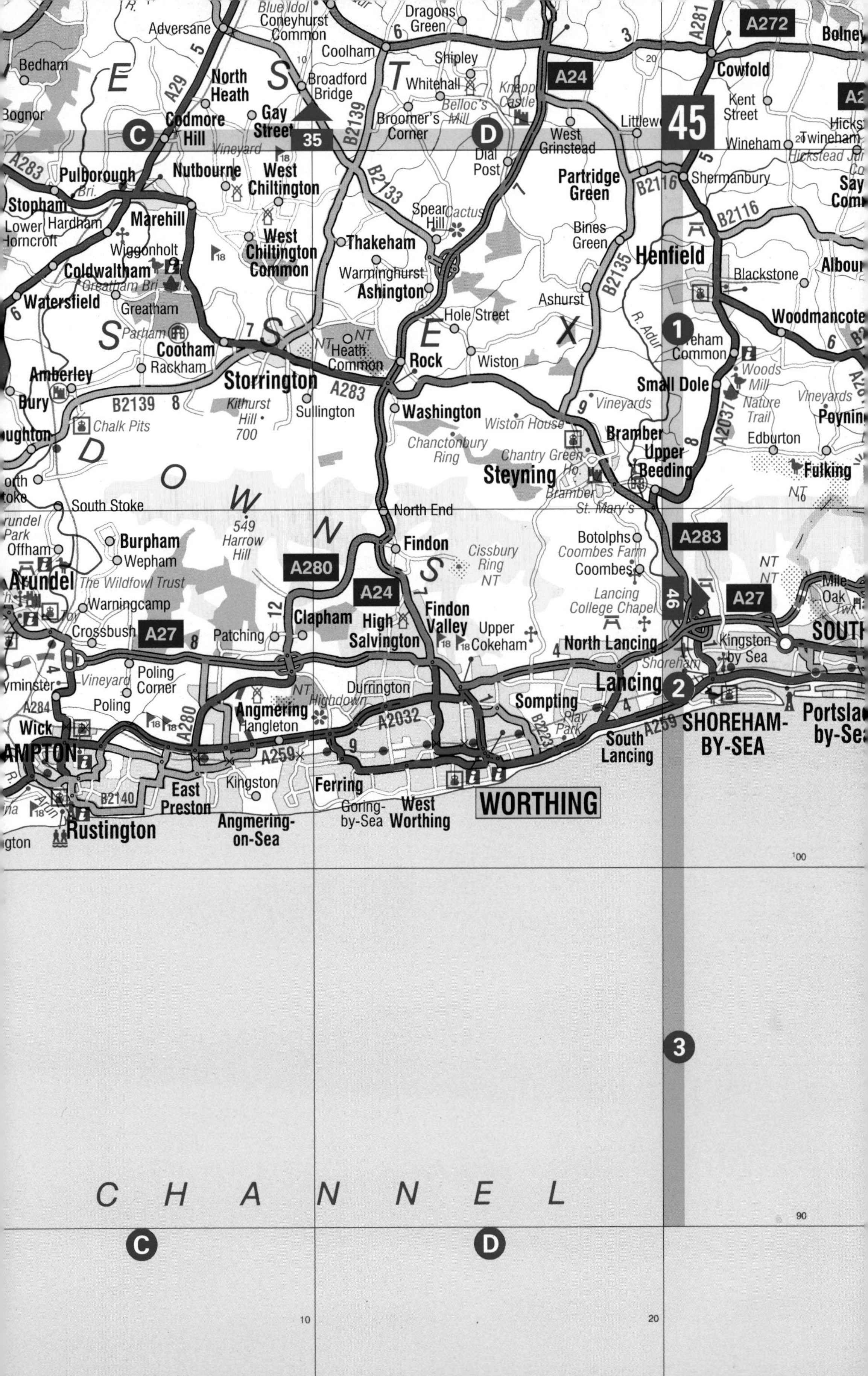

Towns and villages:
Bedham, Adversane, Blue Idol, Coneyhurst Common, Dragons Green, Bognor, North Heath, Broadford Bridge, Coolham, Shipley, Whitehall, Knapp Castle, Cowfold, Kent Street, Hicks, Codmore Hill, Gay Street, Broomer's Corner, Belloc's Mill, West Grinstead, Littlewo..., Wineham, Twineham, Say Com..., Pulborough, Nutbourne, West Chiltington, Dial Post, Partridge Green, Shermanbury, Stopham, Lower Hardham, Marehill, West Chiltington Common, Thakeham, Spear Hill, Cactus, Bines Green, Henfield, Blackstone, Albour..., Coldwaltham, Wiggonholt, Warminghurst, Ashington, Ashurst, Small Dole, Woodmancote, Watersfield, Greatham, Hole Street, Amberley, Cootham, Rackham, Heath Common, Rock, Wiston, Washington, Vineyards, Bramber, Upper Beeding, Edburton, Fulking, Storrington, Sullington, Wiston House, Chantry Green, Steyning, Poynin..., Bury, South Stoke, Chanctonbury Ring, Chantry Green Ho., Bramber, St. Mary's, Arundel Park, Offham, Burpham, Wepham, Harrow Hill, North End, Findon, Cissbury Ring NT, Botolphs, Coombes Farm, Coombes, Lancing College Chapel, Arundel, Warningcamp, Crossbush, Clapham, High Salvington, Findon Valley, Upper Cokeham, North Lancing, Kingston by Sea, South..., Patching, Angmering, Hangleton, Durrington, Sompting, Lancing, Shoreham-by-Sea, Portslade-by-Sea, Wick, Poling Corner, Poling, Play Park, South Lancing, Worthing, Rustington, East Preston, Kingston, Ferring, Goring-by-Sea, West Worthing, Angmering-on-Sea, Wildfowl Trust, Kithurst Hill 700, Chalk Pits, Highdown

Roads:
A29, A281, A272, A24, A283, B2139, B2133, B2116, B2135, B2037, A280, A27, A284, A259, A2032, B2140, B2223, B2139

Grid references: C, D, 35, 45, 46, 1, 2, 3

Other features:
Vineyard, Nature Trail, Woods Mill Nature Trail, The Wildfowl Trust, Chanctonbury Ring, Cissbury Ring, Harrow Hill 549, Mile Oak

CHANNEL

A272
Bolney
Ansty
Scayne's Hill
A24
Cowfold
Rock Lodge Vineyard
North Common
Legh Manor
Kent Street
A23
B2036
BURGESS HILL
A272
Knepp Castle
West Grinstead
Hickstead
Wivelsfield
Dial Post
Wineham
Twineham
Goddards Green
36
World's End
Partridge Green
B2116
Shermanbury
Hickstead Jumping Course
Sayers Common
Wivelsfield Green
Chailey
South Street
Hurstpierpoint
B2113
Ditchling Common
W E S T
S U S S E X
Bines Green
B2116
B2118
Hurst Wickham
Hassocks
Plumpton Green
Henfield
Albourne
B2135
R. Adur
Blackstone
Farm Centre
Keymer
Stoneywish
Ashurst
Woodmancote
Danny
Ditchling
Plumpton
B2117
Streat
East Chiltington
Wiston
Oreham Common
B2112
Farm Cen.
Newtimber Place
Clayton
Vineyards
Westmeston
Woods Mill
Jack
Small Dole
A2037
A281
A273
Jill
Clayton Windmills
813 Ditchling Beacon
Nature Trail
Vineyards
Pyecombe
Plumpton
Wiston House
Vineyards
Poynings
Cross
Mount Harry 639
Bramber
Edburton
NT
Devil's Dyke
Chantry Green Ho.
Upper Beeding
Saddlescombe
A23
Steyning
Fulking
Stanmer Park
Bramber
St. Mary's
S O U T H
Stanmer
University of Sussex
A27
Botolphs
A283
Patcham
Coldean
Cissbury Ring NT
Coombes Farm
Coombes
Hollingbury
Falmer
Kingston
Lancing College Chapel
45
A27
Mile Oak
Hangleton
A2038
Preston Manor
Castle Hill
Upper Cokeham
North Lancing
Kingston by Sea
SOUTHWICK
West Blatchington
Preston
Moulsecoomb
A270
Bevendean
Shoreham
Woodingdean
Lancing
Brighton
B2123
Sompting
Play Park
Royal Pavilion
B2223
South Lancing
A259
SHOREHAM-BY-SEA
Portslade-by-Sea
HOVE
A259
Sea-Life
B2118
Ovingdean
Kemp Town
Saltdean
BRIGHTON
SEE PAGE 62
Marina
Volks Electric Railway
Rottingdean
WORTHING
E N G L I S H
A
B
20
30
100
90

47
Heathfield
Uckfield
Buxted
Pound Green
Pounsley
Cabbages & Kings
Broad Oak
Burwash Common
Paine's Corner
Punnett's Town
Three Cups Corner
Cross in Hand
Rosers Cross
Blackboys
Framfield
Ridgewood
Little London
Old Heathfield
Jack Cade Mon.
Newick
Piltdown
Grisling Common
Shortbridge
Bridge Cot.
Palehouse Common
Little Horsted
Horsted Place
E. Sussex National
Waldron
Maynard's Green
Rushlake Green
Warbleton
Spithurst
Isfield
Lavender Line Steam Railway
Hawkhurst Common
Foxhunt Green
Sussex Fm.
Horam
Merrydown
Vine's Cross
Barcombe Cross
Barcombe Mills
Rose Hill
Bentley Ho.
Shortgate
Halland
East Hoathly
Marle Green
Foul Mile
Chiddingly
Gun Hill
Cuckmere R.
Upper Wellingham
Broyle Side
Laughton
Whitesmith
Cowbeech
Hamsey
Golden Cross
Ringmer
Lower Dicker
Hellingly
Lower Horsebridge
Stunts Green
Herstmonceux
Laughton Place
Horsebridge
Magham Down
The Truggery
South Malling
Cliffe Hill
Glyndebourne
Tunnel
LEWES
Ripe
Upper Dicker
Michelham Priory
HAILSHAM
Herstmonceux Castle
Glynde Place
Glynde
Chalvington
Watermill
Arlington
Heritage Centre
Wartling
Beddingham
Arlington Resr.
Selmeston
Pevensey Levels
Firle Place
West Firle
Charleston Farmhouse
Abbot's Wood Forest Walk
Monk's House
Firle Beacon
Hankham
Alciston
Berwick
Wilmington
Polegate
Westham
Drusillas Park
Priory
Tarring Neville
Winton
Milton Street
The Long Man
Folkington
Stone Cross
Friday Street
South Heighton
Alfriston
Clergy House
Filching Manor
Wannock
Hampden Park
Langney
Piddinghoe
Denton
Planet Earth
Heritage Centre
Willingdon
Ratton Village
Bishopstone
White Horse
Litlington
Lullington Heath
Jevington
The Living World
Charleston Manor
Willingdon Hill
Marina
East Blatchington
Westdean
Sutton
Friston Forest Trails
Old Town
Butterfly Cen.
Combined Services
NEWHAVEN
Exceat
Friston
East Dean
SEAFORD
Martello Tower
Local History
Seven Sisters
Seaford Head
Heritage
Lifeboat
Wish Tower
Sheep Centre
EASTBOURNE
SEE PAGE 63
Newhaven to: Dieppe 4hrs. Dieppe 2hrs. (Fast Ferry, Seasonal)
Birling Gap
BEACHY HEAD
History Centre
CHANNEL
EAST SUSSEX DOWNS
A272
A22
A26
A27
A259
A265
A267
A271
A2270
A2021
A2290
B2102
B2192
B2124
B2203
B2096
B2104
B2191
B2103
37
48
C
D
1
2
3

Paine's Corner
Burwash Common
Burwash Weald
Bateman's NT
Park Mill
Rother Valley Railway
Robertsbridge
Quarry Farm
Heathfield
A265
Broad Oak
Oxley's Green
A21
Cross in Hand
B2096
Punnett's Town
48
Cade Street
Three Cups Corner
A
Obelisk
Brightling
Tower
Pyramid
Darwell Resr.
John's Cross
Vinehall Street
Little London
B2203
Old Heathfield
Sugar Loaf Folly
38
Mountfield
B
Footland Wood
Waldron
Dallington
Netherfield
Maynard's Green
E
A
S
T
S
U
Rushlake Green
Vineyard
A2100
Sussex Fm.
Foxhunt Green
Horam
Merrydown
Warbleton
Vine's Cross
Whatlington
Canadia
Penhurst
B2096
Marle Green
Foul Mile
Pont's Green
Battle
Kent Street
A271
Abbey
Hastings 1066
Brownbread Street
Bodle Street Green
Gun Hill
Cowbeech
Telham
Cuckmere R.
A2100
Catsfield
A271
Stunts Green
Herstmonceux
A269
Henley's Down
B2204
Lower Dicker
A267
Hellingly
Lower Horsebridge
A271
Windmill Hill
Ninfield
Fore Wood
Crowhurst
Hollington
B2092
The Truggery
Horsebridge
Magham Down
Boreham Street
Lunsford's Cross
Michelham Priory
HAILSHAM
Herstmonceux Castle
B2095
Hooe Common
Filsham
Arlington
Heritage Centre
Wartling
Hooe
A269
A2036
Bulverhythe
Sidley
Pevensey Levels
Little Common
47
Cooden
Costume & Social History
Abbot's Wood Forest Walk
A259
BEXHILL
B2182
B2104
Hankham
A27
Polegate
Norman's Bay
Martello Tower
Westham
Pevensey
Folkington
Stone Cross
Pevensey Bay
The Long Man
Wannock
A22
Friday Street
B2191
Filching Manor
A2270
Langney
Martello Tower
Willingdon
Hampden Park
B2104
Lullington Heath
A2021
A2290
Martello Tower
Jevington
Ratton Village
A259
Martello Tower
659
Willingdon Hill
Marina
Langney Point
Old Town
Butterfly Cen.
Combined Services
Friston
East Dean
EASTBOURNE
Heritage
Lifeboat
SEE PAGE 63
Wish Tower
B2103
Sheep Centre
BEACHY HEAD
History Centre
NT
90
A
B
60
70

Peasmarsh
Rye Foreign
Houghton Green
WALLAND MARSH
Clayhill
Brickwall House
Flatropers Wood
Playden
A259
East Guldeford
Rye
Lydd
49
C
River
Tillingham
39
Ypres Tower
D
Denge Marsh
Broad Oak
Udimore
Martello Tower
Lamb House
NT
Camber
B2089
Brede
River
Camber
Rye Harbour
Martello Tower
Rye Harbour
DANGER AREA
Lidham Hill
Winchelsea
Court Hall
Icklesham
Rye Bay
Friary
New Gate
Winchelsea Beach
Westfield
Guestling Thorn
Three Oaks
Pett
Guestling Wood
Guestling Green
Cliff End
A259
The Mens
B2093
Fairlight Cove
Caves
Ore
Fairlight
Hastings
HASTINGS
1
2
3
ENGLISH
CHANNEL
C
D

INDEX TO CITIES, TOWNS, VILLAGES, HAMLETS & LOCATIONS

(1) A strict alphabetical order is used e.g. Abbotstone follows Abbots Langley but precedes Abbots Worthy.

(2) The map reference given refers to the actual map square in which the town spot or built-up area is located and not to the place name.

(3) Where two places of the same name occur in the same County or Unitary Authority, the nearest large town is also given;
e.g. Ash. *Kent* —3C **31** (Sandwich) indicates that Ash is located in square 3C on page **31** and is situated near Sandwich in the County of Kent.

COUNTIES AND UNITARY AUTHORITIES with the abbreviations used in this index.

Bedfordshire : *Beds*
Bracknell Forest : *Brac*
Brighton & Hove (City) : *Brig*
Buckinghamshire : *Buck*
Cambridgeshire : *Cambs*
East Sussex : *E Sus*
Essex : *Essx*
Greater London : *G Lon*
Hampshire : *Hants*
Hertfordshire : *Herts*
Isle of Wight : *IOW*
Kent : *Kent*
Luton : *Lutn*
Medway : *Medw*
Milton Keynes : *Mil*
Northamptonshire : *Nptn*
Oxfordshire : *Oxon*
Portsmouth : *Port*
Reading : *Read*
Slough : *Slo*
Southampton : *Sotn*
Southend-on-Sea : *S'end*
Suffolk : *Suff*
Surrey : *Surr*
Thurrock : *Thur*
Warwickshire : *Warw*
West Berkshire : *W Ber*
West Sussex : *W Sus*
Windsor & Maidenhead : *Wind*
Wokingham : *Wok*

A

Abberton. *Essx* —3A **12**
Abbess Roding. *Essx* —3D **9**
Abbey Wood. *G Lon* —1C **27**
Abbots Langley. *Herts* —1C **17**
Abbotstone. *Hants* —2B **32**
Abbots Worthy. *Hants* —2A **32**
Abingdon. *Oxon* —2A **14**
Abinger Common. *Surr* —1D **35**
Abinger Hammer. *Surr* —1C **35**
Abridge. *Essx* —2C **19**
Acol. *Kent* —2D **31**
Acrise. *Kent* —1B **40**
Acton. *G Lon* —3D **17**
Adderbury. *Oxon* —1A **4**
Addington. *Buck* —2D **5**
Addington. *G Lon* —2B **26**
Addington. *Kent* —3A **28**
Addiscombe. *G Lon* —2B **26**
Addlestone. *Surr* —2C **25**
Adgestone. *IOW* —3B **42**
Adisham. *Kent* —3C **31**
Adstock. *Buck* —1D **5**
Adversane. *W Sus* —3C **35**
Adwell. *Oxon* —2C **15**
Aingers Green. *Essx* —2B **12**
Akeley. *Buck* —1D **5**
Albourne. *W Sus* —1A **46**
Albury. *Herts* —2C **9**
Albury. *Surr* —1C **35**
Alciston. *E Sus* —2D **47**
Aldbury. *Herts* —3B **6**
Aldenham. *Herts* —2D **17**
Aldermaston. *W Ber* —2B **22**
Aldermaston Stoke. *W Ber* —2C **23**
Aldermaston Wharf. *W Ber* —2C **23**
Aldershot. *Hants* —3A **24**
Alderton. *Suff* —1D **13**
Aldham. *Essx* —2D **11**
Aldingbourne. *W Sus* —2B **44**
Aldington. *Kent* —2A **40**
Aldsworth. *W Sus* —2D **43**
Aldwick. *W Sus* —3B **44**
Aldworth. *W Ber* —1B **22**
Aley Green. *Beds* —3C **7**
Alfold. *Surr* —2C **35**
Alfold Bars. *W Sus* —2C **35**
Alfold Crossways. *Surr* —2C **35**
Alfriston. *E Sus* —2D **47**
Alkerton. *Oxon* —1A **4**
Alkham. *Kent* —1C **41**
Allbrook. *Hants* —3A **32**
Allen's Green. *Herts* —3C **9**
Allhallows. *Medw* —1C **29**
Allhallows-on-Sea. *Medw* —1C **29**
Allington. *Kent* —3B **28**
Almodington. *W Sus* —3A **44**
Alphamstone. *Essx* —1C **11**
Alresford. *Essx* —2A **12**
Althorne. *Essx* —2D **21**
Alton. *Hants* —2D **33**
Alverstoke. *Hants* —3C **43**
Amberley. *W Sus* —1C **45**
Ambrosden. *Oxon* —3C **5**
Amersham. *Buck* —2B **16**
Ampfield. *Hants* —3A **32**
Ampthill. *Beds* —1C **7**
Amwell. *Herts* —3D **7**
Ancton. *W Sus* —2B **44**
Andover. *Hants* —1A **32**
Andover Down. *Hants* —1A **32**
Andwell. *Hants* —3C **23**
Angmering. *W Sus* —2C **45**
Angmering-on-Sea. *W Sus* —2C **45**
Anmore. *Hants* —1C **43**
Ansteadbrook. *Surr* —2B **34**
Anstey. *Herts* —1C **9**
Ansty. *W Sus* —3A **36**
Anthill Common. *Hants* —1C **43**
Appledore. *Kent* —3D **39**
Appledore Heath. *Kent* —2D **39**
Appleford. *Oxon* —2B **14**
Applemore. *Hants* —2A **42**
Appleton. *Oxon* —1A **14**
Apsley End. *Beds* —1D **7**
Apuldram. *W Sus* —2A **44**
Arborfield. *Wok* —2D **23**
Arborfield Cross. *Wok* —2D **23**
Arborfield Garrison. *Wok* —2D **23**
Ardeley. *Herts* —2B **8**
Ardingly. *W Sus* —3B **36**
Ardington. *Oxon* —3A **14**
Ardleigh. *Essx* —2A **12**
Ardley. *Oxon* —2B **4**
Arford. *Hants* —2A **34**
Arkesden. *Essx* —1C **9**
Arkley. *G Lon* —2A **18**
Arlesey. *Beds* —1D **7**
Arlington. *E Sus* —2D **47**
Arreton. *IOW* —3B **42**
Arundel. *W Sus* —2C **45**
Ascot. *Wind* —2B **24**
Ash. *Kent* —3C **31**
(Sandwich)
Ash. *Kent* —2A **28**
(Swanley)
Ash. *Surr* —3A **24**
Ashampstead. *W Ber* —1B **22**
Ashdon. *Essx* —1D **9**
Ashe. *Hants* —3B **22**
Asheldham. *Essx* —1D **21**
Ashen. *Essx* —1B **10**
Ashendon. *Buck* —3D **5**
Ashey. *IOW* —3B **42**
Ashfield. *Hants* —1A **42**
Ashfold Crossways. *W Sus* —3A **36**
Ashford. *Kent* —1A **40**
Ashford. *Surr* —1C **25**
Ashford Hill. *Hants* —2B **22**
Ashingdon. *Essx* —2C **21**
Ashington. *W Sus* —1D **45**
Ashlett. *Hants* —2A **42**
Ashley. *Hants* —2A **32**
Ashley. *Kent* —1D **41**
Ashley Green. *Buck* —1B **16**
Ashmansworth. *Hants* —3A **22**
Ashmore Green. *W Ber* —2B **22**
Ashtead. *Surr* —3D **25**
Ashurst. *Hants* —1A **42**
Ashurst. *Kent* —2D **37**
Ashurst. *W Sus* —1D **45**
Ashurstwood. *W Sus* —2C **37**
Ash Vale. *Surr* —3A **24**
Ashwell. *Herts* —1A **8**
Askett. *Buck* —1A **16**
Aspenden. *Herts* —2B **8**
Aspley Guise. *Beds* —1B **6**
Aspley Heath. *Beds* —1B **6**
Assington. *Suff* —1D **11**
Aston. *Herts* —2A **8**
Aston. *Oxon* —1A **14**
Aston. *Wok* —3D **15**
Aston Abbotts. *Buck* —2A **6**
Aston Clinton. *Buck* —3A **6**
Aston End. *Herts* —2A **8**
Aston Rowant. *Oxon* —2D **15**
Aston Sandford. *Buck* —1D **15**
Aston Tirrold. *Oxon* —3B **14**
Aston Upthorpe. *Oxon* —3B **14**
Astrop. *Nptn* —1B **4**
Astwick. *Beds* —1A **8**
Atherington. *W Sus* —2C **45**
Audley End. *Essx* —1D **9**
Aveley. *Thur* —3D **19**
Avington. *Hants* —2B **32**
Axford. *Hants* —1C **33**
Aylesbury. *Buck* —3A **6**
Aylesford. *Kent* —3B **28**
Aylesham. *Kent* —3C **31**
Aynho. *Nptn* —1B **4**
Ayot Green. *Herts* —3A **8**
Ayot St Lawrence. *Herts* —3D **7**
Ayot St Peter. *Herts* —3A **8**

B

Babb's Green. *Herts* —3B **8**
Bacon End. *Essx* —3A **10**
Badgers Mount. *Kent* —2C **27**
Badlesmere. *Kent* —3A **30**
Badshot Lea. *Surr* —1A **34**
Bagham. *Kent* —3A **30**
Bagnor. *W Ber* —2A **22**
Bagshot. *Surr* —2B **24**
Bailey Green. *Hants* —3C **33**
Bainton. *Oxon* —2B **4**
Baker Street. *Thur* —3A **20**
Balcombe. *W Sus* —2B **36**
Balcombe Lane. *W Sus* —2B **36**
Baldock. *Herts* —1A **8**
Baldslow. *E Sus* —1C **49**
Ballards Gore. *Essx* —2D **21**
Ball Hill. *Hants* —2A **22**
Ballingdon. *Suff* —1C **11**
Ballingdon Bulmer. *Essx* —1C **11**
Ballinger Common. *Buck* —1B **16**
Balls Cross. *W Sus* —3B **34**
Ball's Green. *E Sus* —2C **37**
Balscote. *Oxon* —1A **4**
Balstonia. *Thur* —3A **20**
Bamber's Green. *Essx* —2D **9**
Banbury. *Oxon* —1A **4**
Bannister Green. *Essx* —2A **10**
Banstead. *Surr* —3A **26**
Bapchild. *Kent* —2D **29**
Barcombe. *E Sus* —1C **47**
Barcombe Cross. *E Sus* —1C **47**
Bardfield End Green. *Essx* —1A **10**
Bardfield Saling. *Essx* —2A **10**
Barford. *Hants* —2A **34**
Barford St John. *Oxon* —1A **4**
Barford St Michael. *Oxon* —1A **4**
Barfrestone. *Kent* —3C **31**
Barham. *Kent* —3C **31**
Barkham. *Wok* —2D **23**
Barking. *G Lon* —3C **19**
Barkingside. *G Lon* —3C **19**
Barkway. *Herts* —1B **8**
Barlavington. *W Sus* —1B **44**
Barley. *Herts* —1B **8**
Barling. *Essx* —3D **21**
Barming Heath. *Kent* —3B **28**
Barnard Gate. *Oxon* —3A **4**
Barnes. *G Lon* —1A **26**
Barnes Street. *Kent* —1A **38**
Barnet. *G Lon* —2A **18**
Barnham. *W Sus* —2B **44**
Barns Green. *W Sus* —3D **35**
Barnston. *Essx* —3A **10**
Bartholomew Green. *Essx* —2B **10**
Barton. *IOW* —3B **42**
Barton. *Oxon* —1B **14**
Barton Hartshorn. *Buck* —1C **5**
Barton-le-Clay. *Beds* —1C **7**
Barton Stacey. *Hants* —1A **32**
Barwick. *Herts* —3B **8**
Basildon. *Essx* —3B **20**
Basingstoke. *Hants* —3C **23**
Bassett. *Sotn* —1A **42**
Bassingbourn. *Cambs* —1B **8**
Bassus Green. *Herts* —2B **8**
Batchworth. *Herts* —2C **17**
Battersea. *G Lon* —1A **26**
Battle. *E Sus* —1B **48**
Battlesbridge. *Essx* —2B **20**
Battlesden. *Beds* —2B **6**
Batt's Corner. *Surr* —1A **34**
Baughurst. *Hants* —2B **22**
Bawdsey. *Suff* —1D **13**
Bawdsey Manor. *Suff* —1D **13**
Baybridge. *Hants* —3B **32**
Bayford. *Herts* —1B **18**
Baynard's Green. *Oxon* —2B **4**
Baythorn End. *Essx* —1B **10**
Bayworth. *Oxon* —1B **14**
Beachampton. *Buck* —1D **5**
Beacon End. *Essx* —2D **11**
Beacon Hill. *Surr* —2A **34**
Beacon's Bottom. *Buck* —2D **15**
Beaconsfield. *Buck* —2B **16**
Beacontree. *G Lon* —3C **19**
Beamond End. *Buck* —2B **16**
Bean. *Kent* —1D **27**
Beanshanger. *Nptn* —1D **5**
Beare Green. *Surr* —1D **35**
Bearsted. *Kent* —3B **28**
Beauchamp Roding. *Essx* —3D **9**
Beaulieu. *Hants* —2A **42**
Beaumont. *Essx* —2B **12**
Beauworth. *Hants* —3B **32**
Beazley End. *Essx* —2B **10**
Beckenham. *G Lon* —2B **26**
Beckley. *E Sus* —3C **39**
Beckley. *Oxon* —3B **4**
Beckton. *G Lon* —3C **19**
Becontree. *G Lon* —3C **19**
Beddingham. *E Sus* —2C **47**
Beddington. *G Lon* —2A **26**
Bedham. *W Sus* —3C **35**
Bedhampton. *Hants* —2D **43**
Bedlar's Green. *Essx* —2D **9**
Bedmond. *Herts* —1C **17**
Beech. *Hants* —2C **33**
Beech Hill. *W Ber* —2C **23**
Beedon. *W Ber* —1A **22**
Beenham. *W Ber* —2B **22**
Begbroke. *Oxon* —3A **4**
Beggar Hill. *Essx* —1A **20**
Bekesbourne. *Kent* —3B **30**
Belchamp Otten. *Essx* —1C **11**
Belchamp St Paul. *Essx* —1B **10**
Belchamp Walter. *Essx* —1C **11**
Bellingdon. *Buck* —1B **16**
Bells Yew Green. *E Sus* —2A **38**
Belsize. *Herts* —1C **17**
Belstead. *Suff* —1B **12**
Beltinge. *Kent* —2B **30**
Beltring. *Kent* —1A **38**
Belvedere. *G Lon* —1D **27**
Bembridge. *IOW* —3C **43**
Bendish. *Herts* —2D **7**
Benenden. *Kent* —2C **39**
Benington. *Herts* —2B **8**
Benover. *Kent* —1B **38**
Benson. *Oxon* —2C **15**
Bentley. *Hants* —1D **33**
Bentley. *Suff* —1B **12**
Bentley Heath. *Herts* —2A **18**
Bentworth. *Hants* —1C **33**
Bepton. *W Sus* —1A **44**
Berden. *Essx* —2C **9**
Berinsfield. *Oxon* —2B **14**
Berkhamsted. *Herts* —1B **16**
Bermondsey. *G Lon* —1B **26**
Berrick Salome. *Oxon* —2C **15**
Berry's Green. *G Lon* —3C **27**
Berwick. *E Sus* —2D **47**
Bessels Leigh. *Oxon* —1A **14**
Best Beech Hill. *E Sus* —2A **38**
Betchworth. *Surr* —3A **26**
Bethersden. *Kent* —1D **39**
Bethnal Green. *G Lon* —3B **18**
Betsham. *Kent* —1A **28**
Betteshanger. *Kent* —3D **31**
Bevendean. *Brig* —2B **46**
Bexhill. *E Sus* —2B **48**
Bexley. *G Lon* —1C **27**
Bexleyheath. *G Lon* —1C **27**
Bexleyhill. *W Sus* —3B **34**
Bicester. *Oxon* —2B **4**
Bicknacre. *Essx* —1B **20**

:knor. Kent —3C 29
dborough. Kent —1D 37
ddenden. Kent —2C 39
ddenden Green. Kent —1C 39
ddlesden. Buck —1C 5
erton. Buck —3A 6
ggin Hill. G Lon —3C 27
ggin Hill (London) Airport. Kent —2C 27
ghton. Hants —2C 33
gnor. W Sus —1B 44
lericay. Essx —2A 20
lingshurst. W Sus —3C 35
lington. Beds —2B 6
sham. W Sus —2B 44
sington. Kent —2A 40
ting. Kent —1A 40
nes Green. W Sus —1D 45
nfield. Brac —1A 24
nfield Heath. Oxon —1D 23
nley. Hants —3A 22
nstead. IOW —3B 42
nstead. W Sus —2B 44
nsted. Hants —1D 33
rch. Essx —3D 11
rchanger. Essx —2D 9
rch Green. Essx —3D 11
rchington. Kent —2C 31
rchmoor Green. Beds —1B 6
rdbrook. Essx —1B 10
rdham. W Sus —2A 44
rds Green. Essx —1D 19
rling. Kent —2A 28
rling Gap. E Sus —3D 47
sham. Wind —3A 16
shopsbourne. Kent —3B 30
shop's Green. Essx —3A 10
shop's Green. Hants —2B 22
shop's Stortford. Herts —2C 9
shops Sutton. Hants —2C 33
shopstoke. Hants —1A 42
shopstone. Buck —3A 6
shopstone. E Sus —2C 47
shop's Waltham. Hants —1B 42
sley. Surr —3B 24
tterne. Sotn —1A 42
x. Oxon —3D 15
ackboys. E Sus —3D 37
ackbrook. Surr —1D 35
ackditch. Oxon —1A 14
ackfen. G Lon —1C 27
ackfield. Hants —2A 42
ackham. E Sus —2C 37
ackheath. Essx —2A 12
ackheath. G Lon —1B 26
ackheath. Surr —1C 35
ackmoor. Hants —2D 33
ackmore. Essx —1A 20
ackmore End. Essx —1B 10
ackmore End. Herts —3D 7
ackness. Hants —1D 33
ack Notley. Essx —2B 10
ackstone. W Sus —1A 46
ackthorn. Oxon —3C 5
ackwater. Hants —3A 24
ackwater. IOW —3B 42
adon. Oxon —3A 4
ake End. Essx —2B 10
ean. Kent —2B 30
edlow. Buck —1D 15
edlow Ridge. Buck —2D 15
endworth. Hants —1D 43
enheim. Oxon —1B 14
etchingdon. Oxon —3B 4
etchingley. Surr —3B 26
etchley. Mil —1A 6
ewbury. Oxon —3B 14
ndley Heath. Surr —1B 36
oxham. Oxon —1A 4
ue Bell Hill. Kent —2B 28
ue Row. Essx —3A 12
uetown. Kent —3D 29
arhunt. Hants —2C 43
arshead. E Sus —2D 37
ars Hill. Oxon —1A 14
arstall. Buck —3C 5
bbing. Kent —2C 29
bbingworth. Essx —1D 19
cking. Essx —2B 10
cking Churchstreet. Essx —2B 10
diam. E Sus —3B 38
dicote. Oxon —1A 4
dle Street Green. E Sus —1A 48
dsham Green. Kent —1B 40
gnor Regis. W Sus —3B 44
lney. W Sus —3A 36
nnington. Kent —2A 40
oker. Buck —2A 16
orley Green. Hants —1B 42
rden. Kent —2C 29
rden. W Sus —3A 34
rdon. Hants —2A 34
reham. Essx —1B 20
reham Street. E Sus —1A 48
rehamwood. Herts —2D 17
Borley. Essx —1C 11
Borley Green. Essx —1C 11
Borough Green. Kent —3A 28
Borstal. Medw —2B 28
Bosham. W Sus —2A 44
Bossingham. Kent —1B 40
Botany Bay. G Lon —2A 18
Bothampstead. W Ber —1B 22
Botley. Buck —1B 16
Botley. Hants —1B 42
Botley. Oxon —1A 14
Botolph Claydon. Buck —2D 5
Botolphs. W Sus —2D 45
Bough Beech. Kent —1C 37
Boughton Aluph. Kent —1A 40
Boughton Green. Kent —3B 28
Boughton Lees. Kent —1A 40
Boughton Malherbe. Kent —1C 39
Boughton Monchelsea. Kent —3B 28
Boughton under Blean. Kent —3A 30
Bouldnor. IOW —3A 42
Bourne End. Buck —3A 16
Bourne End. Herts —1C 17
Bournes Green. S'end —3D 21
Bourne, The. Surr —1A 34
Boveney. Buck —1B 24
Bovingdon. Herts —1C 17
Bovingdon Green. Buck —3A 16
Bovinger. Essx —1D 19
Bow Brickhill. Mil —1B 6
Bowcombe. IOW —3A 42
Bowers Gifford. Essx —3B 20
Bowlhead Green. Surr —2B 34
Boxford. Suff —1D 11
Boxford. W Ber —1A 22
Boxgrove. W Sus —2B 44
Boxley. Kent —3B 28
Boxted. Essx —1D 11
Boxted Cross. Essx —1A 12
Boyden Gate. Kent —2C 31
Boyton Cross. Essx —1A 20
Boyton End. Essx —1A 10
Brabourne. Kent —1B 40
Brabourne Lees. Kent —1A 40
Bracklesham. W Sus —3A 44
Brackley. Nptn —1B 4
Brackley Hatch. Nptn —1C 5
Bracknell. Brac —2A 24
Bradenham. Buck —2A 16
Bradfield. Essx —1B 12
Bradfield. W Ber —1C 23
Bradfield Heath. Essx —2B 12
Brading. IOW —3C 43
Bradley. Hants —1C 33
Bradwell. Essx —2C 11
Bradwell. Mil —1A 6
Bradwell-on-Sea. Essx —3A 12
Bradwell Waterside. Essx —1D 21
Bragbury End. Herts —2A 8
Braintree. Essx —2B 10
Braishfield. Hants —3A 32
Bramber. W Sus —1D 45
Brambledown. Kent —1D 29
Brambridge. Hants —3A 32
Bramdean. Hants —3C 33
Bramfield. Herts —3A 8
Bramley. Hants —3C 23
Bramley. Surr —1C 35
Bramley Green. Hants —3C 23
Bramling. Kent —3C 31
Bramshill. Hants —2D 23
Bramshott. Hants —2A 34
Bran End. Essx —2A 10
Bransbury. Hants —1A 32
Brantham. Suff —1B 12
Brasted. Kent —3C 27
Brasted Chart. Kent —3C 27
Braughing. Herts —2B 8
Bray. Wind —1B 24
Bray Wick. Wind —1A 24
Breach. W Sus —2D 43
Breachwood Green. Herts —2D 7
Brede. E Sus —1C 49
Bredgar. Kent —2C 29
Bredhurst. Kent —2B 28
Brenchley. Kent —1A 38
Brent Cross. G Lon —3A 18
Brentford. G Lon —1D 25
Brent Pelham. Herts —1C 9
Brentwood. Essx —2A 20
Brenzett. Kent —3A 40
Brewer Street. Surr —3B 26
Bricket Wood. Herts —1D 17
Bridge. Kent —3B 30
Bridge Green. Essx —1C 9
Bridgemary. Hants —2B 42
Brighthampton. Oxon —1A 14
Brightling. E Sus —3A 38
Brightlingsea. Essx —3A 12
Brighton. Brig —2B 46
Brighton Hill. Hants —1C 33
Brightwalton. W Ber —1A 22
Brightwalton Green. W Ber —1A 22
Brightwell. Suff —1C 13
Brightwell Baldwin. Oxon —2C 15
Brightwell-cum-Sotwell. Oxon —2B 14
Brill. Buck —3C 5
Brimpton. W Ber —2B 22
Brissenden Green. Kent —2D 39
Britwell Salome. Oxon —2C 15
Brixton. G Lon —1B 26
Broadbridge. W Sus —2A 44
Broadbridge Heath. W Sus —2D 35
Broadfield. W Sus —2A 36
Broadford Bridge. W Sus —3C 35
Broad Green. Beds —1B 6
Broad Laying. Hants —2A 22
Broadley Common. Essx —1C 19
Broadmere. Hants —1C 33
Broad Oak. E Sus —1C 49 (Hastings)
Broad Oak. E Sus —3A 38 (Heathfield)
Broadoak. Hants —1B 42
Broad Oak. Kent —2B 30
Broad's Green. Essx —3A 10
Broadstairs. Kent —2D 31
Broad Street. Kent —1B 40 (Ashford)
Broad Street. Kent —3C 29 (Maidstone)
Broad Street Green. Essx —1C 21
Brockbridge. Hants —1C 43
Brockham. Surr —1D 35
Brockhurst. Hants —2C 43
Brogborough. Beds —1B 6
Bromley. G Lon —2C 27
Bromley. Herts —2C 9
Bromley Green. Kent —2D 39
Brompton. Medw —2B 28
Brook. Hants —3A 32
Brook. Kent —1A 40
Brook. Surr —1C 35 (Guildford)
Brook. Surr —2B 34 (Haslemere)
Brookland. Kent —3D 39
Brookmans Park. Herts —1A 18
Brooks Green. W Sus —3D 35
Brook Street. Essx —2D 19
Brook Street. Kent —2D 39
Brook Street. W Sus —3B 36
Brookwood. Surr —3B 24
Broom. Beds —1D 7
Broomer's Corner. W Sus —3D 35
Broomfield. Essx —3B 10
Broomfield. Kent —2B 30 (Herne Bay)
Broomfield. Kent —3C 29 (Maidstone)
Broomhall. Surr —2B 24
Broughton. Mil —1A 6
Broughton. Oxon —1A 4
Brownbread Street. E Sus —1A 48
Brown Candover. Hants —2B 32
Broxbourne. Herts —1B 18
Broxted. Essx —2D 9
Broyle Side. E Sus —1C 47
Bryant's Bottom. Buck —2A 16
Buckhurst Hill. Essx —2C 19
Buckingham. Buck —1C 5
Buckland. Buck —3A 6
Buckland. Herts —1B 8
Buckland. Kent —1D 41
Buckland. Oxon —2A 14
Buckland. Surr —3A 26
Buckland Common. Buck —1B 16
Bucklebury. W Ber —1B 22
Bucklers Hard. Hants —3A 42
Bucklesham. Suff —1C 13
Bucknell. Oxon —2B 4
Bucks Green. W Sus —2C 35
Bucks Hill. Herts —1C 17
Bucks Horn Oak. Hants —1A 34
Buffler's Holt. Buck —1C 5
Bulbourne. Herts —3B 6
Bull Hill. Hants —3A 42
Bull's Green. Herts —3A 8
Bulmer. Essx —1C 11
Bulmer Tye. Essx —1C 11
Bulphan. Thur —3A 20
Bulverhythe. E Sus —2B 48
Bumble's Green. Essx —1C 19
Buntingford. Herts —2B 8
Buntings Green. Essx —1C 11
Burchett's Green. Wind —3A 16
Burcot. Oxon —2B 14
Burcott. Buck —2A 6
Burdrop. Oxon —1A 4
Bures. Suff —1D 11
Burgess Hill. W Sus —1B 46
Burghclere. Hants —2A 22
Burghfield. W Ber —2C 23
Burghfield Common. W Ber —2C 23
Burghfield Hill. W Ber —2C 23
Burgh Heath. Surr —3A 26
Burham. Kent —2B 28
Buriton. Hants —3D 33
Burleigh. Brac —1B 24
Burmarsh. Kent —2B 40
Burnham. Buck —3B 16
Burnham Green. Herts —3A 8
Burnham-on-Crouch. Essx —2D 21
Burntcommon. Surr —3C 25
Burnt Heath. Essx —2A 12
Burnt Hill. W Ber —1B 22
Burnt Oak. G Lon —2A 18
Burpham. Surr —3C 25
Burpham. W Sus —2C 45
Burridge. Hants —1B 42
Burrowhill. Surr —2B 24
Bursledon. Hants —2A 42
Burstow. Surr —1B 36
Burton End. Essx —2D 9
Burton's Green. Essx —2C 11
Burwash. E Sus —3A 38
Burwash Common. E Sus —3A 38
Burwash Weald. E Sus —3A 38
Bury. W Sus —1C 45
Bury Green. Herts —2C 9
Busbridge. Surr —1B 34
Bushey. Herts —2D 17
Bushey Heath. Herts —2D 17
Bustard Green. Essx —2A 10
Butcher's Cross. E Sus —3D 37
Buttsash. Hants —2A 42
Butt's Green. Essx —1B 20
Buxted. E Sus —3C 37
Bybrook. Kent —1A 40
Byfleet. Surr —2C 25
Bygrave. Herts —1A 8
Byworth. W Sus —3B 34

C

Caddington. Beds —3C 7
Cade Street. E Sus —3A 38
Cadmore End. Buck —2D 15
Cadwell. Herts —1D 7
Calais Street. Suff —1D 11
Calbourne. IOW —3A 42
Calcot Row. W Ber —1C 23
Calcott. Kent —2B 30
Caldecote. Herts —1A 8
Caldecott. Oxon —2A 14
Calshot. Hants —2A 42
Calvert. Buck —2C 5
Calverton. Mil —1D 5
Camber. E Sus —1D 49
Camberley. Surr —2A 24
Camberwell. G Lon —1B 26
Camden Town. G Lon —3A 18
Camelsdale. Surr —2B 34
Camps End. Cambs —1A 10
Campton. Beds —1D 7
Canadia. E Sus —1B 48
Cane End. Oxon —1C 23
Canewdon. Essx —2C 21
Canterbury. Kent —3B 30
Canvey Island. Essx —3B 20
Capel. Kent —1A 38
Capel. Surr —1D 35
Capel-le-Ferne. Kent —2C 41
Capel St Mary. Suff —1A 12
Carisbrooke. IOW —3A 42
Carshalton. G Lon —2A 26
Cartbridge. Surr —3C 25
Cassington. Oxon —3A 4
Castle Camps. Cambs —1A 10
Castle Green. Surr —2B 24
Castle Hedingham. Essx —1B 10
Castle Hill. Kent —1A 38
Caterham. Surr —3B 26
Catford. G Lon —1B 26
Catherington. Hants —1C 43
Catisfield. Hants —2B 42
Catmore. W Ber —3A 14
Catsfield. E Sus —1B 48
Cattawade. Suff —1B 12
Catteshall. Surr —1B 34
Caulcott. Oxon —2B 4
Caversfield. Oxon —2B 4
Caversham. Read —1D 23
Caversham Heights. Read —1C 23
Chackmore. Buck —1C 5
Chaddleworth. W Ber —1A 22
Chadwell Heath. G Lon —3C 19
Chadwell St Mary. Thur —1A 28
Chafford Hundred. Thur —1A 28
Chailey. E Sus —1B 46
Chainhurst. Kent —1B 38
Chaldon. Surr —3B 26
Chalfont Common. Buck —2C 17
Chalfont St Giles. Buck —2B 16
Chalfont St Peter. Buck —3C 17
Chalgrove. Oxon —2C 15
Chalk. Kent —1A 28
Chalk End. Essx —3A 10
Challock. Kent —3A 30
Chalton. Beds —2C 7
Chalton. Hants —1D 43
Chalvington. E Sus —2D 47

Chandler's Cross. *Herts* —2C **17**
Chandler's Ford. *Hants* —3A **32**
Channel Tunnel. *Kent* —2B **40**
Chantry. *Suff* —1B **12**
Chapel End. *Beds* —1C **7**
Chapel Row. *W Ber* —1B **22**
Chapmore End. *Herts* —3B **8**
Chappel. *Essx* —2C **11**
Charing. *Kent* —1D **39**
Charing Heath. *Kent* —1D **39**
Charlbury. *Oxon* —3A **4**
Charleshill. *Surr* —1A **34**
Charlton. *G Lon* —1C **27**
Charlton. *Herts* —2D **7**
Charlton. *Nptn* —1B **4**
Charlton. *Oxon* —3A **14**
Charlton. *W Sus* —1A **44**
Charlton-on-Otmoor. *Oxon* —3B **4**
Charlwood. *Hants* —2C **33**
Charlwood. *Surr* —1B **36**
Charndon. *Buck* —2C **5**
Charney Bassett. *Oxon* —2A **14**
Chart Corner. *Kent* —3B **28**
Charter Alley. *Hants* —3B **22**
Chartham. *Kent* —3B **30**
Chartham Hatch. *Kent* —3B **30**
Chartridge. *Buck* —1B **16**
Chart Sutton. *Kent* —3B **28**
Chart, The. *Kent* —3C **27**
Charvil. *Wok* —1D **23**
Chatham. *Medw* —2B **28**
Chatham Green. *Essx* —3B **10**
Chattenden. *Medw* —1B **28**
Chattisham. *Suff* —1A **12**
Chaulden. *Herts* —1C **17**
Chaul End. *Beds* —2C **7**
Chawley. *Oxon* —1A **14**
Chawton. *Hants* —2D **33**
Cheam. *Surr* —2A **26**
Cheapside. *Wind* —2B **24**
Chearsley. *Buck* —3D **5**
Checkendon. *Oxon* —3C **15**
Cheddington. *Buck* —3B **6**
Cheeseman's Green. *Kent* —2A **40**
Chelmondiston. *Suff* —1C **13**
Chelmsford. *Essx* —1B **20**
Chelsea. *G Lon* —1A **26**
Chelsfield. *G Lon* —2C **27**
Chelsham. *Surr* —3B **26**
Chelwood Common. *E Sus* —3C **37**
Chelwood Gate. *E Sus* —3C **37**
Chenies. *Buck* —2C **17**
Cheriton. *Hants* —3B **32**
Cheriton. *Kent* —2C **41**
Cherry Green. *Herts* —2B **8**
Chertsey. *Surr* —2C **25**
Chesham. *Buck* —1B **16**
Chesham Bois. *Buck* —2B **16**
Cheshunt. *Herts* —1B **18**
Chessington. *G Lon* —2D **25**
Chesterton. *Oxon* —2B **4**
Chestfield. *Kent* —2B **30**
Chetwode. *Buck* —2C **5**
Chevening. *Kent* —2D **27**
Chichester. *W Sus* —2A **44**
Chidden. *Hants* —1C **43**
Chiddingfold. *Surr* —2B **34**
Chiddingly. *E Sus* —1D **47**
Chiddingstone. *Kent* —1D **37**
Chiddingstone Causeway. *Kent* —1D **37**
Chiddingstone Hoath. *Kent* —1C **37**
Chidham. *W Sus* —2D **43**
Chieveley. *W Ber* —1A **22**
Chignall Smealy. *Essx* —3A **10**
Chignall St James. *Essx* —1A **20**
Chigwell. *Essx* —2C **19**
Chigwell Row. *Essx* —2C **19**
Chilbolton. *Hants* —1A **32**
Chilcomb. *Hants* —3B **32**
Childrey. *Oxon* —3A **14**
Childwick Green. *Herts* —3D **7**
Chilgrove. *W Sus* —1A **44**
Chilham. *Kent* —3A **30**
Chilland. *Hants* —2B **32**
Chillenden. *Kent* —3C **31**
Chilmington Green. *Kent* —1D **39**
Chiltern Green. *Beds* —3D **7**
Chilton. *Buck* —3C **5**
Chilton. *Oxon* —3A **14**
Chilton Candover. *Hants* —1B **32**
Chilworth. *Hants* —1A **42**
Chilworth. *Surr* —1C **35**
Chimney. *Oxon* —1A **14**
Chineham. *Hants* —3C **23**
Chingford. *G Lon* —2B **18**
Chinnor. *Oxon* —1D **15**
Chipperfield. *Herts* —1C **17**
Chipping. *Herts* —1B **8**
Chipping Hill. *Essx* —3C **11**
Chipping Ongar. *Essx* —1D **19**
Chipstead. *Kent* —3D **27**
Chipstead. *Surr* —3A **26**
Chisbridge Cross. *Buck* —3A **16**
Chislehampton. *Oxon* —2B **14**

Chislehurst. *G Lon* —2C **27**
Chislet. *Kent* —2C **31**
Chiswell Green. *Herts* —1D **17**
Chiswick. *G Lon* —1A **26**
Chitcombe. *E Sus* —3C **39**
Chithurst. *W Sus* —3A **34**
Chobham. *Surr* —2B **24**
Cholesbury. *Buck* —1B **16**
Cholsey. *Oxon* —3B **14**
Chorleywood. *Herts* —2C **17**
Chrishall. *Essx* —1C **9**
Christmas Common. *Oxon* —2D **15**
Chuck Hatch. *E Sus* —2C **37**
Church Common. *Hants* —3D **33**
Church Crookham. *Hants* —3A **24**
Church End. *Beds* —2B **6**
  (Dunstable)
Church End. *Beds* —1D **7**
  (Stotfold)
Church End. *Beds* —1B **6**
  (Woburn)
Church End. *Essx* —2B **10**
  (Braintree)
Church End. *Essx* —2A **10**
  (Great Dunmow)
Church End. *Essx* —1D **9**
  (Saffron Walden)
Churchend. *Essx* —2D **21**
  (Southend)
Church End. *Hants* —3C **23**
Church Enstone. *Oxon* —2A **4**
Church Hanborough. *Oxon* —3A **4**
Church Hougham. *Kent* —1C **41**
Church Langley. *Essx* —1C **19**
Church Norton. *W Sus* —3A **44**
Church Street. *Kent* —1B **28**
Churt. *Surr* —2A **34**
Cippenham. *Slo* —3B **16**
City (London) Airport. *G Lon* —3C **19**
City of London. *G Lon* —3B **18**
City, The. *Buck* —2D **5**
Clacton-on-Sea. *Essx* —3B **12**
Clanfield. *Hants* —1C **43**
Clapgate. *Herts* —2C **9**
Clapham. *G Lon* —1A **26**
Clapham. *W Sus* —2C **45**
Clap Hill. *Kent* —2A **40**
Clark's Green. *Surr* —2D **35**
Clatterford. *IOW* —3A **42**
Clavering. *Essx* —1C **9**
Clay End. *Herts* —2B **8**
Claygate. *Kent* —1B **38**
Claygate. *Surr* —2D **25**
Claygate Cross. *Kent* —3A **28**
Clayhall. *Kent* —1C **43**
Clayhill. *E Sus* —3C **39**
Clayton. *W Sus* —1B **46**
Cleeve. *Oxon* —3C **15**
Cleveley. *Oxon* —2A **4**
Cliddesden. *Hants* —1C **33**
Cliffe. *Medw* —1B **28**
Cliff End. *E Sus* —1C **49**
Cliffe Woods. *Medw* —1B **28**
Cliffs End. *Kent* —2D **31**
Clifton. *Beds* —1D **7**
Clifton. *Oxon* —1A **4**
Clifton Hampden. *Oxon* —2B **14**
Cliftonville. *Kent* —1D **31**
Climping. *W Sus* —2B **44**
Clophill. *Beds* —1C **7**
Clothall. *Herts* —1A **8**
Coalhill. *Essx* —2B **20**
Coates. *W Sus* —1B **44**
Cobham. *Kent* —2A **28**
Cobham. *Surr* —2D **25**
Cock Clarks. *Essx* —1C **21**
Cockernhoe. *Herts* —2D **7**
Cockfosters. *G Lon* —2A **18**
Cock Green. *Essx* —3A **10**
Cocking. *W Sus* —1A **44**
Cocking Causeway. *W Sus* —1A **44**
Cockpole Green. *Wind* —3A **16**
Codicote. *Herts* —3A **8**
Codmore Hill. *W Sus* —3C **35**
Cogges. *Oxon* —1A **14**
Coggeshall. *Essx* —2C **11**
Coggeshall Hamlet. *Essx* —2C **11**
Coggins Mill. *E Sus* —3D **37**
Colchester. *Essx* —2A **12**
Cold Ash. *W Ber* —2B **22**
Coldean. *Brig* —2B **46**
Colden Common. *Hants* —3A **32**
Coldharbour. *Kent* —3D **27**
Coldharbour. *Surr* —1D **35**
Cold Norton. *Essx* —1C **21**
Coldred. *Kent* —1C **41**
Coldwaltham. *W Sus* —1C **45**
Cole Green. *Herts* —3A **8**
Cole Henley. *Hants* —3A **22**
Coleman Green. *Herts* —3D **7**
Coleman's Hatch. *E Sus* —2C **37**
Colemore. *Hants* —2D **33**
Coleshill. *Buck* —2B **16**
Colgate. *W Sus* —2A **36**

Collier Row. *G Lon* —2C **19**
Colliers End. *Herts* —2B **8**
Collier Street. *Kent* —1B **38**
Colnbrook. *Buck* —1C **25**
Colne Engaine. *Essx* —1C **11**
Colney Heath. *Herts* —1A **18**
Colney Street. *Herts* —1D **17**
Colt's Hill. *Kent* —1B **38**
Colworth. *W Sus* —2B **44**
Combe. *Oxon* —3A **4**
Combe. *W Ber* —2A **22**
Combe Common. *Surr* —2B **34**
Compton. *Hants* —3A **32**
Compton. *Surr* —1B **34**
Compton. *W Ber* —1B **22**
Compton. *W Sus* —1D **43**
Coneyhurst Common. *W Sus* —3D **35**
Conford. *Hants* —2A **34**
Conyer. *Kent* —2D **29**
Cooden. *E Sus* —2B **48**
Cookham. *Wind* —3A **16**
Cookham Dean. *Wind* —3A **16**
Cookham Rise. *Wind* —3A **16**
Cookley Green. *Oxon* —2C **15**
Cooksbridge. *E Sus* —1C **47**
Cooksmill Green. *Essx* —1A **20**
Coolham. *W Sus* —3D **35**
Cooling. *Medw* —1B **28**
Cooling Street. *Medw* —1B **28**
Coombe. *Hants* —3C **33**
Coombes. *W Sus* —2D **45**
Coopersale Common. *Essx* —1C **19**
Coopersale Street. *Essx* —1C **19**
Cooper's Corner. *Kent* —1C **37**
Cooper Street. *Kent* —3D **31**
Cootham. *W Sus* —1C **45**
Copdock. *Suff* —1B **12**
Copford. *Essx* —2D **11**
Copford Green. *Essx* —2D **11**
Copsale. *W Sus* —3D **35**
Copthall Green. *Essx* —1C **19**
Copthorne. *W Sus* —2B **36**
Corhampton. *Hants* —1C **43**
Cornish Hall End. *Essx* —1A **10**
Corringham. *Thur* —3B **20**
Coryton. *Thur* —3B **20**
Coscote. *Oxon* —3B **14**
Cosgrove. *Nptn* —1D **5**
Cosham. *Port* —2C **43**
Cote. *Oxon* —1A **14**
Cothill. *Oxon* —2A **14**
Cottered. *Herts* —2B **8**
Cottisford. *Oxon* —1B **4**
Coulsdon. *Surr* —3A **26**
Coultershaw Bridge. *W Sus* —1B **44**
Countess Cross. *Essx* —1C **11**
Court-at-Street. *Kent* —2A **40**
Courtsend. *Essx* —2D **21**
Cousley Wood. *E Sus* —2A **38**
Cove. *Hants* —3A **24**
Cowbeech. *E Sus* —1A **48**
Cowden. *Kent* —1C **37**
Cowes. *IOW* —3A **42**
Cowfold. *W Sus* —3A **36**
Cowley. *G Lon* —3C **17**
Cowley. *Oxon* —1B **14**
Cowplain. *Hants* —1C **43**
Cox Green. *Surr* —2C **35**
Coxheath. *Kent* —3B **28**
Crabtree. *W Sus* —3A **36**
Crafton. *Buck* —3A **6**
Cranbourne. *Brac* —1B **24**
Cranbrook. *Kent* —2B **38**
Cranbrook Common. *Kent* —2B **38**
Cranfield. *Beds* —1B **6**
Cranford. *G Lon* —1C **25**
Cranham. *G Lon* —3D **19**
Cranleigh. *Surr* —2C **35**
Cranmore. *IOW* —3A **42**
Crawley. *Hants* —2A **32**
Crawley. *W Sus* —2A **36**
Crawley Down. *W Sus* —2B **36**
Crayford. *G Lon* —1D **27**
Crays Hill. *Essx* —2B **20**
Cray's Pond. *Oxon* —3C **15**
Crazies Hill. *Wok* —3D **15**
Creekmouth. *G Lon* —3C **19**
Cressing. *Essx* —2B **10**
Crews Hill. *G Lon* —1B **18**
Cricket Hill. *Hants* —2A **24**
Cricklewood. *G Lon* —3A **18**
Cripp's Corner. *E Sus* —3B **38**
Crockenhill. *Kent* —2D **27**
Crocker End. *Oxon* —3D **15**
Crockerhill. *Hants* —2B **42**
Crockham Hill. *Kent* —3C **27**
Crockhurst Street. *Kent* —1A **38**
Crockleford Heath. *Essx* —2A **12**
Cromer. *Herts* —2A **8**
Crondall. *Hants* —1D **33**
Crookham. *W Ber* —2B **22**
Crookham Village. *Hants* —3D **23**
Cross-at-Hand. *Kent* —1B **38**
Crossbush. *W Sus* —2C **45**

Cross End. *Essx* —1C **11**
Cross in Hand. *E Sus* —3D **37**
Crouch. *Kent* —3A **28**
Croughton. *Nptn* —1B **4**
Crowborough. *E Sus* —2D **37**
Crowdhill. *Hants* —1A **42**
Crowfield. *Nptn* —1C **5**
Crow Green. *Essx* —2D **19**
Crowhurst. *E Sus* —1B **48**
Crowhurst. *Surr* —1B **36**
Crowhurst Lane End. *Surr* —1B **36**
Crowmarsh Gifford. *Oxon* —3C **15**
Crowthorne. *Brac* —2A **24**
Croxley Green. *Herts* —2C **17**
Croydon. *G Lon* —2B **26**
Crundale. *Kent* —1A **40**
Crux Easton. *Hants* —3A **22**
Cryers Hill. *Buck* —2A **16**
Crystal Palace. *G Lon* —1B **26**
Cublington. *Buck* —2A **6**
Cuckfield. *W Sus* —3B **36**
Cuddesdon. *Oxon* —1C **15**
Cuddington. *Buck* —3D **5**
Cudham. *G Lon* —3C **27**
Cudworth. *Surr* —1A **36**
Cuffley. *Herts* —1B **18**
Culham. *Oxon* —2B **14**
Culverstone Green. *Kent* —2A **28**
Cumberlow Green. *Herts* —1B **8**
Cumnor. *Oxon* —1A **14**
Cupernham. *Hants* —3A **32**
Curbridge. *Hants* —1B **42**
Curdridge. *Hants* —1B **42**
Curridge. *W Ber* —1A **22**
Curtisden Green. *Kent* —1B **38**
Cutlers Green. *Essx* —1D **9**
Cuxham. *Oxon* —2C **15**
Cuxton. *Medw* —2B **28**

D

Dadford. *Buck* —1C **5**
Dagenham. *G Lon* —3C **19**
Dagnall. *Buck* —3B **6**
Dallington. *E Sus* —1A **48**
Danaway. *Kent* —2C **29**
Danbury. *Essx* —1B **20**
Dane End. *Herts* —2B **8**
Danehill. *E Sus* —3C **37**
Daneshill. *Hants* —3C **23**
Daniel's Water. *Kent* —1D **39**
Darenth. *Kent* —1D **27**
Dargate. *Kent* —2A **30**
Dartford. *Kent* —1D **27**
Dartford Crossing. *Kent* —1D **27**
Dassels. *Herts* —2B **8**
Datchet. *Wind* —1B **24**
Datchworth. *Herts* —3A **8**
Datchworth Green. *Herts* —3A **8**
Dawesgreen. *Surr* —1A **36**
Daws Heath. *Essx* —3C **21**
Deal. *Kent* —3D **31**
Dean. *Hants* —1B **42**
  (Bishop's Waltham)
Dean. *Hants* —2A **32**
  (Winchester)
Deane. *Hants* —3B **22**
Deanlane End. *W Sus* —1D **43**
Deanshanger. *Nptn* —1D **5**
Debden. *Essx* —1D **9**
Debden Green. *Essx* —2C **19**
  (Loughton)
Debden Green. *Essx* —1D **9**
  (Saffron Walden)
Deddington. *Oxon* —1A **4**
Dedham. *Essx* —1A **12**
Dedham Heath. *Essx* —1A **12**
Deepcut. *Surr* —3B **24**
Delly End. *Oxon* —3A **4**
Delvin End. *Essx* —1B **10**
Denchworth. *Oxon* —2A **14**
Dengie. *Essx* —1D **21**
Denham. *Buck* —3C **17**
Denham Green. *Buck* —3C **17**
Denmead. *Hants* —1C **43**
Densole. *Kent* —1C **41**
Denstroude. *Kent* —2B **30**
Denton. *E Sus* —2C **47**
Denton. *Kent* —1C **41**
Denton. *Oxon* —1B **14**
Deptford. *G Lon* —1B **26**
Derringstone. *Kent* —1C **41**
Detling. *Kent* —3B **28**
Dial Green. *W Sus* —3B **34**
Dial Post. *W Sus* —1D **45**
Dibden. *Hants* —2A **42**
Dibden Purlieu. *Hants* —2A **42**
Didcot. *Oxon* —2B **14**
Didling. *W Sus* —1A **44**
Digswell. *Herts* —3A **8**
Dingleden. *Kent* —2C **39**
Dinton. *Buck* —3D **5**
Dipley. *Hants* —3D **23**

Dippenhall. *Surr* —1A **34**
Ditchling. *E Sus* —1B **46**
Ditton. *Kent* —3B **28**
Doddinghurst. *Essx* —2D **19**
Doddington. *Kent* —3D **29**
Dogmersfield. *Hants* —3D **23**
Donkey Town. *Surr* —3D **23**
Donnington. *W Ber* —2A **22**
Donnington. *W Sus* —2B **20**
Doomsday Green. *W Sus* —2D **35**
Dorchester. *Oxon* —2B **14**
Dorking. *Surr* —1D **35**
Dorking Tye. *Suff* —1D **11**
Dormansland. *Surr* —1C **37**
Dormans Park. *Surr* —1B **36**
Dorney. *Buck* —1B **24**
Dorton. *Buck* —3C **5**
Dover. *Kent* —1D **41**
Dovercourt. *Essx* —1C **13**
Doversgreen. *Surr* —1A **36**
Dowlesgreen. *Wok* —2A **24**
Downe. *G Lon* —2C **27**
Downend. *IOW* —3B **42**
Downend. *W Ber* —1A **22**
Downham. *Essx* —2B **20**
Downley. *Buck* —2A **16**
Downside. *Surr* —3D **25**
Dragons Green. *W Sus* —3D **35**
Draycot. *Oxon* —1C **15**
Drayton. *Oxon* —2A **14**
(Abingdon)
Drayton. *Oxon* —1A **4**
(Banbury)
Drayton. *Port* —2C **43**
Drayton Beauchamp. *Buck* —3B **6**
Drayton Parslow. *Buck* —2A **6**
Drayton St Leonard. *Oxon*
—2B **14**
Drellingore. *Kent* —1C **41**
Droxford. *Hants* —1C **43**
Dry Sandford. *Oxon* —1A **14**
Dry Street. *Essx* —3A **20**
Duck End. *Essx* —2A **10**
Ducklington. *Oxon* —1A **14**
Duddenhoe End. *Essx* —1C **9**
Dulwich. *G Lon* —1B **26**
Dummer. *Hants* —1B **32**
Dumpford. *W Sus* —3A **34**
Duncton. *W Sus* —1B **44**
Dundridge. *Hants* —1B **42**
Dungate. *Kent* —3D **29**
Dungeness. *Kent* —3A **40**
Dunkirk. *Kent* —3A **30**
Dunk's Green. *Kent* —3A **28**
Dunley. *Hants* —3A **22**
Dunsden Green. *Oxon* —1D **23**
Dunsfold. *Surr* —2C **35**
Dunsmore. *Buck* —1A **16**
Dunstable. *Beds* —2C **7**
Duns Tew. *Oxon* —2A **4**
Dunton. *Buck* —2A **6**
Dunton Green. *Kent* —3D **27**
Durgates. *E Sus* —2A **38**
Durley. *Hants* —1B **42**
Durley Street. *Hants* —1B **42**
Durrant Green. *Kent* —2C **39**
Durrants. *Hants* —1D **43**
Durrington. *W Sus* —2D **45**
Duton Hill. *Essx* —2A **10**
Duxford. *Oxon* —2A **14**
Dymchurch. *Kent* —3B **40**

E

Ealing. *G Lon* —3D **17**
Earley. *Wok* —1D **23**
Earls Colne. *Essx* —2C **11**
Earnley. *W Sus* —3A **44**
Eartham. *W Sus* —2B **44**
Easebourne. *W Sus* —3A **34**
Eashing. *Surr* —1B **34**
Easington. *Buck* —3C **5**
Easington. *Oxon* —1A **4**
(Banbury)
Easington. *Oxon* —2C **15**
(Watlington)
Easole Street. *Kent* —3C **31**
East Anton. *Hants* —1A **32**
East Ashling. *W Sus* —2A **44**
East Aston. *Hants* —1A **32**
East Barming. *Kent* —3B **28**
East Barnet. *G Lon* —2A **18**
East Beach. *W Sus* —3A **44**
East Bedfont. *G Lon* —1C **25**
East Bergholt. *Suff* —1A **12**
East Blatchington. *E Sus* —3C **47**
East Boldre. *Hants* —2A **42**
Eastbourne. *E Sus* —3A **48**
East Burnham. *Buck* —3B **16**
Eastbury. *Herts* —2C **17**
Eastbury. *W Ber* —1A **22**
East Challow. *Oxon* —3A **14**
East Chiltington. *E Sus* —1B **46**
Eastchurch. *Kent* —1D **29**

East Clandon. *Surr* —3C **25**
East Claydon. *Buck* —2D **5**
Eastcote. *G Lon* —3D **17**
East Cowes. *IOW* —3B **42**
East Dean. *E Sus* —3D **47**
East Dean. *W Sus* —1B **44**
East End. *Hants* —3A **42**
(Lymington)
East End. *Hants* —2A **22**
(Newbury)
East End. *Herts* —2C **9**
East End. *Kent* —1D **29**
(Minster)
East End. *Kent* —2C **39**
(Tenterden)
East End. *Oxon* —3A **4**
East End. *Suff* —1B **12**
Eastergate. *W Sus* —2B **44**
East Farleigh. *Kent* —3B **28**
East Garston. *W Ber* —1A **22**
East Ginge. *Oxon* —3A **14**
East Gores. *Essx* —2C **11**
East Grinstead. *W Sus* —2B **36**
East Guldeford. *E Sus* —3D **39**
East Hagbourne. *Oxon* —3B **14**
East Ham. *G Lon* —3C **19**
Easthampstead. *Brac* —2A **24**
East Hanney. *Oxon* —2A **14**
East Hanningfield. *Essx* —1B **20**
East Harting. *W Sus* —1A **44**
Eastheath. *Wok* —2A **24**
East Hendred. *Oxon* —3A **14**
East Hoathly. *E Sus* —1D **47**
Easthorpe. *Essx* —2D **11**
East Horsley. *Surr* —3C **25**
East Hyde. *Beds* —3D **7**
East Ilsley. *W Ber* —3A **14**
East Langdon. *Kent* —1D **41**
East Lavant. *W Sus* —2A **44**
East Lavington. *W Sus* —1B **44**
Eastleigh. *Hants* —1A **42**
Eastling. *Kent* —3D **29**
East Liss. *Hants* —1D **33**
East Lockinge. *Oxon* —3A **14**
East Malling. *Kent* —3B **28**
East Marden. *W Sus* —1A **44**
East Meon. *Hants* —3C **33**
East Mersea. *Essx* —3A **12**
East Molesey. *Surr* —2D **25**
Eastney. *Port* —3C **43**
East Oakley. *Hants* —3B **22**
Easton. *Hants* —2B **32**
East Peckham. *Kent* —1A **38**
East Preston. *W Sus* —2C **45**
Eastry. *Kent* —3D **31**
East Shefford. *W Ber* —1A **22**
East Stourmouth. *Kent* —2C **31**
East Stratton. *Hants* —1B **32**
East Studdal. *Kent* —1D **41**
East Tilbury. *Thur* —1A **28**
East Tisted. *Hants* —2D **33**
Eastwick. *Herts* —3C **9**
East Wittering. *W Sus* —3D **43**
Eastwood. *S'end* —3C **21**
East Woodhay. *Hants* —2A **22**
East Worldham. *Hants* —2D **33**
Eaton. *Oxon* —1A **14**
Eaton Bray. *Beds* —2B **6**
Eaton Green. *Beds* —2B **6**
Ecchinswell. *Hants* —3B **22**
Eccles. *Kent* —2B **28**
Edburton. *W Sus* —1A **46**
Eddington. *W Ber* —2A **22**
Edenbridge. *Kent* —1C **37**
Edgcott. *Buck* —2C **5**
Edgware. *G Lon* —2D **17**
Edlesborough. *Buck* —3B **6**
Edmonton. *G Lon* —2B **18**
Edney Common. *Essx* —1A **20**
Edwardstone. *Suff* —1D **11**
Edworth. *Beds* —1A **8**
Effingham. *Surr* —3D **25**
Effingham Common. *Surr*
—3D **25**
Egbury. *Hants* —3A **22**
Egerton. *Kent* —1D **39**
Egerton Forstal. *Kent* —1C **39**
Eggington. *Beds* —2B **6**
Egham. *Surr* —1C **25**
Egham Hythe. *Surr* —1C **25**
Egypt. *Buck* —3B **16**
Egypt. *Hants* —1A **32**
Eight Ash Green. *Essx* —2D **11**
Elbridge. *W Sus* —2B **44**
Elcot. *W Ber* —1A **22**
Elder Street. *Essx* —1D **9**
Elham. *Kent* —1B **40**
Eling. *Hants* —1A **42**
Eling. *W Ber* —1D **23**
Elkins Green. *Essx* —1A **20**
Ellenbrook. *Herts* —1A **18**
Ellen's Green. *Surr* —2C **35**
Ellesborough. *Buck* —1A **16**
Ellisfield. *Hants* —1C **33**
Elmdon. *Essx* —1C **9**

Elmfield. *IOW* —3B **42**
Elm Park. *G Lon* —3D **19**
Elmstead. *Essx* —2A **12**
Elmstead Heath. *Essx* —2A **12**
Elmstead Market. *Essx* —2A **12**
Elmsted. *Kent* —1B **40**
Elmstone. *Kent* —2C **31**
Elsenham. *Essx* —2D **9**
Elsfield. *Oxon* —3A **4**
Elstead. *Surr* —1B **34**
Elsted. *W Sus* —1A **44**
Elsted Marsh. *W Sus* —3A **34**
Elstree. *Herts* —2D **17**
Eltham. *G Lon* —1C **27**
Elvington. *Kent* —3C **31**
Emmbrook. *Wok* —2D **23**
Emmer Green. *Read* —1D **23**
Emmington. *Oxon* —1D **15**
Empshott. *Hants* —2D **33**
Emsworth. *Hants* —2D **43**
Enborne. *W Ber* —2A **22**
Enborne Row. *W Ber* —2A **22**
Enfield. *G Lon* —2B **18**
Enfield Wash. *G Lon* —2B **18**
Englefield. *W Ber* —1C **23**
Englefield Green. *Surr* —1B **24**
Enham Alamein. *Hants* —1A **32**
Enstone. *Oxon* —2A **4**
Epping. *Essx* —1C **19**
Epping Green. *Essx* —1C **19**
Epping Green. *Herts* —1A **18**
Epping Upland. *Essx* —1C **19**
Epsom. *Surr* —2A **26**
Epwell. *Oxon* —1A **4**
Eridge Green. *E Sus* —2D **37**
Erith. *G Lon* —1D **27**
Erriottwood. *Kent* —3D **29**
Erwarton. *Suff* —1C **13**
Esher. *Surr* —2D **25**
Essendon. *Herts* —1A **18**
Etchingham. *E Sus* —3B **38**
Etchinghill. *Kent* —2B **40**
Eton. *Wind* —1B **24**
Eton Wick. *Wind* —1B **24**
Evenley. *Nptn* —1B **4**
Evershot. *Beds* —1B **6**
Eversley. *Hants* —2D **23**
Eversley Cross. *Hants* —2D **23**
Ewell. *Surr* —2A **26**
Ewell Minnis. *Kent* —1C **41**
Ewelme. *Oxon* —2C **15**
Ewhurst. *Surr* —1C **35**
Ewhurst Green. *E Sus* —3B **38**
Ewhurst Green. *Surr* —2C **35**
Ewshot. *Hants* —1A **34**
Exbury. *Hants* —2A **42**
Exceat. *E Sus* —3D **47**
Exlade Street. *Oxon* —3C **15**
Exton. *Hants* —3C **33**
Eyhorne Street. *Kent* —3C **29**
Eynsford. *Kent* —2D **27**
Eynsham. *Oxon* —1A **14**
Eythorne. *Kent* —1C **41**

F

Faccombe. *Hants* —3A **22**
Fairbourne Heath. *Kent* —3C **29**
Fairfield. *Kent* —3D **39**
Fairlands. *Surr* —3B **24**
Fairlight. *E Sus* —1C **49**
Fairlight Cove. *E Sus* —1C **49**
Fairmile. *Surr* —2D **25**
Fair Oak. *Hants* —1A **42**
(Eastleigh)
Fair Oak. *Hants* —2B **22**
(Kingsclere)
Fair Oak Green. *Hants* —2C **23**
Fairseat. *Kent* —2A **28**
Fairstead. *Essx* —3B **10**
Fairwarp. *E Sus* —3C **37**
Falkenham. *Suff* —1C **13**
Falmer. *E Sus* —2B **46**
Fancott. *Beds* —2C **7**
Fanner's Green. *Essx* —3A **10**
Fareham. *Hants* —2B **42**
Farleigh. *Surr* —2B **26**
Farleigh Wallop. *Hants* —1C **33**
Farley Green. *Surr* —1C **35**
Farley Hill. *Wok* —2D **23**
Farlington. *Port* —2C **43**
Farmoor. *Oxon* —1A **14**
Farnborough. *G Lon* —2C **27**
Farnborough. *Hants* —3A **24**
Farnborough. *W Ber* —3A **14**
Farncombe. *Surr* —1B **34**
Farnham. *Essx* —2C **9**
Farnham. *Surr* —1A **34**
Farnham Common. *Buck*
—3B **16**
Farnham Green. *Essx* —2C **9**
Farnham Royal. *Buck* —3B **16**
Farningham. *Kent* —2D **27**
Farthinghoe. *Nptn* —1B **4**

Faulkbourne. *Essx* —3B **10**
Faversham. *Kent* —2A **30**
Fawkham Green. *Kent* —2D **27**
Fawler. *Oxon* —3A **4**
Fawley. *Buck* —3D **15**
Fawley. *Hants* —2A **42**
Fawley. *W Ber* —3A **14**
Faygate. *W Sus* —2A **36**
Feering. *Essx* —2C **11**
Felbridge. *Surr* —2B **36**
Felcourt. *Surr* —1B **36**
Felden. *Herts* —1C **17**
Felixstowe. *Suff* —1C **13**
Felixstowe Ferry. *Suff* —1D **13**
Felpham. *W Sus* —3B **44**
Felsted. *Essx* —2A **10**
Feltham. *G Lon* —1D **25**
Felthamhill. *G Lon* —1C **25**
Fencott. *Oxon* —3B **4**
Fenn Street. *Medw* —1B **28**
Fenny Stratford. *Mil* —1A **6**
Fernhill. *Hants* —1A **36**
Fernhurst. *W Sus* —3A **34**
Ferring. *W Sus* —2D **45**
Fetcham. *Surr* —3D **25**
Fewcott. *Oxon* —2B **4**
Fiddlers Hamlet. *Essx* —1C **19**
Fifield. *Wind* —1B **24**
Finchampstead. *Wok* —2D **23**
Finchdean. *Hants* —1D **43**
Finchingfield. *Essx* —1A **10**
Finchley. *G Lon* —2A **18**
Findon. *W Sus* —2D **45**
Findon Valley. *W Sus* —2D **45**
Fingest. *Buck* —2D **15**
Finglesham. *Kent* —3D **31**
Fingringhoe. *Essx* —2A **12**
Finmere. *Oxon* —1C **5**
Finsbury. *G Lon* —3B **18**
Finstock. *Oxon* —3A **4**
Fishbourne. *IOW* —3B **42**
Fishbourne. *W Sus* —2A **44**
Fisher's Pond. *Hants* —3A **32**
Fisherstreet. *W Sus* —2B **34**
Fittleworth. *W Sus* —1C **45**
Five Ash Down. *E Sus* —3C **37**
Five Ashes. *E Sus* —3D **37**
Five Oak Green. *Kent* —1A **38**
Five Oaks. *W Sus* —3C **35**
Flack's Green. *Essx* —3B **10**
Flackwell Heath. *Buck* —3A **16**
Flamstead. *Herts* —3C **7**
Flansham. *W Sus* —3B **44**
Flaunden. *Herts* —1C **17**
Fleet. *Hants* —3A **24**
(Farnborough)
Fleet. *Hants* —2D **43**
(South Hayling)
Fleetville. *Herts* —1D **17**
Fletcher's Green. *Kent* —1D **37**
Fletching. *E Sus* —3C **37**
Flexford. *Surr* —3B **24**
Flimwell. *E Sus* —2B **38**
Flishinghurst. *Kent* —2B **38**
Flitton. *Beds* —1C **7**
Flitwick. *Beds* —1C **7**
Fobbing. *Thur* —3B **20**
Folkestone. *Kent* —2C **41**
Folkington. *E Sus* —2D **47**
Folly, The. *Herts* —3D **7**
Folly, The. *W Ber* —2C **23**
Fontwell. *W Sus* —2B **44**
Foots Cray. *G Lon* —1C **27**
Ford. *Buck* —1D **15**
Ford. *W Sus* —2C **45**
Fordcombe. *Kent* —1D **37**
Ford End. *Essx* —3A **10**
Fordham. *Essx* —2D **11**
Fordham Heath. *Essx* —2D **11**
Ford Street. *Essx* —2D **11**
Fordwich. *Kent* —3B **30**
Forest Green. *Surr* —1D **35**
Forest Hill. *Oxon* —1B **14**
Forest Row. *E Sus* —2C **37**
Forestside. *W Sus* —1D **43**
Forstal, The. *Kent* —2A **40**
Forton. *Hants* —1A **32**
Forty Green. *Buck* —2B **16**
Forty Hill. *G Lon* —2B **18**
Foster Street. *Essx* —1C **19**
Foul Mile. *E Sus* —1A **48**
Four Elms. *Kent* —1C **37**
Four Marks. *Hants* —2C **33**
Four Oaks. *E Sus* —3C **39**
Four Throws. *Kent* —3B **38**
Foxcombe Hill. *Oxon* —1A **14**
Fox Corner. *Surr* —3B **24**
Fox Hatch. *Essx* —2D **19**
Foxhunt Green. *E Sus* —1D **47**
Fox Lane. *Hants* —3A **24**
Fox Street. *Essx* —2A **12**
Framfield. *E Sus* —3C **37**
Frant. *E Sus* —2D **37**
Frating Green. *Essx* —2A **12**
Fratton. *Port* —2C **43**

Freefolk Priors. *Hants* —1A **32**
Freeland. *Oxon* —3A **4**
French Street. *Kent* —3C **27**
Frensham. *Surr* —1A **34**
Freshwater. *IOW* —3A **42**
Freshwater Bay. *IOW* —3A **42**
Freston. *Suff* —1B **12**
Friar's Gate. *E Sus* —2C **37**
Friday Street. *E Sus* —2A **48**
Friday Street. *Surr* —1D **35**
Friern Barnet. *G Lon* —2A **18**
Frieth. *Buck* —2D **15**
Frilford. *Oxon* —2A **14**
Frilsham. *W Ber* —1B **22**
Frimley. *Surr* —3A **24**
Frimley Green. *Surr* —3A **24**
Frindsbury. *Medw* —2B **28**
Fringford. *Oxon* —2C **5**
Frinsted. *Kent* —3C **29**
Frinton-on-Sea. *Essx* —3C **13**
Friston. *E Sus* —3D **47**
Frithsden. *Herts* —3C **7**
Frittenden. *Kent* —1C **39**
Fritwell. *Oxon* —2B **4**
Frogham. *Kent* —3C **31**
Frogmore. *Hants* —2A **24**
Frogmore. *Herts* —1D **17**
Froxfield. *Beds* —1B **6**
Froxfield Green. *Hants* —3D **33**
Fryern Hill. *Hants* —3A **32**
Fryerning. *Essx* —1A **20**
Fulflood. *Hants* —3A **32**
Fulham. *G Lon* —1A **26**
Fulking. *W Sus* —1A **46**
Fuller Street. *Essx* —3B **10**
Fullerton. *Hants* —2A **32**
Fulmer. *Buck* —3B **16**
Funtington. *W Sus* —2A **44**
Funtley. *Hants* —2B **42**
Furner's Green. *E Sus* —3C **37**
Furneux Pelham. *Herts* —2C **9**
Furzeley Corner. *Hants* —1C **43**
Furzey Lodge. *Hants* —2A **42**
Fyfield. *Essx* —1D **19**
Fyfield. *Oxon* —2A **14**
Fyning. *W Sus* —3A **34**

G

Gadbrook. *Surr* —1A **36**
Gagingwell. *Oxon* —2A **4**
Gainsborough. *Suff* —1B **12**
Gainsford End. *Essx* —1B **10**
Galleyend. *Essx* —1B **20**
Galleywood. *Essx* —1B **20**
Gallowstree Common. *Oxon* —3C **15**
Gardeners Green. *Wok* —2A **24**
Garford. *Oxon* —2A **14**
Garlinge Green. *Kent* —3B **30**
Garsington. *Oxon* —1B **14**
Gatton. *Surr* —3A **26**
Gatwick (London) Airport. *W Sus* —1A **36**
Gawcott. *Buck* —1C **5**
Gay Bowers. *Essx* —1B **20**
Gay Street. *W Sus* —3C **35**
George Green. *Buck* —3B **16**
Gerrards Cross. *Buck* —3B **16**
Gestingthorpe. *Essx* —1C **11**
Gibralter. *Buck* —1D **5**
Gidea Park. *G Lon* —3D **19**
Gillingham. *Medw* —2B **28**
Gill's Green. *Kent* —2B **38**
Glassenbury. *Kent* —2B **38**
Glympton. *Oxon* —2A **4**
Glynde. *E Sus* —2C **47**
Glyndebourne. *E Sus* —1C **47**
Goathurst Common. *Kent* —3C **27**
Goat Lees. *Kent* —1A **40**
Godalming. *Surr* —1B **34**
Goddard's Green. *Kent* —2C **39**
  (Benenden)
Goddard's Green. *Kent* —2B **38**
  (Cranbrook)
Goddards Green. *W Sus* —3A **36**
Godmersham. *Kent* —3A **30**
Godstone. *Surr* —3B **26**
Goff's Oak. *Herts* —1B **18**
Golden Cross. *E Sus* —1D **47**
Golden Green. *Kent* —1A **38**
Golden Pot. *Hants* —3A **24**
Golders Green. *G Lon* —3A **18**
Goldhanger. *Essx* —1D **21**
Goldstone. *Kent* —2C **31**
Gomshall. *Surr* —1C **35**
Good Easter. *Essx* —3A **10**
Goodmayes. *G Lon* —3C **19**
Goodnestone. *Kent* —3C **31**
  (Aylesham)
Goodnestone. *Kent* —2A **30**
  (Faversham)
Goodworth Clatford. *Hants* —1A **32**
Goosey. *Oxon* —2A **14**
Goring. *Oxon* —3C **15**

Goring-by-Sea. *W Sus* —2D **45**
Goring Heath. *Oxon* —1C **23**
Gosfield. *Essx* —2B **10**
Gosford. *Oxon* —2C **3**
Gosmore. *Herts* —2D **7**
Gosport. *Hants* —2B **42**
Gossops Green. *W Sus* —2A **36**
Goudhurst. *Kent* —2B **38**
Graffham. *W Sus* —1B **44**
Grafham. *Surr* —1C **35**
Grafty Green. *Kent* —1C **39**
Grain. *Medw* —1C **29**
Granborough. *Buck* —2D **5**
Grandpont. *Oxon* —1B **14**
Grange Hill. *G Lon* —2C **19**
Graveley. *Herts* —2A **8**
Graveney. *Kent* —2A **30**
Gravesend. *Kent* —1A **28**
Grays. *Thur* —1A **28**
Grayshott. *Hants* —2A **34**
Grayswood. *Surr* —2B **34**
Grazeley. *Wok* —2C **23**
Great Amwell. *Herts* —3B **8**
Great Baddow. *Essx* —1B **20**
Great Bardfield. *Essx* —1A **10**
Great Bentley. *Essx* —2B **12**
Great Bookham. *Surr* —3D **25**
Great Braxted. *Essx* —3C **11**
Great Brickhill. *Buck* —1B **6**
Great Bromley. *Essx* —2A **12**
Great Burstead. *Essx* —2A **20**
Great Canfield. *Essx* —3D **9**
Great Chart. *Kent* —1D **39**
Great Chesterford. *Essx* —1D **9**
Great Chishill. *Cambs* —1C **9**
Great Clacton. *Essx* —3B **12**
Great Cornard. *Suff* —1C **11**
Great Dunmow. *Essx* —2A **10**
Great Easton. *Essx* —2A **10**
Great Gaddesden. *Herts* —3C **7**
Great Hallingbury. *Essx* —3D **9**
Greatham. *Hants* —2D **33**
Greatham. *W Sus* —1C **45**
Great Hampden. *Buck* —1A **16**
Great Haseley. *Oxon* —1C **15**
Great Henny. *Essx* —1C **11**
Great Holland. *Essx* —3C **13**
Great Horkesley. *Essx* —1D **11**
Great Hormead. *Herts* —1C **9**
Great Horwood. *Buck* —1D **5**
Great Kimble. *Buck* —1A **16**
Great Kingshill. *Buck* —2A **16**
Great Leighs. *Essx* —3B **10**
Great Linford. *Mil* —1A **6**
Great Maplestead. *Essx* —1C **11**
Great Milton. *Oxon* —1C **15**
Great Missenden. *Buck* —1A **16**
Great Mongeham. *Kent* —3D **31**
Great Munden. *Herts* —2B **8**
Great Notley. *Essx* —2B **10**
Great Oakley. *Essx* —2B **12**
Great Offley. *Herts* —2D **7**
Great Oxney Green. *Essx* —1A **20**
Great Parndon. *Essx* —1C **19**
Great Saling. *Essx* —2A **10**
Great Sampford. *Essx* —1A **10**
Great Shefford. *W Ber* —1A **22**
Great Stambridge. *Essx* —2C **21**
Great Stonar. *Kent* —3D **31**
Greatstone-on-Sea. *Kent* —3A **40**
Great Tew. *Oxon* —2A **4**
Great Tey. *Essx* —2C **11**
Great Thorness. *IOW* —3A **42**
Great Totham North. *Essx* —3C **11**
Great Totham South. *Essx* —3C **11**
Great Wakering. *Essx* —3D **21**
Great Waldingfield. *Suff* —1D **11**
Great Waltham. *Essx* —3A **10**
Great Warley. *Essx* —2D **19**
Great Wenham. *Suff* —1A **12**
Great Wigborough. *Essx* —3D **11**
Greatworth. *Nptn* —1B **4**
Great Wymondley. *Herts* —2A **8**
Great Yeldham. *Essx* —1B **10**
Green End. *Herts* —1B **8**
  (Buntingford)
Green End. *Herts* —2B **8**
  (Stevenage)
Greenfield. *Beds* —1C **7**
Greenfield. *Oxon* —2D **15**
Greenford. *G Lon* —3D **17**
Greenham. *W Ber* —2A **22**
Greenhill. *Kent* —2B **30**
Greenhithe. *Kent* —1D **27**
Greenstead Green. *Essx* —2C **11**
Greensted Green. *Essx* —1D **19**
Green Street. *Herts* —2D **17**
Green Street Green. *G Lon* —2C **27**
Green Street Green. *Kent* —1D **27**
Green Tye. *Herts* —3C **9**
Greenwich. *G Lon* —1B **26**
Grendon Underwood. *Buck* —2C **5**
Greywell. *Hants* —3D **23**
Griggs Green. *Hants* —2A **34**

Grisling Common. *E Sus* —3C **37**
Groombridge. *E Sus* —2D **37**
Groton. *Suff* —1D **11**
Grove. *Kent* —2C **31**
Grove. *Oxon* —2A **14**
Grove Park. *G Lon* —1B **26**
Gubblecote. *Herts* —3B **6**
Guestling Green. *E Sus* —1C **49**
Guestling Thorn. *E Sus* —1C **49**
Guildford. *Surr* —1B **34**
Gundleton. *Hants* —2C **33**
Gun Green. *Kent* —2B **38**
Gun Hill. *E Sus* —1D **47**
Gunville. *IOW* —3A **42**
Gurnard. *IOW* —3A **42**
Guston. *Kent* —1D **41**

H

Habin. *W Sus* —3A **34**
Hackney. *G Lon* —3B **18**
Haddenham. *Buck* —1D **15**
Hadham Cross. *Herts* —3C **9**
Hadham Ford. *Herts* —2C **9**
Hadleigh. *Essx* —3C **21**
Hadleigh. *Suff* —1A **12**
Hadleigh Heath. *Suff* —1D **11**
Hadley Wood. *G Lon* —2A **18**
Hadlow. *Kent* —1A **38**
Hadlow Down. *E Sus* —3D **37**
Haffenden Quarter. *Kent* —1C **39**
Hailey. *Oxon* —3B **8**
Hailsham. *E Sus* —2D **47**
Hainault. *G Lon* —2C **19**
Hale. *Surr* —1A **34**
Hale Street. *Kent* —1A **38**
Halfway. *W Ber* —2A **22**
Halfway Houses. *Kent* —1D **29**
Halland. *E Sus* —1D **47**
Halley. *Herts* —3B **8**
Halling. *Medw* —2B **28**
Hall's Green. *Herts* —2A **8**
Halnaker. *W Sus* —2B **44**
Halse. *Nptn* —1B **4**
Halstead. *Essx* —1C **11**
Halstead. *Kent* —2C **27**
Halton. *Buck* —1A **16**
Ham. *G Lon* —1D **25**
Ham. *Kent* —3D **31**
Hambleden. *Buck* —3D **15**
Hambledon. *Hants* —1C **43**
Hambledon. *Surr* —2B **34**
Hamble-le-Rice. *Hants* —2A **42**
Hambrook. *W Sus* —2D **43**
Ham Green. *Kent* —2C **29**
Ham Hill. *Kent* —2A **28**
Hammer. *W Sus* —2A **34**
Hammersmith. *G Lon* —1A **26**
Hammerwood. *E Sus* —2C **37**
Hammill. *Kent* —3C **31**
Hammond Street. *Herts* —1B **18**
Hampden Park. *E Sus* —2A **48**
Hamperden End. *Essx* —1D **9**
Hampstead. *G Lon* —3A **18**
Hampstead Norreys. *W Ber* —1B **22**
Hampton. *G Lon* —1D **25**
Hampton. *Kent* —2B **30**
Hampton Poyle. *Oxon* —3B **4**
Hampton Wick. *G Lon* —2D **25**
Hamsey. *E Sus* —1C **47**
Hamsey Green. *Surr* —3B **26**
Hamstead. *IOW* —3A **42**
Hamstead Marshall. *W Ber* —2A **22**
Hamstreet. *Kent* —2A **40**
Handcross. *W Sus* —3A **36**
Handy Cross. *Buck* —2A **16**
Hangleton. *Brig* —2A **46**
Hangleton. *W Sus* —2C **45**
Hankham. *E Sus* —2A **48**
Hannington. *Hants* —3B **22**
Hanscombe End. *Beds* —1D **7**
Hanwell. *G Lon* —3D **17**
Hanwell. *Oxon* —1A **4**
Hanworth. *G Lon* —1D **25**
Harbledown. *Kent* —3B **30**
Hardham. *W Sus* —1C **45**
Hardley. *Hants* —2A **42**
Hardway. *Hants* —2C **43**
Hardwick. *Buck* —3A **6**
Hardwick. *Oxon* —2B **4**
  (Bicester)
Hardwick. *Oxon* —1A **14**
  (Witney)
Hardy's Green. *Essx* —2D **11**
Harefield. *G Lon* —2C **17**
Hare Green. *Essx* —2A **12**
Hare Hatch. *Wok* —1A **24**
Hareplain. *Kent* —2C **39**
Hare Street. *Essx* —1C **19**
Hare Street. *Herts* —2B **8**
Harkstead. *Suff* —1B **12**
Harlington. *Beds* —1C **7**
Harlington. *G Lon* —1C **25**

Harlow. *Essx* —1C **19**
Harmer Green. *Herts* —3A **8**
Harmondsworth. *G Lon* —1C **25**
Harold Hill. *G Lon* —2D **19**
Harold Wood. *G Lon* —2D **19**
Harpenden. *Herts* —3D **7**
Harpsden. *Oxon* —3D **15**
Harrietsham. *Kent* —3C **29**
Harrow. *G Lon* —3D **17**
Harrow on the Hill. *G Lon* —3D **17**
Harrow Weald. *G Lon* —2D **17**
Hartfield. *E Sus* —2C **37**
Hartfordbridge. *Hants* —3D **23**
Hartford End. *Essx* —3A **10**
Hartley. *Kent* —2B **38**
  (Cranbrook)
Hartley. *Kent* —2A **28**
  (Dartford)
Hartley Mauditt. *Hants* —2D **33**
Hartley Wespall. *Hants* —3C **23**
Hartley Wintney. *Hants* —3D **23**
Hartlip. *Kent* —2C **29**
Harvel. *Kent* —2A **28**
Harwell. *Oxon* —3A **14**
Harwich. *Essx* —1C **13**
Hascombe. *Surr* —1B **34**
Haslemere. *Surr* —2B **34**
Hassell Street. *Kent* —1A **40**
Hassocks. *W Sus* —1B **46**
Haste Hill. *Surr* —2B **34**
Hastingleigh. *Kent* —1A **40**
Hastings. *E Sus* —2C **49**
Hastingwood. *Essx* —1C **19**
Hastoe. *Herts* —1B **16**
Hatch End. *G Lon* —2D **17**
Hatching Green. *Herts* —3D **7**
Hatch Warren. *Hants* —1C **33**
Hatfield. *Herts* —1A **18**
Hatfield Broad Oak. *Essx* —3D **9**
Hatfield Heath. *Essx* —3D **9**
Hatfield Hyde. *Herts* —3A **8**
Hatfield Peverel. *Essx* —3B **10**
Hatford. *Oxon* —2A **14**
Hatherden. *Hants* —3A **22**
Hattingley. *Hants* —2C **33**
Hatton. *G Lon* —1C **25**
Haultwick. *Herts* —2B **8**
Havant. *Hants* —2D **43**
Havenstreet. *IOW* —3B **42**
Haven, The. *W Sus* —2C **35**
Havering-atte-Bower. *G Lon* —2D **19**
Havering's Grove. *Essx* —2A **20**
Haversham. *Mil* —1A **6**
Hawkenbury. *Kent* —1C **39**
Hawkhurst. *Kent* —2B **38**
Hawkhurst Common. *E Sus* —1D **47**
Hawkinge. *Kent* —1C **41**
Hawkley. *Hants* —3D **33**
Hawkwell. *Essx* —2C **21**
Hawley. *Hants* —3A **24**
Hawley. *Kent* —1D **27**
Hawthorn Hill. *Brac* —1A **24**
Hayes. *G Lon* —2C **27**
  (Bromley)
Hayes. *G Lon* —3C **17**
  (Uxbridge)
Haylands. *IOW* —3B **42**
Haynes. *Beds* —1C **7**
Haynes West End. *Beds* —1C **7**
Haysden. *Kent* —1D **37**
Hay Street. *Herts* —2B **8**
Haywards Heath. *W Sus* —3B **36**
Hazeleigh. *Essx* —1C **21**
Hazeley. *Hants* —3D **23**
Hazel Street. *Kent* —2A **38**
Hazlemere. *Buck* —2A **16**
Headbourne Worthy. *Hants* —2A **32**
Headcorn. *Kent* —1C **39**
Headington. *Oxon* —1B **14**
Headley. *Hants* —2A **34**
  (Haslemere)
Headley. *Hants* —2B **22**
  (Kingsclere)
Headley. *Surr* —3A **26**
Headley Down. *Hants* —2A **34**
Heath and Reach. *Beds* —2B **6**
Heath Common. *W Sus* —1D **45**
Heath End. *Hants* —2B **22**
Heathfield. *E Sus* —3D **37**
Heathrow (London) Airport. *G Lon* —1C **25**
Heathton. *Suff* —1B **12**
Heaverham. *Kent* —3D **27**
Hebing End. *Herts* —2B **8**
Heckfield. *Hants* —2D **23**
Heckfordbridge. *Essx* —2D **11**
Hedge End. *Hants* —1A **42**
Hedgerley. *Buck* —3B **16**
Helions Bumpstead. *Essx* —1A **10**
Hellingly. *E Sus* —1D **47**
Helmdon. *Nptn* —1B **4**
Hemel Hempstead. *Herts* —1C **17**
Hemley. *Suff* —1C **13**
Hemp's Green. *Essx* —2D **11**
Hempstead. *Essx* —1A **10**

Hempstead. *Medw* —2B **28**
Hempton. *Oxon* —1A **4**
Hendon. *G Lon* —3A **18**
Henfield. *W Sus* —1A **46**
Henham. *Essx* —2D **9**
Henley. *W Sus* —3A **34**
Henley-on-Thames. *Oxon* —3D **15**
Henley's Down. *E Sus* —1B **48**
Henley Street. *Kent* —2A **28**
Henlow. *Beds* —1D **7**
Henny Street. *Essx* —1C **11**
Hensting. *Hants* —3A **32**
Henton. *Oxon* —1D **15**
Hermitage. *W Ber* —1B **22**
Hermitage. *W Sus* —2D **43**
Herne. *Kent* —2B **30**
Herne Bay. *Kent* —2B **30**
Herne Common. *Kent* —2B **30**
Herne Pound. *Kent* —3A **28**
Hernhill. *Kent* —2A **30**
Heronden. *Kent* —3C **31**
Herongate. *Essx* —2A **20**
Heronsgate. *Herts* —2C **17**
Heron's Ghyll. *E Sus* —3C **37**
Herriard. *Hants* —1C **33**
Hersden. *Kent* —2C **31**
Hersham. *Surr* —2D **25**
Herstmonceux. *E Sus* —1A **48**
Hertford. *Herts* —3B **8**
Hertford Heath. *Herts* —3B **8**
Hertingfordbury. *Herts* —3B **8**
Heston. *G Lon* —1D **25**
Hethe. *Oxon* —2B **4**
Hever. *Kent* —1C **37**
Hextable. *Kent* —1D **27**
Hexton. *Herts* —1D **7**
Heybridge. *Essx* —2A **20**
 (Brentwood)
Heybridge. *Essx* —1C **21**
 (Maldon)
Heybridge Basin. *Essx* —1C **21**
Heydon. *Cambs* —1C **9**
Heyshott. *W Sus* —1A **44**
Heythrop. *Oxon* —2A **4**
Hickstead. *W Sus* —3A **36**
Higham. *Kent* —1B **28**
Higham. *Suff* —1A **12**
Higham Gobion. *Beds* —1D **7**
Higham Wood. *Kent* —1D **37**
High Barnet. *G Lon* —2A **18**
High Beech. *Essx* —2C **19**
Highbrook. *W Sus* —2B **36**
High Brooms. *Kent* —1D **37**
Highclere. *Hants* —2A **22**
High Cogges. *Oxon* —1A **14**
High Cross. *Hants* —3D **33**
High Cross. *Herts* —3B **8**
High Easter. *Essx* —3A **10**
High Garrett. *Essx* —2B **10**
Highgate. *G Lon* —3A **18**
High Halden. *Kent* —2C **39**
High Halstow. *Medw* —1B **28**
High Hurstwood. *E Sus* —3C **37**
High Laver. *Essx* —1D **19**
Highleigh. *W Sus* —3A **44**
Highmoor. *Oxon* —3D **15**
High Ongar. *Essx* —1D **19**
High Roding. *Essx* —3A **10**
High Salvington. *W Sus* —2D **45**
Highsted. *Kent* —2D **29**
Highstreet Green. *Essx* —1B **10**
Highstreet Green. *Surr* —2B **34**
High Wych. *Herts* —3C **9**
High Wycombe. *Buck* —2A **16**
Hildenborough. *Kent* —1D **37**
Hillborough. *Kent* —2C **31**
Hill Brow. *Hants* —3D **33**
Hillesden. *Buck* —2C **5**
Hill Green. *Essx* —1C **9**
Hillgreen. *W Ber* —1A **22**
Hill Head. *Hants* —2B **42**
Hillingdon. *G Lon* —3C **17**
Hillside. *Hants* —3D **23**
Hillstreet. *Hants* —1A **42**
Hill Top. *Hants* —2A **42**
Hilsea. *Port* —2C **43**
Hiltingbury. *Hants* —3A **32**
Hindhead. *Surr* —2A **34**
Hintlesham. *Suff* —1A **12**
Hinton Ampner. *Hants* —3B **32**
Hinton-in-the-Hedges. *Nptn* —1B **4**
Hinton Waldrist. *Oxon* —2A **14**
Hinxhill. *Kent* —1A **40**
Hinxworth. *Herts* —1A **8**
Hipley. *Hants* —1C **43**
Hitchin. *Herts* —2D **7**
Hoaden. *Kent* —3C **31**
Hoath. *Kent* —2C **31**
Hobbs Cross. *Essx* —2C **19**
Hockley. *Essx* —2C **21**
Hockliffe. *Beds* —2B **6**
Hoddesdon. *Herts* —1B **18**
Hodsoll Street. *Kent* —2A **28**
Hoe Gate. *Hants* —1C **43**

Hogben's Hill. *Kent* —3A **30**
Hoggeston. *Buck* —2A **6**
Holborn. *G Lon* —3B **18**
Holbrook. *Suff* —1B **12**
Holbury. *Hants* —2A **42**
Holder's Green. *Essx* —2A **10**
Hole Street. *W Sus* —1D **45**
Holland-on-Sea. *Essx* —3B **12**
Hollingbourne. *Kent* —3C **29**
Hollingbury. *Brig* —2B **46**
Hollingdon. *Buck* —2A **6**
Hollingrove. *E Sus* —3A **38**
Hollington. *E Sus* —1B **48**
Holmbury St Mary. *Surr* —1D **35**
Holmer Green. *Buck* —2A **16**
Holt End. *Hants* —2C **33**
Holton. *Oxon* —1C **15**
Holton St Mary. *Suff* —1A **12**
Holt Pound. *Hants* —1A **34**
Holtsmere End. *Herts* —3C **7**
Holtye. *E Sus* —2D **37**
Holwell. *Herts* —1D **7**
Holybourne. *Hants* —1D **33**
Holyfield. *Essx* —1B **18**
Holyport. *Wind* —3A **24**
Honey Hill. *Kent* —2B **30**
Honey Tye. *Suff* —1D **11**
Hooe. *E Sus* —2A **48**
Hooe Common. *E Sus* —1A **48**
Hook. *G Lon* —1D **25**
Hook. *Hants* —3D **23**
 (Basingstoke)
Hook. *Hants* —2B **42**
 (Fareham)
Hook Green. *Kent* —2A **38**
 (Lamberhurst)
Hook Green. *Kent* —1A **28**
 (Longfield)
Hook Green. *Kent* —2A **28**
 (Meopham)
Hook Norton. *Oxon* —1A **4**
Hook's Cross. *Herts* —2A **8**
Hookwood. *Surr* —1A **36**
Hooley. *Surr* —3A **26**
Hoo St Werburgh. *Medw* —1B **28**
Hope's Green. *Essx* —3B **20**
Horam. *E Sus* —1D **47**
Horkesley Heath. *Essx* —2D **11**
Horley. *Oxon* —1A **4**
Horley. *Surr* —1A **36**
Hornchurch. *G Lon* —3D **19**
Horndean. *Hants* —1C **43**
Horndon on the Hill. *Thur* —3A **20**
Horne. *Surr* —1B **36**
Horns Corner. *Kent* —3B **38**
Hornsey. *G Lon* —3B **18**
Horsell. *Surr* —3B **24**
Horsenden. *Buck* —1A **16**
Horsham. *W Sus* —2D **35**
Horsley Cross. *Essx* —2B **12**
Horsleycross Street. *Essx* —2B **12**
Horsmonden. *Kent* —1A **38**
Horspath. *Oxon* —1B **14**
Horsted Keynes. *W Sus* —3B **36**
Horton. *Buck* —3B **6**
Horton. *Wind* —1C **25**
Horton-cum-Studley. *Oxon* —3B **4**
Horton Heath. *Hants* —1A **42**
Horton Kirby. *Kent* —2D **27**
Hothfield. *Kent* —1D **39**
Houghton. *Hants* —2A **32**
Houghton. *W Sus* —1C **45**
Houghton Conquest. *Beds* —1C **7**
Houghton Green. *E Sus* —3D **39**
Houghton Regis. *Beds* —2C **7**
Hound. *Hants* —2A **42**
Hound Green. *Hants* —3D **23**
Hounslow. *G Lon* —1D **25**
Hove. *Brig* —2A **46**
Howe Green. *Essx* —1B **20**
 (Chelmsford)
Howegreen. *Essx* —1C **21**
 (Maldon)
How End. *Beds* —1C **7**
Howe Street. *Essx* —3A **10**
 (Chelmsford)
Howe Street. *Essx* —1A **10**
 (Finchingfield)
How Green. *Kent* —1C **37**
Howlett End. *Essx* —1D **9**
Howt Green. *Kent* —2C **29**
Hoyle. *W Sus* —1B **44**
Hucking. *Kent* —3C **29**
Hughenden Valley. *Buck* —2A **16**
Hulcott. *Buck* —3A **6**
Hullbridge. *Essx* —2C **21**
Hundred Acres. *Hants* —1B **42**
Hungerford. *W Ber* —2A **22**
Hungerford Newtown. *W Ber* —1A **22**
Hunny Hill. *IOW* —3A **42**
Hunsdon. *Herts* —3C **9**
Hunston. *W Sus* —2A **44**
Hunton. *Hants* —2A **32**
Hunton. *Kent* —1B **38**

Hunton Bridge. *Herts* —1C **17**
Hurley. *Wind* —3A **16**
Hursley. *Hants* —3A **32**
Hurst. *Wok* —1D **23**
Hurstbourne Priors. *Hants* —1A **32**
Hurstbourne Tarrant. *Hants* —3A **22**
Hurst Green. *E Sus* —3B **38**
Hurst Green. *Essx* —3A **12**
Hurst Green. *Surr* —2B **36**
Hurstpierpoint. *W Sus* —1A **46**
Hurst Wickham. *W Sus* —1A **46**
Hurtmore. *Surr* —1B **34**
Husborne Crawley. *Beds* —1B **6**
Hutton. *Essx* —2A **20**
Hyde Heath. *Buck* —1B **16**
Hydestile. *Surr* —1B **34**
Hythe. *Hants* —2A **42**
Hythe. *Kent* —2B **40**
Hythe End. *Wind* —1C **25**

I

Ibstone. *Buck* —2D **15**
Ibthorpe. *Hants* —3A **22**
Ibworth. *Hants* —3B **22**
Ickenham. *G Lon* —3C **17**
Ickford. *Buck* —1C **15**
Ickham. *Kent* —3C **31**
Ickleford. *Herts* —1D **7**
Icklesham. *E Sus* —1C **49**
Ide Hill. *Kent* —3C **27**
Iden. *E Sus* —3D **39**
Iden Green. *Kent* —2C **39**
 (Benenden)
Iden Green. *Kent* —2B **38**
 (Goudhurst)
Iffley. *Oxon* —1B **14**
Ifield. *W Sus* —2A **36**
Ifieldwood. *W Sus* —2A **36**
Ifold. *W Sus* —2C **35**
Iford. *E Sus* —2C **47**
Ightham. *Kent* —3D **27**
Ilford. *G Lon* —3C **19**
Ilmer. *Buck* —1D **15**
Ingatestone. *Essx* —2A **20**
Ingrave. *Essx* —2A **20**
Inkpen. *W Ber* —2A **22**
Inworth. *Essx* —3C **11**
Iping. *W Sus* —3A **34**
Ipsden. *Oxon* —3C **15**
Ipswich. *Suff* —1B **12**
Isfield. *E Sus* —1C **47**
Isle of Thanet. *Kent* —2D **31**
Isleworth. *G Lon* —1D **25**
Islington. *G Lon* —3B **18**
Islip. *Oxon* —3B **4**
Istead Rise. *Kent* —2A **28**
Itchen. *Sotn* —1A **42**
Itchen Abbas. *Hants* —2B **32**
Itchen Stoke. *Hants* —2B **32**
Itchingfield. *W Sus* —3D **35**
Iver. *Buck* —3C **17**
Iver Heath. *Buck* —3C **17**
Ivinghoe. *Buck* —3B **6**
Ivinghoe Aston. *Buck* —3B **6**
Ivychurch. *Kent* —3A **40**
Ivy Hatch. *Kent* —3D **27**
Iwade. *Kent* —2D **29**

J

Jacobswell. *Surr* —3B **24**
Jarvis Brook. *E Sus* —3D **37**
Jasper's Green. *Essx* —2B **10**
Jaywick. *Essx* —3B **12**
Jevington. *E Sus* —2D **47**
Jockey End. *Herts* —3C **7**
John's Cross. *E Sus* —3B **38**
Jordans. *Buck* —2B **16**

K

Kearsney. *Kent* —1C **41**
Kelshall. *Herts* —1B **8**
Kelvedon. *Essx* —3C **11**
Kelvedon Hatch. *Essx* —2D **19**
Kempshott. *Hants* —3C **23**
Kemp Town. *Brig* —2B **46**
Kemsing. *Kent* —3D **27**
Kemsley. *Kent* —2D **29**
Kenardington. *Kent* —2D **39**
Kennington. *Kent* —1A **40**
Kennington. *Oxon* —1B **14**
Kensington. *G Lon* —1A **26**
Kensworth. *Beds* —3C **7**
Kensworth Common. *Beds* —3C **7**
Kenton. *G Lon* —3D **17**
Kent Street. *E Sus* —1B **48**
Kent Street. *Kent* —3A **28**
Kent Street. *W Sus* —3A **36**
Kersey. *Suff* —1A **12**
Keston. *G Lon* —2C **27**

Kew. *G Lon* —1D **25**
Keymer. *W Sus* —1B **46**
Key Street. *Kent* —2C **29**
Kidbrooke. *G Lon* —1C **27**
Kiddington. *Oxon* —2A **4**
Kidlington. *Oxon* —3A **4**
Kidmore End. *Oxon* —1C **23**
Kilburn. *G Lon* —3A **18**
Killinghurst. *Surr* —2B **34**
Kilmeston. *Hants* —3B **32**
Kilndown. *Kent* —2B **38**
Kiln Green. *Wind* —1A **24**
Kimble Wick. *Buck* —1A **16**
Kimpton. *Herts* —3D **7**
Kingsash. *Buck* —1A **16**
Kingsbury. *G Lon* —3D **17**
Kingsclere. *Hants* —3B **22**
Kingsdown. *Kent* —1D **41**
Kingsey. *Buck* —1D **15**
Kingsfold. *W Sus* —2D **35**
Kingsgate. *Kent* —1D **31**
Kings Hill. *Kent* —3A **28**
Kings Langley. *Herts* —1C **17**
Kingsley. *Hants* —2D **33**
Kingsley Green. *W Sus* —2A **34**
Kingsnorth. *Kent* —2A **40**
Kingsnorth. *Medw* —1C **29**
King's Somborne. *Hants* —2A **32**
King's Sutton. *Nptn* —1A **4**
Kingston. *Kent* —3B **30**
Kingston. *W Sus* —2C **45**
Kingston Bagpuize. *Oxon* —2A **14**
Kingston Blount. *Oxon* —2D **15**
Kingston by Sea. *W Sus* —2A **46**
Kingston near Lewes. *E Sus* —2B **46**
Kingston Stert. *Oxon* —1D **15**
Kingston upon Thames. *G Lon* —2D **25**
King's Walden. *Herts* —2D **7**
Kingswood. *Buck* —3C **5**
Kingswood. *Kent* —3C **29**
Kingswood. *Surr* —3A **26**
Kings Worthy. *Hants* —2A **32**
Kinsbourne Green. *Herts* —3D **7**
Kintbury. *W Ber* —2A **22**
Kipping's Cross. *Kent* —1A **38**
Kirby Cross. *Essx* —2C **13**
Kirby-le-Soken. *Essx* —2C **13**
Kirdford. *W Sus* —3C **35**
Kirtlington. *Oxon* —3A **4**
Kirton. *Suff* —1C **13**
Kitwood. *Hants* —2C **33**
Knaphill. *Surr* —3B **24**
Knapp. *Hants* —3A **32**
Knatts Valley. *Kent* —2D **27**
Knebworth. *Herts* —2A **8**
Knockholt. *Kent* —3C **27**
Knockholt Pound. *Kent* —3C **27**
Knotty Green. *Buck* —2B **16**
Knowl Hill. *Wind* —1A **24**
Knowlton. *Kent* —3C **31**

L

Lacey Green. *Buck* —1A **16**
Laddingford. *Kent* —1A **38**
Lagness. *W Sus* —2A **44**
Laindon. *Essx* —3A **20**
Laleham. *Surr* —2C **25**
Lamarsh. *Essx* —1C **11**
Lamb Corner. *Essx* —1A **12**
Lamberhurst. *Kent* —2A **38**
Lamberhurst Quarter. *Kent* —2A **38**
Lambeth. *G Lon* —1B **26**
Lambourne End. *Essx* —2C **19**
Lambs Green. *W Sus* —2A **36**
Lancing. *W Sus* —2D **45**
Landport. *Port* —2C **43**
Lane End. *Buck* —2A **16**
Lane End. *Hants* —3B **32**
Lane End. *IOW* —3C **43**
Langdon Hills. *Essx* —3A **20**
Langdown. *Hants* —2A **42**
Langenhoe. *Essx* —3A **12**
Langford. *Beds* —1D **7**
Langford. *Essx* —1C **21**
Langham. *Essx* —1A **12**
Langley. *Essx* —1C **9**
Langley. *Hants* —2A **42**
Langley. *Herts* —2A **8**
Langley. *Kent* —3C **29**
Langley. *W Sus* —3A **34**
Langley. *Wind* —1C **25**
Langleybury. *Herts* —1C **17**
Langley Green. *W Sus* —2A **36**
Langley Heath. *Kent* —3C **29**
Langney. *E Sus* —2A **48**
Langrish. *Hants* —3D **33**
Langstone. *Hants* —2D **43**
Langton Green. *Kent* —2D **37**
Larkfield. *Kent* —3A **28**
Lasham. *Hants* —1C **33**
Lashenden. *Kent* —1C **39**
Latchford. *Herts* —2B **8**

Latchford—Mimbridge

Latchford. *Oxon* —1C **15**
Latchingdon. *Essx* —1C **21**
Latchmere Green. *Hants* —2C **23**
Latimer. *Buck* —2C **17**
Laughton. *E Sus* —1D **47**
Launton. *Oxon* —2C **5**
Laverstoke. *Hants* —1A **32**
Lawford. *Essx* —1A **12**
Layer Breton. *Essx* —3D **11**
Layer-de-la-Haye. *Essx* —2D **11**
Layer Marney. *Essx* —3D **11**
Layland's Green. *W Ber* —2A **22**
Layter's Green. *Buck* —2B **16**
Leaden Roding. *Essx* —3D **9**
Leadingcross Green. *Kent* —3C **29**
Leagrave. *Lutn* —2C **7**
Leatherhead. *Surr* —3D **25**
Leaveland. *Kent* —3A **30**
Leavenheath. *Suff* —1D **11**
Leaves Green. *G Lon* —2C **27**
Leckford. *Hants* —2A **32**
Leckhampstead. *Buck* —1D **5**
Leckhampstead. *W Ber* —1A **22**
Leckhampstead Street. *W Ber* —1A **22**
Ledburn. *Buck* —2B **6**
Ledwell. *Oxon* —2A **4**
Lee. *G Lon* —1C **27**
Lee. *Hants* —1A **42**
Lee Clump. *Buck* —1B **16**
Leeds. *Kent* —3C **29**
Lee-on-the-Solent. *Hants* —2B **42**
Lees, The. *Kent* —3A **30**
Lee, The. *Buck* —1B **16**
Leigh. *Kent* —1D **37**
Leigh. *Surr* —1A **36**
Leigh Beck. *Essx* —3C **21**
Leigh Green. *Kent* —2D **39**
Leigh-on-Sea. *S'end* —3C **21**
Leigh Park. *Hants* —2D **43**
Leighton Buzzard. *Beds* —2B **6**
Lemsford. *Herts* —3A **8**
Lenham. *Kent* —3C **29**
Lenham Heath. *Kent* —1D **39**
Lepe. *Hants* —3A **42**
Letchmore Heath. *Herts* —2D **17**
Letchworth. *Herts* —1A **8**
Letcombe Bassett. *Oxon* —3A **14**
Letcombe Regis. *Oxon* —3A **14**
Letty Green. *Herts* —3A **8**
Levens Green. *Herts* —2B **8**
Levington. *Suff* —1C **13**
Lewes. *E Sus* —1C **47**
Lewisham. *G Lon* —1B **26**
Lewknor. *Oxon* —2D **15**
Lewson Street. *Kent* —2D **29**
Leybourne. *Kent* —3A **28**
Ley Green. *Herts* —2D **7**
Ley Hill. *Buck* —1B **16**
Leysdown-on-Sea. *Kent* —1A **30**
Leyton. *G Lon* —3B **18**
Leytonstone. *G Lon* —3C **19**
Lickfold. *W Sus* —3B **34**
Lidham Hill. *E Sus* —1C **49**
Lidlington. *Beds* —1B **6**
Lidsey. *W Sus* —2B **44**
Lidstone. *Oxon* —2A **4**
Lightwater. *Surr* —2B **24**
Lilley. *Herts* —2D **7**
Lillingstone Dayrell. *Buck* —1D **5**
Lillingstone Lovell. *Buck* —1D **5**
Limbury. *Lutn* —2C **7**
Limpsfield. *Surr* —3B **26**
Linchmere. *W Sus* —2A **34**
Lindfield. *W Sus* —3B **36**
Lindford. *Hants* —2A **34**
Lindsell. *Essx* —2A **10**
Linford. *Thur* —1A **28**
Lingfield. *Surr* —1B **36**
Linkenholt. *Hants* —3A **22**
Linslade. *Beds* —2B **6**
Linton. *Kent* —3B **28**
Liphook. *Hants* —2A **34**
Lisle Court. *Hants* —3A **42**
Liss. *Hants* —3D **33**
Liss Forest. *Hants* —3D **33**
Litchfield. *Hants* —3A **22**
Litlington. *Cambs* —1B **8**
Litlington. *E Sus* —2D **47**
Little Baddow. *Essx* —1B **20**
Little Bardfield. *Essx* —1A **10**
Little Bentley. *Essx* —2B **12**
Little Berkhamsted. *Herts* —1A **18**
Little Billington. *Beds* —2B **6**
Little Bognor. *W Sus* —3C **35**
Little Bookham. *Surr* —3D **25**
Littlebourne. *Kent* —3C **31**
Little Brickhill. *Buck* —1B **6**
Little Bromley. *Essx* —2A **12**
Little Burstead. *Essx* —2A **20**
Littlebury. *Essx* —1D **9**
Littlebury Green. *Essx* —1C **9**
Little Canfield. *Essx* —2D **9**
Little Chalfont. *Buck* —2B **16**
Little Chart. *Kent* —1D **39**
Little Chesterford. *Essx* —1D **9**
Little Chishill. *Cambs* —1C **9**
Little Clacton. *Essx* —3B **12**
Little Common. *E Sus* —2B **48**
Little Cornard. *Suff* —1C **11**
Littlecote. *Buck* —2A **6**
Little Down. *Hants* —3A **22**
Little Dunmow. *Essx* —2A **10**
Little Easton. *Essx* —2A **10**
Little End. *Essx* —1D **19**
Little Gaddesden. *Herts* —3B **6**
Little Hadham. *Herts* —2C **9**
Little Hallingbury. *Essx* —3C **9**
Little Hampden. *Buck* —1A **16**
Littlehampton. *W Sus* —2C **45**
Little Haseley. *Oxon* —1C **15**
Little Horkesley. *Essx* —1D **11**
Little Hormead. *Herts* —2C **9**
Little Horsted. *E Sus* —1C **47**
Little Horwood. *Buck* —1D **5**
Little Kimble. *Buck* —1A **16**
Little Kingshill. *Buck* —2A **16**
Little Laver. *Essx* —1D **19**
Little Leighs. *Essx* —3B **10**
Little London. *Buck* —3C **5**
Little London. *E Sus* —1D **47**
Little London. *Hants* —1A **32**
(Andover)
Little London. *Hants* —3C **23**
(Basingstoke)
Little Maplestead. *Essx* —1C **11**
Little Marlow. *Buck* —3A **16**
Little Milton. *Oxon* —1C **15**
Little Missenden. *Buck* —2B **16**
Littlemore. *Oxon* —1B **14**
Little Oakley. *Essx* —2C **13**
Little Posbrook. *Hants* —2B **42**
Little Sampford. *Essx* —1A **10**
Little Sandhurst. *Brac* —2A **24**
Little Somborne. *Hants* —2A **32**
Littlestone-on-Sea. *Kent* —3A **40**
Little Tew. *Oxon* —2A **4**
Little Tey. *Essx* —2C **11**
Little Thurrock. *Thur* —1A **28**
Littleton. *G Lon* —2C **25**
Littleton. *Hants* —2A **32**
Littleton. *Surr* —1B **34**
Little Totham. *Essx* —3C **11**
Little Wakering. *Essx* —3D **21**
Little Walden. *Essx* —1D **9**
Little Waltham. *Essx* —3B **10**
Little Warley. *Essx* —2A **20**
Little Wenham. *Suff* —1A **12**
Littlewick Green. *Wind* —1A **24**
Little Wittenham. *Oxon* —2B **14**
Littleworth. *W Sus* —3D **35**
Little Wymondley. *Herts* —2A **8**
Little Yeldham. *Essx* —1B **10**
Littley Green. *Essx* —3A **10**
Locksgreen. *IOW* —3A **42**
Locks Heath. *Hants* —2B **42**
Lodsworth. *W Sus* —3B **34**
London. *G Lon* —3B **18**
London Biggin Hill Airport. *Kent* —2C **27**
London City Airport. *G Lon* —3C **19**
London Colney. *Herts* —1D **17**
London Gatwick Airport. *W Sus* —1A **36**
London Heathrow Airport. *G Lon* —1C **25**
London Luton Airport. *Beds* —2D **7**
London Southend Airport. *Essx* —3C **21**
London Stansted Airport. *Essx* —2D **9**
Long Common. *Hants* —1B **42**
Long Crendon. *Buck* —1C **15**
Longcross. *Surr* —2B **24**
Long Ditton. *Surr* —2D **25**
Longfield. *Kent* —2A **28**
Longfield Hill. *Kent* —2A **28**
Longford. *G Lon* —1C **25**
Long Gardens. *Essx* —1C **11**
Long Hanborough. *Oxon* —3A **4**
Longlane. *W Ber* —1A **22**
Long Marston. *Herts* —3A **6**
Longmoor Camp. *Hants* —2D **33**
Longparish. *Hants* —1A **32**
Longstock. *Hants* —2A **32**
Long Sutton. *Hants* —1D **33**
Longwick. *Buck* —1D **15**
Long Wittenham. *Oxon* —2B **14**
Longworth. *Oxon* —2A **14**
Loose. *Kent* —3B **28**
Loosley Row. *Buck* —1A **16**
Lordington. *W Sus* —2D **43**
Loudwater. *Buck* —2B **16**
Loughton. *Essx* —2C **19**
Loughton. *Mil* —1A **6**
Lovedean. *Hants* —1C **43**
Loves Green. *Essx* —1A **20**
Lower Arncott. *Oxon* —3C **5**
Lower Assendon. *Oxon* —3D **15**
Lower Basildon. *W Ber* —1C **23**
Lower Beeding. *W Sus* —3A **36**
Lower Bordean. *Hants* —3C **33**
Lower Bullington. *Hants* —1A **32**
Lower Common. *Hants* —1C **33**
Lower Dicker. *E Sus* —1D **47**
Lower Farringdon. *Hants* —2D **33**
Lower Froyle. *Hants* —1D **33**
Lower Gravenhurst. *Beds* —1D **7**
Lower Green. *Essx* —1C **9**
Lower Green. *W Ber* —2A **22**
Lower Halstow. *Kent* —2C **29**
Lower Hardres. *Kent* —3B **30**
Lower Heyford. *Oxon* —2A **4**
Lower Higham. *Kent* —1B **28**
Lower Holbrook. *Suff* —1B **12**
Lower Horncroft. *W Sus* —1C **45**
Lower Horsebridge. *E Sus* —1D **47**
Lower Kingswood. *Surr* —3A **26**
Lower Layham. *Suff* —1A **12**
Lower Nazeing. *Essx* —1B **18**
Lower Rainham. *Medw* —2C **29**
Lower Raydon. *Suff* —1A **12**
Lower Shelton. *Beds* —1B **6**
Lower Shiplake. *Oxon* —1D **23**
Lower Stoke. *Medw* —1C **29**
Lower Sundon. *Beds* —2C **7**
Lower Swanwick. *Hants* —2A **42**
Lower Upham. *Hants* —1B **42**
Lower Upnor. *Medw* —1B **28**
Lower Wield. *Hants* —1C **33**
Lower Winchendon. *Buck* —3D **5**
Lower Woodend. *Buck* —3A **16**
Lowfield Heath. *W Sus* —1A **36**
Lowford. *Hants* —1A **42**
Loxhill. *Surr* —2C **35**
Loxwood. *W Sus* —2C **35**
Luddenham. *Kent* —2D **29**
Luddesdown. *Kent* —2A **28**
Ludgershall. *Buck* —3C **5**
Luffenhall. *Herts* —2A **8**
Lunsford. *Kent* —3B **28**
Lunsford's Cross. *E Sus* —1B **48**
Lurgashall. *W Sus* —3B **34**
Luton. *Lutn* —2C **7**
Luton. *Medw* —2B **28**
Luton (London) Airport. *Beds* —2D **7**
Lydd. *Kent* —3A **40**
Lydden. *Kent* —1C **41**
Lydd-on-Sea. *Kent* —3A **40**
Lyde Green. *Hants* —3D **23**
Lye Green. *Buck* —1B **16**
Lye Green. *E Sus* —2D **37**
Lyford. *Oxon* —2A **14**
Lymbridge Green. *Kent* —1B **40**
Lyminge. *Kent* —1B **40**
Lyminster. *W Sus* —2C **45**
Lympne. *Kent* —2B **40**
Lyne. *Surr* —2C **25**
Lynsted. *Kent* —2D **29**

M

Mackerye End. *Herts* —3D **7**
Madehurst. *W Sus* —1B **44**
Magdalen Laver. *Essx* —1D **19**
Magham Down. *E Sus* —1A **48**
Maidenbower. *W Sus* —2A **36**
Maidenhead. *Wind* —3A **16**
Maiden's Green. *Brac* —1A **24**
Maidensgrove. *Oxon* —3D **15**
Maid's Moreton. *Buck* —1D **5**
Maidstone. *Kent* —3B **28**
Malden Rushett. *Surr* —2D **25**
Maldon. *Essx* —1C **21**
Mallows Green. *Essx* —2C **9**
Maltman's Hill. *Kent* —1D **39**
Mannings Heath. *W Sus* —3A **36**
Manningtree. *Essx* —1B **12**
Manor Park. *G Lon* —3C **19**
Manston. *Kent* —2D **31**
Manuden. *Essx* —2C **9**
Maple Cross. *Herts* —2C **17**
Mapledurham. *Oxon* —1C **23**
Mapledurwell. *Hants* —3C **23**
Maplehurst. *W Sus* —3D **35**
Maplescombe. *Kent* —2D **27**
Marcham. *Oxon* —2A **14**
Marchwood. *Hants* —1A **42**
Marden. *Kent* —1B **38**
Marden Beech. *Kent* —1B **38**
Marden Thorn. *Kent* —1B **38**
Marehill. *W Sus* —1C **45**
Maresfield. *E Sus* —3C **37**
Margaret Roding. *Essx* —3D **9**
Margaretting. *Essx* —1A **20**
Margaretting Tye. *Essx* —1A **20**
Margate. *Kent* —1D **31**
Margery. *Surr* —3A **26**
Marine Town. *Kent* —1D **29**
Markbeech. *Kent* —1C **37**
Mark Cross. *E Sus* —2D **37**
Mark's Corner. *IOW* —3A **42**
Marks Tey. *Essx* —2D **11**
Markyate. *Herts* —3C **7**
Marle Green. *E Sus* —1D **47**
Marlow. *Buck* —3A **16**
Marlow Bottom. *Buck* —3A **16**
Marlpit Hill. *Kent* —1C **37**
Marlpits. *E Sus* —3C **37**
Marsh. *Buck* —1A **16**
Marshalswick. *Herts* —1D **17**
Marsh Baldon. *Oxon* —2B **14**
Marsh Benham. *W Ber* —2A **22**
Marshborough. *Kent* —3D **31**
Marsh Gibbon. *Buck* —2C **5**
Marsh Green. *Kent* —1C **37**
Marston. *Oxon* —1B **14**
Marston Moretaine. *Beds* —1B **6**
Marston St Lawrence. *Nptn* —1B **4**
Marsworth. *Buck* —3B **6**
Martin. *Kent* —1D **41**
Martin Mill. *Kent* —1D **41**
Martyr's Green. *Surr* —3C **25**
Martyr Worthy. *Hants* —2B **32**
Marylebone. *G Lon* —3A **18**
Mashbury. *Essx* —3A **10**
Matching. *Essx* —3D **9**
Matching Green. *Essx* —3D **9**
Matching Tye. *Essx* —3D **9**
Matfield. *Kent* —1A **38**
Mattingley. *Hants* —3D **23**
Maulden. *Beds* —1C **7**
Maxton. *Kent* —1D **41**
Maybush. *Sotn* —1A **42**
Mayes Green. *Surr* —2D **35**
Mayfield. *E Sus* —3D **37**
Mayford. *Surr* —3B **24**
Mayland. *Essx* —1D **21**
Maylandsea. *Essx* —1D **21**
Maynard's Green. *E Sus* —1D **47**
Maypole. *Kent* —2C **31**
Meadle. *Buck* —1A **16**
Meath Green. *Surr* —1A **36**
Medmenham. *Buck* —3A **16**
Medstead. *Hants* —2C **33**
Medway Towns. *Medw* —2B **28**
Meesden. *Herts* —1C **9**
Mentmore. *Buck* —3B **6**
Meon. *Hants* —2B **42**
Meonstoke. *Hants* —1C **43**
Meopham. *Kent* —2A **28**
Meopham Green. *Kent* —2A **28**
Meopham Station. *Kent* —2A **28**
Meppershall. *Beds* —1D **7**
Mereworth. *Kent* —3A **28**
Merrow. *Surr* —3C **25**
Mersham. *Kent* —2A **40**
Merstham. *Surr* —3A **26**
Merston. *W Sus* —2A **44**
Merton. *G Lon* —2A **26**
Merton. *Oxon* —3B **4**
Messing. *Essx* —3C **11**
Micheldever. *Hants* —2B **32**
Micheldever Station. *Hants* —1B **32**
Michelmersh. *Hants* —3A **32**
Micklefield Green. *Herts* —2C **17**
Mickleham. *Surr* —3D **25**
Middle Assendon. *Oxon* —3D **15**
Middle Aston. *Oxon* —2A **4**
Middle Barton. *Oxon* —2A **4**
Middle Claydon. *Buck* —2D **5**
Middleton. *Essx* —1C **11**
Middleton. *Hants* —1A **32**
Middleton Cheney. *Nptn* —1B **4**
Middleton-on-Sea. *W Sus* —2B **44**
Middleton Stoney. *Oxon* —2B **4**
Middle Tysoe. *Warw* —1A **4**
Midgham. *W Ber* —2B **22**
Midhurst. *W Sus* —3A **34**
Mid Lavant. *W Sus* —2A **44**
Milcombe. *Oxon* —1A **4**
Milebush. *Kent* —1B **38**
Mile End. *Essx* —2D **11**
Mile Oak. *Brig* —2A **46**
Mile Town. *Kent* —1D **29**
Milford. *Surr* —1B **34**
Milland. *W Sus* —3A **34**
Millbridge. *Surr* —1A **34**
Millbrook. *Beds* —1C **7**
Millbrook. *Sotn* —1A **42**
Mill Corner. *E Sus* —3C **39**
Mill End. *Buck* —3D **15**
Mill End. *Herts* —1B **8**
Mill Green. *Suff* —1D **11**
Mill Greep. *Essx* —1A **20**
Mill Hill. *G Lon* —2A **18**
Mill Lane. *Hants* —3D **23**
Millow. *Beds* —1A **8**
Milstead. *Kent* —3D **29**
Milton. *Oxon* —1A **4**
(Banbury)
Milton. *Oxon* —2A **14**
(Didcot)
Milton. *Port* —3C **43**
Milton Bryan. *Beds* —1B **6**
Milton Hill. *Oxon* —2A **14**
Milton Keynes. *Mil* —1A **6**
Milton Keynes Village. *Mil* —1A **6**
Milton Regis. *Kent* —2C **29**
Milton Street. *E Sus* —2D **47**
Mimbridge. *Surr* —2B **24**

Minsted. W Sus —3A 34
Minster. Kent —2D 31
(Ramsgate)
Minster. Kent —1D 29
(Sheerness)
Mistley. Essx —1B 12
Mistley Heath. Essx —1B 12
Mitcham. G Lon —2A 26
Mixbury. Oxon —1C 5
Molash. Kent —3A 30
Molehill Green. Essx —2D 9
Moneyrow Green. Wind —1A 24
Monken Hadley. G Lon —2A 18
Monk's Gate. W Sus —3A 36
Monk Sherborne. Hants —3C 23
Monks Risborough. Buck —1A 16
Monk Street. Essx —2A 10
Monkton. Kent —2C 31
Monkwood. Hants —2C 33
Moon's Green. Kent —3C 39
Moorgreen. Hants —1A 42
Moorhouse. Surr —3C 27
Moor, The. Kent —3B 38
Morden. G Lon —2A 26
Morestead. Hants —3B 32
Moreton. Essx —1D 19
Moreton. Oxon —1C 15
Morris Green. Essx —1B 10
Mortimer Common. W Ber —2C 23
Mortimer West End. Hants —2C 23
Mottingham. G Lon —1C 27
Mott's Mill. E Sus —2D 37
Moulsecoomb. Brig —2B 46
Moulsford. Oxon —3B 14
Moulsoe. Mil —1B 6
Mount Bures. Essx —1D 11
Mountfield. E Sus —3B 38
Mountnessing. Essx —2A 20
Mount Pleasant. Buck —1C 5
Mount Pleasant. E Sus —1C 47
Much Hadham. Herts —3C 9
Mucking. Thur —3A 20
Mugswell. Surr —3A 26
Mundon. Essx —1C 21
Murcott. Oxon —3B 4
Murrell Green. Hants —3D 23
Mursley. Buck —2A 6
Muswell Hill. G Lon —3A 18
Mytchett. Surr —3A 24

N

Nackington. Kent —3B 30
Nacton. Suff —1C 13
Nalderswood. Surr —1A 36
Naphill. Buck —2A 16
Nash. Buck —1D 5
Nash. Kent —3C 31
Nash Lee. Buck —1A 16
Nasty. Herts —2B 8
Nately Scures. Hants —3D 23
Navestock Heath. Essx —2D 19
Navestock Side. Essx —2D 19
Nayland. Suff —1D 11
Nazeing. Essx —1C 19
Neasden. G Lon —3A 18
Neithrop. Oxon —1A 4
Nethercott. Oxon —2A 4
Netherfield. E Sus —1B 48
Nether Street. Essx —3D 9
Netherton. Hants —3A 22
Nether Worton. Oxon —1A 4
Netley. Hants —2A 42
Nettlebed. Oxon —3D 15
Nettleden. Herts —3C 7
Nettlestead. Kent —3A 28
Nettlestead Green. Kent —3A 28
Nettlestone. IOW —3C 43
Nevendon. Essx —2B 20
New Addington. G Lon —2B 26
New Alresford. Hants —2B 32
New Ash Green. Kent —2A 28
New Barn. Kent —2A 28
Newbottle. Nptn —1B 4
Newbourne. Suff —1C 13
Newbridge. IOW —3A 42
New Brighton. Hants —2D 43
Newbury. W Ber —2A 22
Newchapel. Surr —1B 36
New Cheriton. Hants —3B 32
Newchurch. Kent —2A 40
New Denham. Buck —3C 17
Newdigate. Surr —1D 35
Newell Green. Brac —1A 24
New Eltham. G Lon —1C 27
Newenden. Kent —3C 39
New England. Essx —1B 10
Newfound. Hants —3B 22
Newgate Street. Herts —1B 18
New Greens. Herts —1D 17
Newhaven. E Sus —2C 47
New Haw. Surr —2C 25
New Hythe. Kent —3B 28
Newick. E Sus —3C 37
Newington. Kent —2B 40
(Folkestone)
Newington. Kent —2C 29
(Sittingbourne)
Newington. Oxon —2C 15
Newlands. Essx —3C 21
New Malden. G Lon —2A 26
Newman's Green. Suff —1C 11
New Mill. Herts —3B 6
New Mistley. Essx —1B 12
Newnham. Hants —3D 23
Newnham. Herts —1A 8
Newnham. Kent —3D 29
Newport. Essx —1D 9
Newport. IOW —3B 42
Newpound Common. W Sus —3C 35
New Romney. Kent —3A 40
Newton. Suff —1D 11
Newton Longville. Buck —1A 6
Newton Purcell. Oxon —1C 5
Newton Stacey. Hants —1A 32
Newton Valence. Hants —2D 33
Newtown. Hants —1B 42
(Bishop's Waltham)
Newtown. Hants —2A 22
(Newbury)
Newtown. Hants —2A 42
(Warsash)
Newtown. Hants —1C 43
(Wickham)
Newtown. IOW —3A 42
New Town. Lutn —2C 7
New Yatt. Oxon —3A 4
Newyears Green. G Lon —3C 17
Nine Ashes. Essx —1D 19
Ninfield. E Sus —1B 48
Ningwood. IOW —3A 42
Noak Hill. G Lon —2D 19
Noke. Oxon —3B 4
Nonington. Kent —3C 31
Norleywood. Hants —3A 42
Normandy. Surr —3B 24
Norman's Bay. E Sus —2A 48
Northall. Buck —2B 6
Northam. Sotn —1A 42
North Ascot. Brac —2B 24
North Aston. Oxon —2A 4
Northaw. Herts —1A 18
North Baddesley. Hants —3A 32
North Benfleet. Essx —3B 20
North Bersted. W Sus —2B 44
North Boarhunt. Hants —1C 43
Northbourne. Kent —3D 31
Northbourne. Oxon —3B 14
Northbrook. Oxon —2A 4
North Chailey. E Sus —3B 36
Northchapel. W Sus —3B 34
Northchurch. Herts —1B 16
North Common. E Sus —3B 36
Northcourt. Oxon —2B 14
North Cray. G Lon —1C 27
North End. Essx —3A 10
(Great Dunmow)
North End. Essx —1B 10
(Great Yeldham)
North End. Hants —2A 22
Northend. Oxon —2D 15
North End. Port —2C 43
North End. W Sus —2D 45
North Fambridge. Essx —2C 21
Northfleet. Kent —1A 28
North Halling. Medw —2B 28
North Hayling. Hants —2D 43
North Heath. W Sus —3C 35
North Hinksey Village. Oxon —1A 14
North Holmwood. Surr —1D 35
Northiam. E Sus —3C 39
Northington. Hants —2B 32
North Lancing. W Sus —2D 45
North Lee. Buck —1A 16
North Leigh. Kent —1B 40
North Leigh. Oxon —3A 4
North Marden. W Sus —1A 44
North Marston. Buck —2D 5
Northmoor. Oxon —1A 14
North Moreton. Oxon —3B 14
North Mundham. W Sus —2A 44
North Newington. Oxon —1A 4
Northney. Hants —2D 43
North Oakley. Hants —3B 22
North Ockendon. G Lon —3D 19
Northolt. G Lon —3D 17
North Sheen. G Lon —1D 25
North Shoebury. Essx —3D 21
North Stifford. Thur —3A 20
North Stoke. Medw —1C 29
North Stoke. Oxon —3C 15
North Stoke. W Sus —1C 45
North Street. Hants —2C 33
North Street. Kent —3A 30
North Street. Medw —1C 29
North Street. W Ber —1C 23
North Waltham. Hants —1B 32
North Warnborough. Hants —3D 23
North Weald Bassett. Essx —1D 19
Northwood. G Lon —2C 17
Northwood. IOW —3A 42
Northwood. Kent —2D 31
Norton. Herts —1A 8
Norton. W Sus —2B 44
(Arundel)
Norton. W Sus —3A 44
(Selsey)
Norton Heath. Essx —1A 20
Norton Mandeville. Essx —1D 19
Norwood Hill. Surr —1A 36
Nounsley. Essx —3B 10
Nuffield. Oxon —3C 15
Nuneham Courtenay. Oxon —2B 14
Nursling. Hants —1A 42
Nursted. Hants —3D 33
Nutbourne. W Sus —2D 43
(Chichester)
Nutbourne. W Sus —1C 45
(Pulborough)
Nutfield. Surr —3B 26
Nuthampstead. Herts —1C 9
Nuthurst. W Sus —3D 35
Nutley. E Sus —3C 37
Nyetimber. W Sus —3A 44
Nyewood. W Sus —3A 34
Nyton. W Sus —2B 44

O

Oad Street. Kent —2C 29
Oakhanger. Hants —2D 33
Oakley. Buck —3C 5
Oakley. Hants —3B 22
Oakley Green. Wind —1B 24
Oakshott. Hants —3D 33
Oakwoodhill. Surr —2D 35
Oare. Kent —2A 30
Oare. W Ber —1B 22
Ockham. Surr —3C 25
Ockley. Surr —1D 35
Oddington. Oxon —3B 4
Odiham. Hants —3D 23
Odsey. Cambs —1A 8
Offham. E Sus —1C 47
Offham. Kent —3A 28
Offham. W Sus —2C 45
Offley Hoo. Herts —2D 7
Old Alresford. Hants —2B 32
Old Basing. Hants —3C 23
Old Bexley. G Lon —1C 27
Old Burghclere. Hants —3A 22
Old Coulsdon. G Lon —3B 26
Old Felixstowe. Suff —1D 13
Old Grimsbury. Oxon —1A 4
Old Heathfield. E Sus —3D 37
Old Knebworth. Herts —2A 8
Old Romney. Kent —3A 40
Old Stratford. Nptn —1D 5
Old Town. E Sus —3D 47
Old Warden. Beds —1D 7
Old Windsor. Wind —1B 24
Old Wives Lees. Kent —3A 30
Old Woking. Surr —3C 25
Old Woodstock. Oxon —3A 4
Oliver's Battery. Hants —3A 32
Olmstead Green. Cambs —1A 10
Onslow Green. Essx —3A 10
Onslow Village. Surr —1B 34
Ore. E Sus —1C 49
Oreham Common. W Sus —1A 46
Orlestone. Kent —2D 39
Orpington. G Lon —2C 27
Orsett. Thur —3A 20
Ospringe. Kent —2A 30
Ostend. Essx —2D 21
Osterley. G Lon —1D 25
Otford. Kent —3D 27
Otham. Kent —3B 28
Otterbourne. Hants —3A 32
Otterham Quay. Kent —2C 29
Ottershaw. Surr —2C 25
Otterwood. Hants —2A 42
Ottinge. Kent —1B 40
Outwood. Surr —1B 36
Over Kiddington. Oxon —2A 4
Oversland. Kent —3A 30
Overthorpe. Nptn —1A 4
Overton. Hants —1B 32
Over Worton. Oxon —2A 4
Oving. Buck —2D 5
Oving. W Sus —2B 44
Ovingdean. Brig —2B 46
Ovington. Essx —1B 10
Ovington. Hants —2B 32
Ower. Hants —2A 42
Owlswick. Buck —1D 15
Ownham. W Ber —1A 22
Owslebury. Hants —3B 32
Oxen End. Essx —2A 10
Oxford. Oxon —1B 14
Oxhey. Herts —2D 17
Oxley Green. Essx —3D 11
Oxley's Green. E Sus —3A 38
Oxshott. Surr —2D 25
Oxted. Surr —3B 26

P

Pachesham. Surr —3D 25
Padbury. Buck —1D 5
Paddington. G Lon —3A 18
Paddlesworth. Kent —2B 40
Paddock. Kent —3D 29
Paddock Wood. Kent —1A 38
Padworth. W Ber —2C 23
Pagham. W Sus —3A 44
Paglesham Churchend. Essx —2D 21
Paglesham Eastend. Essx —2D 21
Paine's Corner. E Sus —3A 38
Painter's Forstal. Kent —3D 29
Palehouse Common. E Sus —1C 47
Paley Street. Wind —1A 24
Palmarsh. Kent —2B 40
Pamber End. Hants —3C 23
Pamber Green. Hants —3C 23
Pamber Heath. Hants —2C 23
Panfield. Essx —2B 10
Pangbourne. W Ber —1C 23
Paramour Street. Kent —2C 31
Parbrook. W Sus —3C 35
Pardown. Hants —1B 32
Park Corner. E Sus —2D 37
Park Corner. Oxon —3C 15
Parkeston. Essx —1C 13
Park Gate. Hants —2B 42
Parkgate. Surr —1A 36
Parkhurst. IOW —3A 42
Park Street. Herts —1D 17
Park Street. W Sus —2D 35
Park Town. Oxon —1B 14
Parmoor. Buck —3D 15
Parsonage Green. Essx —3B 10
Partridge Green. W Sus —1D 45
Passenham. Nptn —1D 5
Passfield. Hants —2A 34
Passingford Bridge. Essx —2D 19
Patcham. Brig —2B 46
Patchetts Green. Herts —2D 17
Patching. W Sus —2C 45
Patmore Heath. Herts —2C 9
Patrixbourne. Kent —3B 30
Pattiswick. Essx —2C 11
Peacehaven. E Sus —2C 47
Peasemore. W Ber —1A 22
Pease Pottage. W Sus —2A 36
Peaslake. Surr —1C 35
Peasmarsh. E Sus —3C 39
Peasmarsh. Surr —1B 34
Pebmarsh. Essx —1C 11
Peckham Bush. Kent —3A 28
Pedlinge. Kent —2B 40
Peel Common. Hants —2B 42
Peening Quarter. Kent —3C 39
Pegsdon. Beds —1D 7
Peldon. Essx —3D 11
Pembury. Kent —1A 38
Penge. G Lon —1B 26
Penhurst. E Sus —1A 48
Penn. Buck —2B 16
Penn Street. Buck —2B 16
Penshurst. Kent —1D 37
Peper Harow. Surr —1B 34
Perry Green. Essx —2C 11
Perry Green. Herts —3C 9
Perry Street. Kent —1A 28
Perrywood. Kent —3A 30
Petersfield. Hants —3D 33
Peter's Green. Herts —3D 7
Petham. Kent —3B 30
Pett. E Sus —1C 49
Petteridge. Kent —1A 38
Petts Wood. G Lon —2C 27
Petworth. W Sus —3B 34
Pevensey. E Sus —2A 48
Pevensey Bay. E Sus —2A 48
Pheasant's Hill. Buck —3D 15
Phoenix Green. Hants —3D 23
Piccotts End. Herts —1C 17
Picket Piece. Hants —1A 32
Piddinghoe. E Sus —2C 47
Piddington. Buck —2A 16
Piddington. Oxon —3C 5
Pilgrims Hatch. Essx —2D 19
Piltdown. E Sus —3C 37
Pinkneys Green. Wind —3A 16
Pin Mill. Suff —1C 13
Pinner. G Lon —3D 17
Pirbright. Surr —3B 24
Pirton. Herts —1D 7
Pishill. Oxon —3D 15
Pitchcott. Buck —2D 5
Pitch Green. Buck —1D 15
Pitch Place. Surr —3B 24

Pitsea. *Essx* —3B **20**
Pitstone. *Buck* —3B **6**
Pitstone Green. *Buck* —3B **6**
Pitt. *Hants* —3A **32**
Pittswood. *Kent* —1A **38**
Plaistow. *W Sus* —2C **35**
Plastow Green. *Hants* —2B **22**
Platt. *Kent* —3A **28**
Platt's Heath. *Kent* —3C **29**
Platt, The. *E Sus* —2D **37**
Plaxtol. *Kent* —3A **28**
Playden. *E Sus* —3D **39**
Play Hatch. *Oxon* —1D **23**
Pledgdon Green. *Essx* —2D **9**
Pleshey. *Essx* —3A **10**
Pluckley. *Kent* —1D **39**
Plummers Plain. *W Sus* —3A **36**
Plumpton. *E Sus* —1A **46**
Plumpton Green. *E Sus* —1B **46**
Plumstead. *G Lon* —1C **27**
Poffley End. *Oxon* —3A **4**
Point Clear. *Essx* —3A **12**
Polegate. *E Sus* —2D **47**
Poling. *W Sus* —2C **45**
Poling Corner. *W Sus* —2C **45**
Pollicott. *Buck* —3D **5**
Polstead. *Suff* —1D **11**
Polstead Heath. *Suff* —1D **11**
Ponders End. *G Lon* —2B **18**
Pond Street. *Essx* —1C **9**
Pondtail. *Hants* —3A **24**
Ponts Green. *E Sus* —1A **48**
Pooksgreen. *Hants* —1A **42**
Pool Street. *Essx* —1B **10**
Pootings. *Kent* —1C **37**
Popeswood. *Brac* —2A **24**
Popham. *Hants* —1B **32**
Poplar. *G Lon* —3B **18**
Popley. *Hants* —3C **23**
Porchfield. *IOW* —3A **42**
Portchester. *Hants* —2C **43**
Portsea. *Port* —2C **43**
Portslade-by-Sea. *Brig* —2A **46**
Portsmouth. *Port* —3C **43**
Port Solent. *Hants* —2C **43**
Portswood. *Sotn* —1A **42**
Postcombe. *Oxon* —2D **15**
Postling. *Kent* —2B **40**
Potsgrove. *Beds* —2B **6**
Potten End. *Herts* —1C **17**
Potters Bar. *Herts* —1A **18**
Potters Crouch. *Herts* —1D **17**
Potterspury. *Nptn* —1A **5**
Potter Street. *Essx* —1C **19**
Poundfield. *E Sus* —2D **37**
Poundgate. *E Sus* —3C **37**
Pound Green. *E Sus* —3D **37**
Pound Hill. *W Sus* —3A **36**
Poundon. *Buck* —2C **5**
Pound Street. *Hants* —2A **22**
Pounsley. *E Sus* —3D **37**
Poyle. *Buck* —1C **25**
Poynings. *W Sus* —1A **46**
Pratt's Bottom. *G Lon* —2C **27**
Preston. *Brig* —2B **46**
Preston. *Herts* —2D **7**
Preston. *Kent* —2C **31**
  (Canterbury)
Preston. *Kent* —2A **30**
  (Faversham)
Preston Bissett. *Buck* —2C **5**
Preston Candover. *Hants* —1C **33**
Prestwood. *Buck* —1A **16**
Priestwood. *Brac* —2A **24**
Priestwood. *Kent* —2A **28**
Princes Risborough. *Buck* —1A **16**
Prinsted. *W Sus* —2D **43**
Prittlewell. *S'end* —3C **21**
Privett. *Hants* —3C **33**
Puckeridge. *Herts* —2B **8**
Pulborough. *W Sus* —1C **45**
Pulloxhill. *Beds* —1C **7**
Punnett's Town. *E Sus* —3A **38**
Purbrook. *Hants* —2C **43**
Purfleet. *Thur* —1D **27**
Purleigh. *Essx* —1C **21**
Purley. *G Lon* —2B **26**
Purley on Thames. *W Ber* —1C **23**
Pusey. *Oxon* —2A **14**
Putney. *G Lon* —1A **26**
Puttenham. *Herts* —3A **6**
Puttenham. *Surr* —1B **34**
Puttock End. *Essx* —1C **11**
Puttock's End. *Essx* —3D **9**
Pyecombe. *W Sus* —1A **46**
Pye Corner. *Herts* —3C **9**
Pyrford. *Surr* —3C **25**
Pyrton. *Oxon* —2C **15**

Q

Quainton. *Buck* —2D **5**
Quarrendon. *Buck* —3A **6**
Queenborough. *Kent* —1D **29**
Queen Street. *Kent* —1A **38**
Quendon. *Essx* —1D **9**
Quick's Green. *W Ber* —1B **22**
Quidhampton. *Hants* —3B **22**

R

Rableyheath. *Herts* —3A **8**
Rackham. *W Sus* —1C **45**
Radclive. *Buck* —1C **5**
Radlett. *Herts* —2D **17**
Radley. *Oxon* —2B **14**
Radnage. *Buck* —2D **15**
Radstone. *Nptn* —1B **4**
Radwell. *Herts* —1A **8**
Radwinter. *Essx* —1A **10**
Rainham. *G Lon* —3D **19**
Rainham. *Medw* —2C **29**
Rake. *W Sus* —3A **34**
Ram Lane. *Kent* —1D **39**
Ramsdean. *Hants* —3D **33**
Ramsdell. *Hants* —3B **22**
Ramsden. *Oxon* —3A **4**
Ramsden Bellhouse. *Essx* —2B **20**
Ramsden Heath. *Essx* —2B **20**
Ramsey. *Essx* —1C **13**
Ramsey Island. *Essx* —1D **21**
Ramsgate. *Kent* —2D **31**
Ramsnest Common. *Surr* —2B **34**
Rank's Green. *Essx* —3B **10**
Ranmore Common. *Surr* —3D **25**
Ratton Village. *E Sus* —2D **47**
Rawreth. *Essx* —2B **20**
Raydon. *Suff* —1A **12**
Rayleigh. *Essx* —2C **21**
Rayne. *Essx* —2B **10**
Rayners Lane. *G Lon* —3D **17**
Reading. *Read* —1D **23**
Reading Street. *Kent* —2D **39**
Reculver. *Kent* —2C **31**
Redbourn. *Herts* —3D **7**
Redford. *W Sus* —3A **34**
Redhill. *Herts* —1A **8**
Redhill. *Surr* —3A **26**
Reed. *Herts* —1B **8**
Reed End. *Herts* —1B **8**
Reigate. *Surr* —3A **26**
Remenham. *Wok* —3D **15**
Remenham Hill. *Wok* —3D **15**
Rettendon. *Essx* —2B **20**
Rew Street. *IOW* —3A **42**
Rhodes Minnis. *Kent* —1B **40**
Richborough Port. *Kent* —2D **31**
Richings Park. *Buck* —1C **25**
Richmond. *G Lon* —1D **25**
Rickling. *Essx* —1C **9**
Rickling Green. *Essx* —2D **9**
Rickmansworth. *Herts* —2C **17**
Ridge. *Herts* —1A **18**
Ridgewell. *Essx* —1B **10**
Ridgewood. *E Sus* —3C **37**
Ridgmont. *Beds* —1B **6**
Ridley. *Kent* —2A **28**
Ringlestone. *Kent* —3C **29**
Ringmer. *E Sus* —1C **47**
Ringshall. *Buck* —3B **6**
Ringwould. *Kent* —1D **41**
Ripe. *E Sus* —1D **47**
Ripley. *Surr* —3C **25**
Riplington. *Hants* —3C **33**
Ripple. *Kent* —1D **41**
Riseden. *E Sus* —2A **38**
Riseden. *Kent* —2B **38**
Riseley. *Wok* —2D **23**
Rivenhall. *Essx* —3C **11**
Rivenhall End. *Essx* —3C **11**
River. *Kent* —1C **41**
River. *W Sus* —3B **34**
Riverhead. *Kent* —3D **27**
Robertsbridge. *E Sus* —3B **38**
Robinhood End. *Essx* —1B **10**
Rochester. *Medw* —2B **28**
Rochford. *Essx* —2C **21**
Rock. *W Sus* —1D **45**
Rockwell End. *Buck* —3D **15**
Rodmell. *E Sus* —2C **47**
Rodmersham. *Kent* —2D **29**
Rodmersham Green. *Kent* —2D **29**
Roe Green. *Herts* —1B **8**
Roehampton. *G Lon* —1A **26**
Roffey. *W Sus* —2D **35**
Rogate. *W Sus* —3A **34**
Roke. *Oxon* —2C **15**
Rokemarsh. *Oxon* —2C **15**
Rolvenden. *Kent* —2C **39**
Rolvenden Layne. *Kent* —2C **39**
Romford. *G Lon* —3D **19**
Romsey. *Hants* —3A **32**
Rookwood. *W Sus* —3D **43**
Ropley. *Hants* —2C **33**
Ropley Dean. *Hants* —2C **33**
Rose Green. *Essx* —2C **11**

Rose Hill
Rose Hill. *E Sus* —1C **47**
Roser's Cross. *E Sus* —3D **37**
Rotherfield. *E Sus* —3D **37**
Rotherfield Greys. *Oxon* —3D **15**
Rotherfield Peppard. *Oxon* —3D **15**
Rotherwick. *Hants* —3D **23**
Rotten Row. *W Ber* —1B **22**
Rottingdean. *Brig* —2B **46**
Rough Common. *Kent* —3B **30**
Roundbush Green. *Essx* —3D **9**
Roundhurst Common. *W Sus* —2B **34**
Roundstreet Common. *W Sus* —3C **35**
Rousham. *Oxon* —2A **4**
Rout's Green. *Buck* —2D **15**
Row Ash. *Hants* —1B **42**
Row Green. *Essx* —2B **10**
Row Heath. *Essx* —3B **12**
Rowhedge. *Essx* —2C **11**
Rowhook. *W Sus* —2D **35**
Rowland's Castle. *Hants* —1D **43**
Rowledge. *Surr* —1A **34**
Rowly. *Surr* —1C **35**
Rowner. *Hants* —2B **42**
Rownhams. *Hants* —1A **42**
Rowsham. *Buck* —3A **6**
Rowstock. *Oxon* —3A **14**
Row Town. *Surr* —2C **25**
Roxwell. *Essx* —1A **20**
Royal Tunbridge Wells. *Kent* —2D **37**
Roydon. *Essx* —3C **9**
Roydon Hamlet. *Essx* —1C **19**
Royston. *Herts* —1B **8**
Ruckinge. *Kent* —2A **40**
Rucklers Lane. *Herts* —1C **17**
Rudgwick. *W Sus* —2C **35**
Rudley Green. *Essx* —1C **21**
Ruislip. *G Lon* —3C **17**
Ruislip Common. *G Lon* —3C **17**
Runcton. *W Sus* —2A **44**
Runfold. *Surr* —1A **34**
Runwell. *Essx* —2B **20**
Ruscombe. *Wok* —1D **23**
Rushden. *Herts* —1B **8**
Rushenden. *Kent* —1D **29**
Rush Green. *Herts* —2A **8**
Rushlake Green. *E Sus* —1A **48**
Rushmoor. *Surr* —1A **34**
Rusper. *W Sus* —2A **36**
Russell's Water. *Oxon* —3D **15**
Russ Hill. *Surr* —1A **36**
Rusthall. *Kent* —2D **37**
Rustington. *W Sus* —2C **45**
Ryarsh. *Kent* —3A **28**
Ryde. *IOW* —3B **42**
Rye. *E Sus* —3D **39**
Rye Foreign. *E Sus* —3D **39**
Rye Harbour. *E Sus* —1D **49**

S

Sacombe. *Herts* —3B **8**
Saddlescombe. *W Sus* —1A **46**
Saffron Walden. *Essx* —1D **9**
St Albans. *Herts* —1D **17**
St Cross. *Hants* —3A **32**
St Gile's Hill. *Hants* —3A **32**
St Helens. *E Sus* —1C **49**
St Helens. *IOW* —3C **43**
Saint Hill. *W Sus* —2B **36**
St Ippollitts. *Herts* —2D **7**
St Lawrence. *Essx* —1D **21**
St Leonards. *Buck* —1B **16**
St Leonards. *E Sus* —2B **48**
St Margaret's. *Herts* —3C **7**
  (Hemel Hempstead)
St Margarets. *Herts* —3B **8**
  (Hoddesdon)
St Margaret's at Cliffe. *Kent* —1D **41**
St Mary Bourne. *Hants* —3A **22**
St Mary Cray. *G Lon* —2C **27**
St Mary Hoo. *Medw* —1C **29**
St Mary in the Marsh. *Kent* —3A **40**
St Mary's Bay. *Kent* —3A **40**
St Michaels. *Kent* —2C **39**
St Nicholas at Wade. *Kent* —2C **31**
St Osyth. *Essx* —3B **12**
St Osyth Heath. *Essx* —3B **12**
St Paul's Cray. *G Lon* —2C **27**
St Paul's Walden. *Herts* —2D **7**
St Peter's. *Kent* —2D **31**
Salcott. *Essx* —3D **11**
Salehurst. *E Sus* —3B **38**
Salford. *Beds* —1B **6**
Salfords. *Surr* —1A **36**
Saltdean. *Brig* —2B **46**
Saltwood. *Kent* —2B **40**
Sanderstead. *G Lon* —2B **26**
Sandford-on-Thames. *Oxon* —1B **14**
Sandford St Martin. *Oxon* —2A **4**
Sandgate. *Kent* —2B **40**
Sandhills. *Surr* —2B **34**
Sandhurst. *Brac* —2A **24**
Sandhurst. *Kent* —3B **38**

Sandhurst Cross. *Kent* —3B **38**
Sandling. *Kent* —3B **28**
Sandon. *Essx* —1B **20**
Sandon. *Herts* —1B **8**
Sandridge. *Herts* —3D **7**
Sands, The. *Surr* —1A **34**
Sandway. *Kent* —3C **29**
Sandwich. *Kent* —3D **31**
Sarisbury. *Hants* —1B **42**
Sarratt. *Herts* —2C **17**
Sarre. *Kent* —2C **31**
Satwell. *Oxon* —3D **15**
Saunderton. *Buck* —1D **15**
Saunderton Lee. *Buck* —2A **16**
Sawbridgeworth. *Herts* —3C **9**
Sayers Common. *W Sus* —1A **46**
Scayne's Hill. *W Sus* —3B **36**
School Green. *Essx* —1B **10**
Seabrook. *Kent* —2B **40**
Seaford. *E Sus* —3C **47**
Seal. *Kent* —3D **27**
Seale. *Surr* —1A **34**
Seasalter. *Kent* —2A **30**
Seaview. *IOW* —3C **43**
Seawick. *Essx* —3B **12**
Sedlescombe. *E Sus* —1B **48**
Seer Green. *Buck* —2B **16**
Selborne. *Hants* —2D **33**
Selham. *W Sus* —3B **34**
Sellindge. *Kent* —2A **40**
Selling. *Kent* —3A **30**
Selmeston. *E Sus* —2D **47**
Selsdon. *G Lon* —2B **26**
Selsey. *W Sus* —3A **44**
Selsfield Common. *W Sus* —2B **36**
Selsted. *Kent* —1C **41**
Send. *Surr* —3C **25**
Send Marsh. *Surr* —3C **25**
Sennicotts. *W Sus* —2A **44**
Sevenoaks. *Kent* —3D **27**
Sevenoaks Weald. *Kent* —3D **27**
Sevington. *Kent* —1A **40**
Sewards End. *Essx* —1D **9**
Sewardstone. *Essx* —2B **18**
Sewell. *Beds* —2B **6**
Shabbington. *Buck* —1C **15**
Shackleford. *Surr* —1B **34**
Shadoxhurst. *Kent* —2D **39**
Shalden. *Hants* —1C **33**
Shalfleet. *IOW* —3A **42**
Shalford. *Essx* —2B **10**
Shalford. *Surr* —1C **35**
Shalford Green. *Essx* —2B **10**
Shalmsford Street. *Kent* —3A **30**
Shalstone. *Buck* —1C **5**
Shamley Green. *Surr* —1C **35**
Sharnal Street. *Medw* —1B **28**
Sharpenhoe. *Beds* —1C **7**
Sharpthorne. *W Sus* —2B **36**
Shaw. *W Ber* —2A **22**
Shawford. *Hants* —3A **32**
Shedfield. *Hants* —1B **42**
Sheering. *Essx* —3D **9**
Sheerness. *Kent* —1D **29**
Sheerwater. *Surr* —2C **25**
Sheet. *Hants* —3D **33**
Sheffield Bottom. *W Ber* —2C **23**
Sheffield Green. *E Sus* —3C **37**
Shefford. *Beds* —1D **7**
Shefford Woodlands. *W Ber* —1A **22**
Sheldwich. *Kent* —3A **30**
Sheldwich Lees. *Kent* —3A **30**
Shelley. *Suff* —1A **12**
Shellow Bowells. *Essx* —1A **20**
Shenfield. *Essx* —2A **20**
Shenington. *Oxon* —1A **4**
Shenley. *Herts* —1D **17**
Shenley Brook End. *Mil* —1A **6**
Shenleybury. *Herts* —1D **17**
Shenley Church End. *Mil* —1A **6**
Shephall. *Herts* —2A **8**
Shepherd's Bush. *G Lon* —3A **18**
Shepherd's Green. *Oxon* —3D **15**
Shepherdswell. *Kent* —1C **41**
Shepperton. *Surr* —2C **25**
Shepway. *Kent* —3B **28**
Sherborne St John. *Hants* —3C **23**
Shere. *Surr* —1C **35**
Sherfield on Loddon. *Hants* —3C **23**
Shermanbury. *W Sus* —1A **46**
Shillingford. *Oxon* —2B **14**
Shillington. *Beds* —1D **7**
Shinfield. *Wok* —2D **23**
Shingle Street. *Suff* —1D **13**
Shipbourne. *Kent* —3D **27**
Shiplake. *Oxon* —1D **23**
Shipley. *W Sus* —3D **35**
Shipley Bridge. *Surr* —1B **36**
Shippon. *Oxon* —2D **5**
Shipton. *Buck* —2D **5**
Shipton Green. *W Sus* —3A **44**
Shipton-on-Cherwell. *Oxon* —3A **4**
Shirburn. *Oxon* —2C **15**
Shirkoak. *Kent* —2D **39**

Shirley. Sotn —1A 42
Shirrell Heath. Hants —1B 42
Shoeburyness. S'end —3D 21
Sholden. Kent —3D 31
Sholing. Sotn —1A 42
Shoreditch. G Lon —3B 18
Shoreham. Kent —2D 27
Shoreham-by-Sea. W Sus —2A 46
Shorne. Kent —1A 28
Shorne Ridgeway. Kent —1A 28
Shortbridge. E Sus —3C 37
Shortgate. E Sus —1C 47
Shotgate. Essx —2B 20
Shotley. Suff —1C 13
Shotley Gate. Suff —1C 13
Shottenden. Kent —3A 30
Shottermill. Surr —2A 34
Shreding Green. Buck —3C 17
Shripney. W Sus —2B 44
Shrub End. Essx —2D 11
Shurlock Row. Wind —1A 24
Shutford. Oxon —1A 4
Sibertswold. Kent —1C 41
Sibford Ferris. Oxon —1A 4
Sibford Gower. Oxon —1A 4
Sible Hedingham. Essx —1B 10
Sidcup. G Lon —1C 27
Sidlesham. W Sus —3A 44
Sidley. E Sus —2B 48
Sidlowbridge. Surr —1A 36
Silchester. Hants —2C 23
Silsoe. Beds —1C 7
Silver End. Essx —3C 11
Sindlesham. Wok —2D 23
Singleborough. Buck —1D 5
Singleton. Kent —1D 39
Singleton. W Sus —1A 44
Singlewell. Kent —1A 28
Sinkhurst Green. Kent —1C 39
Sipson. G Lon —1C 25
Sissinghurst. Kent —2B 38
Sittingbourne. Kent —2D 29
Skirmett. Buck —2D 15
Skittle Green. Buck —1D 15
Skye Green. Essx —2C 11
Slade End. Oxon —2B 14
Slade Green. G Lon —1D 27
Slade, The. W Ber —1B 22
Slapton. Buck —2B 6
Slaugham. W Sus —3A 36
Sleaford. Hants —2A 34
Slindon. W Sus —2B 44
Slinfold. W Sus —2D 35
Slip End. Herts —3C 7
Slough. Slo —1B 24
Slough Green. W Sus —3A 36
Small Dole. W Sus —1A 46
Smallfield. Surr —1B 36
Small Hythe. Kent —2C 39
Smannell. Hants —1A 32
Smarden. Kent —1C 39
Smarden Bell. Kent —1C 39
Smart's Hill. Kent —1D 37
Smeeth. Kent —2A 40
Smith's Green. Essx —2D 9
Smyth's Green. Essx —3D 11
Snargate. Kent —3D 39
Snave. Kent —3A 40
Snodland. Kent —2A 28
Soake. Hants —1C 43
Soberton. Hants —1C 43
Soberton Heath. Hants —1C 43
Soldridge. Hants —2C 33
Solent Breezes. Hants —2B 42
Sole Street. Kent —2A 28
(Meopham)
Sole Street. Kent —1A 40
(Waltham)
Somerley. W Sus —3A 44
Somerton. Oxon —2A 4
Sompting. W Sus —2D 45
Sonning. Wok —1D 23
Sonning Common. Oxon —3D 15
Soulbury. Buck —2A 6
Souldern. Oxon —1B 4
Southall. G Lon —1D 25
South Ambersham. W Sus —3B 34
Southampton. Sotn —1A 42
Southampton Airport. Hants —1A 42
South Ascot. Wind —2B 24
South Baddesley. Hants —3A 42
South Benfleet. Essx —3B 20
South Bersted. W Sus —2B 44
Southborough. Kent —1D 37
Southbourne. W Sus —2D 43
Southchurch. S'end —3D 21
South Common. E Sus —1B 46
Southcourt. Buck —3A 6
South Darenth. Kent —2D 27
Southease. E Sus —2C 47
South End. W Ber —1B 22
Southend (London) Airport. Essx —3C 21
Southend-on-Sea. S'end —3C 21
Southernden. Kent —1C 39
Southey Green. Essx —1B 10
South Fambridge. Essx —2C 21
South Fawley. W Ber —3A 14
Southfleet. Kent —1A 28
Southgate. G Lon —2B 18
South Godstone. Surr —1B 36
South Green. Essx —2A 20
(Billericay)
South Green. Essx —3A 12
(Colchester)
South Green. Kent —2C 29
South Hanningfield. Essx —2B 20
South Harting. W Sus —1D 43
South Hayling. Hants —3D 43
South Heath. Buck —1B 16
South Heath. Essx —3B 12
South Heighton. E Sus —2C 47
South Hinksey. Oxon —1B 14
South Holmwood. Surr —1D 35
South Hornchurch. G Lon —3D 19
Southill. Beds —1D 7
Southington. Hants —1B 32
South Lancing. W Sus —2D 45
South Leigh. Oxon —1A 14
South Malling. E Sus —1C 47
South Mimms. Herts —1A 18
Southminster. Essx —2D 21
Southmoor. Oxon —2A 14
South Moreton. Oxon —3B 14
South Mundham. W Sus —2A 44
South Newington. Oxon —1A 4
South Norwood. G Lon —2B 26
South Nutfield. Surr —1B 36
South Ockendon. Thur —3D 19
South Oxhey. Herts —2D 17
Southrope. Hants —1C 33
Southsea. Port —3C 43
South Stifford. Thur —1D 27
South Stoke. Oxon —3B 14
South Stoke. W Sus —1C 45
South Street. E Sus —1B 46
South Street. Kent —3A 30
(Faversham)
South Street. Kent —2B 30
(Whitstable)
South Town. Hants —2C 33
South Warnborough. Hants —1D 33
Southwater. W Sus —3D 35
Southwater Street. W Sus —3D 35
South Weald. Essx —2D 19
South Weston. Oxon —2D 15
Southwick. Hants —2C 43
Southwick. W Sus —2A 46
South Wonston. Hants —2A 32
South Woodham Ferrers. Essx —2C 21
Sparrow's Green. E Sus —2A 38
Sparsholt. Hants —2A 32
Sparsholt. Oxon —3A 14
Spear Hill. W Sus —1D 45
Speen. Buck —2A 16
Speen. W Ber —2A 22
Speldhurst. Kent —1D 37
Spellbrook. Herts —3C 9
Spencers Wood. Wok —2D 23
Spithurst. E Sus —1C 47
Spreakley. Surr —1A 34
Spring Vale. IOW —3C 43
Stadhampton. Oxon —2C 15
Stagden Cross. Essx —3A 10
Staines. Surr —1C 25
Stakes. Hants —2C 43
Stalisfield Green. Kent —3D 29
Stambourne. Essx —1B 10
Stanborough. Herts —3A 8
Stanbridge. Beds —2B 6
Standen. Kent —1C 39
Standen Street. Kent —2C 39
Standford. Hants —2A 34
Standlake. Oxon —1A 14
Standon. Hants —3A 32
Standon. Herts —2B 8
Standon Green End. Herts —3B 8
Stanford. Beds —1D 7
Stanford. Kent —2B 40
Stanford Dingley. W Ber —1B 22
Stanford in the Vale. Oxon —2A 14
Stanford-le-Hope. Thur —3A 20
Stanford Rivers. Essx —1D 19
Stanmer. Brig —2B 46
Stanmore. G Lon —2D 17
Stanmore. Hants —3A 32
Stanmore. W Ber —1A 22
Stanstead Abbotts. Herts —3B 8
Stansted. Kent —2A 28
Stansted (London) Airport. Essx —2D 9
Stansted Mountfitchet. Essx —2D 9
Stanton Harcourt. Oxon —1A 14
Stanton St John. Oxon —1B 14
Stanway. Essx —2D 11
Stanwell. Surr —1C 25
Stanwell Moor. Surr —1C 25
Staple. Kent —3C 31
Staplecross. E Sus —3B 38
Staplefield. W Sus —3A 36
Stapleford. Herts —3B 8
Stapleford Abbotts. Essx —2D 19
Stapleford Tawney. Essx —2D 19
Staplehurst. Kent —1B 38
Staplers. IOW —3B 42
Starling's Green. Essx —1C 9
Start Hill. Essx —2D 9
Stebbing. Essx —2A 10
Stebbing Green. Essx —2A 10
Stedham. W Sus —3A 34
Steel Cross. E Sus —2D 37
Steep. Hants —3D 33
Steeple. Essx —1D 21
Steeple Aston. Oxon —2A 4
Steeple Barton. Oxon —2A 4
Steeple Bumpstead. Essx —1A 10
Steeple Claydon. Buck —2C 5
Steeple Morden. Cambs —1A 8
Stelling Minnis. Kent —1B 40
Stepney. G Lon —3B 18
Steppingley. Beds —1C 7
Stevenage. Herts —2A 8
Steventon. Hants —1B 32
Steventon. Oxon —2A 14
Stevington End. Cambs —1D 9
Stewartby. Beds —1C 7
Stewkley. Buck —2A 6
Stewkley Dean. Buck —2A 6
Steyning. W Sus —1D 45
Stickling Green. Essx —1C 9
Stisted. Essx —2B 10
Stock. Essx —2A 20
Stockbridge. Hants —2A 32
Stockbury. Kent —2C 29
Stockcross. W Ber —2A 22
Stocker's Head. Kent —3D 29
Stocking Green. Essx —1D 9
Stocking Pelham. Herts —2C 9
Stocks, The. Kent —3D 39
Stockstreet. Essx —2C 11
Stodmarsh. Kent —2C 31
Stoke. Hants —3A 22
(Andover)
Stoke. Hants —2D 43
(South Hayling)
Stoke. Medw —1C 29
Stoke-by-Nayland. Suff —1D 11
Stoke Charity. Hants —2A 32
Stoke D'Abernon. Surr —3D 25
Stoke Hammond. Buck —2A 6
Stoke Lyne. Oxon —2B 4
Stoke Mandeville. Buck —3A 6
Stokenchurch. Buck —2D 15
Stoke Newington. G Lon —3B 18
Stoke Poges. Buck —3B 16
Stoke Row. Oxon —3C 15
Stoke Talmage. Oxon —2C 15
Stondon Massey. Essx —1D 19
Stone. Buck —3D 5
Stone. Kent —1D 27
Stonebridge. Surr —1D 35
Stone Cross. E Sus —2A 48
Stone Cross. Kent —2D 37
Stonegate. E Sus —3A 38
Stone Hill. Kent —2A 40
Stone in Oxney. Kent —3D 39
Stoner Hill. Hants —3D 33
Stonesfield. Oxon —3A 4
Stones Green. Essx —2B 12
Stone Street. Kent —3D 27
Stone Street. Suff —1D 11
Stoneyhills. Essx —2D 21
Stonor. Oxon —3D 15
Stony Stratford. Mil —1D 5
Stopham. W Sus —1C 45
Stopsley. Lutn —2D 7
Storrington. W Sus —1C 45
Stotfold. Beds —1A 8
Stoughton. Surr —3B 24
Stoughton. W Sus —1A 44
Stow Maries. Essx —2C 21
Stowting. Kent —1B 40
Stratfield Mortimer. W Ber —2C 23
Stratfield Saye. Hants —2C 23
Stratfield Turgis. Hants —3C 23
Stratford. G Lon —3B 18
Stratford St Mary. Suff —1A 12
Stratton Audley. Oxon —2C 5
Streat. E Sus —1B 46
Streatham. G Lon —1A 26
Streatley. Beds —2C 7
Streatley. W Ber —3B 14
Street End. W Sus —3A 44
Strethall. Essx —1C 9
Strood. Kent —2C 39
Strood. Medw —2B 28
Strood Green. Surr —1A 36
Strood Green. W Sus —3C 35
(Billingshurst)
Strood Green. W Sus —2D 35
(Horsham)
Stroud. Hants —3D 33
Stroud Green. Essx —2C 21
Stubbington. Hants —2B 42
Stubb's Cross. Kent —2D 39
Studham. Beds —3C 7
Stunts Green. E Sus —1A 48
Sturmer. Essx —1A 10
Sturry. Kent —2B 30
Stutton. Suff —1B 12
Sudbury. Suff —1C 11
Sulham. W Ber —1C 23
Sulhamstead. W Ber —2C 23
Sullington. W Sus —1C 45
Summersdale. W Sus —2A 44
Sunbury. Surr —2D 25
Sundon Park. Lutn —2C 7
Sundridge. Kent —3C 27
Sunningdale. Wind —2B 24
Sunninghill. Wind —2B 24
Sunningwell. Oxon —1A 14
Sunnymead. Oxon —1B 14
Sunnyside. W Sus —2B 36
Surbiton. G Lon —2D 25
Surrex. Essx —2C 11
Sutton. Buck —1C 25
Sutton. E Sus —3C 47
Sutton. G Lon —2A 26
Sutton. Kent —1D 41
Sutton. Oxon —1A 14
Sutton. W Sus —1B 44
Sutton Abinger. Surr —1D 35
Sutton at Hone. Kent —2D 27
Sutton Courtenay. Oxon —2B 14
Sutton Green. Surr —3C 25
Sutton Scotney. Hants —2A 32
Sutton Valence. Kent —1C 39
Swalcliffe. Oxon —1A 4
Swalecliffe. Kent —2B 30
Swallowfield. Wok —2D 23
Swampton. Hants —3A 22
Swanbourne. Buck —2A 6
Swanley. Kent —2D 27
Swanmore. Hants —1B 42
Swanscombe. Kent —1D 27
Swan Street. Essx —2C 11
Swanton Street. Kent —3C 29
Swanwick. Hants —2B 42
Swarraton. Hants —2B 32
Swaythling. Sotn —1A 42
Swerford. Oxon —1A 4
Swiftsden. E Sus —3B 38
Swinford. Oxon —1B 14
Swingfield Minnis. Kent —1C 41
Swingfield Street. Kent —1C 41
Sydenham. G Lon —1B 26
Sydenham. Oxon —1D 15
Sydmonton. Hants —3A 22
Syresham. Nptn —1C 5

T

Tackley. Oxon —2A 4
Tadley. Hants —2C 23
Tadmarton. Oxon —1A 4
Tadworth. Surr —3A 26
Takeley. Essx —2D 9
Takeley Street. Essx —2D 9
Tandridge. Surr —3B 26
Tangmere. W Sus —2B 44
Tankerton. Kent —2B 30
Taplow. Buck —3B 16
Tarpots. Essx —3B 20
Tarring Neville. E Sus —2C 47
Taston. Oxon —2A 4
Tatling End. Buck —3C 17
Tatsfield. Surr —3C 27
Tattingstone. Suff —1B 12
Tattingstone White Horse. Suff —1B 12
Taverners Green. Essx —3D 9
Tebworth. Beds —2B 6
Teddington. G Lon —1D 25
Telham. E Sus —1B 48
Telscombe. E Sus —2C 47
Telscombe Cliffs. E Sus —2B 46
Temple Ewell. Kent —1C 41
Templeton. W Ber —2A 22
Tendring. Essx —2B 12
Tendring Green. Essx —2B 12
Tenterden. Kent —2C 39
Terling. Essx —3B 10
Terrick. Buck —1A 16
Teston. Kent —3B 28
Testwood. Hants —1A 42
Tetsworth. Oxon —1C 15
Tewin. Herts —3A 8
Teynham. Kent —2D 29
Teynham Street. Kent —2D 29
Thakeham. W Sus —1D 45
Thame. Oxon —1D 15
Thames Ditton. Surr —2D 25
Thames Haven. Thur —3B 20
Thamesmead. G Lon —1C 27
Thamesport. Medw —1C 29
Thanington Without. Kent —3B 30
Thatcham. W Ber —2B 22
Thaxted. Essx —1A 10

Theale. *W Ber* —1C **23**
Thenford. *Nptn* —1B **4**
Therfield. *Herts* —1B **8**
Theydon Bois. *Essx* —2C **19**
Thong. *Kent* —1A **28**
Thorington Street. *Suff* —1A **12**
Thorley. *Herts* —3C **9**
Thorley Street. *Herts* —3C **9**
Thorley Street. *IOW* —3A **42**
Thornborough. *Buck* —1D **5**
Thorncombe Street. *Surr* —1B **34**
Thornhill. *Sotn* —1A **42**
Thornton. *Buck* —1D **5**
Thornton Heath. *G Lon* —2B **26**
Thornwood Common. *Essx* —1C **19**
Thorpe. *Surr* —2C **25**
Thorpe Bay. *S'end* —3D **21**
Thorpe Common. *Suff* —1C **13**
Thorpe Green. *Essx* —2B **12**
Thorpe-le-Soken. *Essx* —2B **12**
Thorrington. *Essx* —2A **12**
Three Bridges. *W Sus* —2A **36**
Three Chimneys. *Kent* —2C **39**
Three Cups Corner. *E Sus* —3A **38**
Three Leg Cross. *E Sus* —2A **38**
Three Mile Cross. *Wok* —2D **23**
Three Oaks. *E Sus* —1C **49**
Throcking. *Herts* —1B **8**
Throwley. *Kent* —3D **29**
Throwley Forstal. *Kent* —3D **29**
Thrupp. *Oxon* —3A **4**
Thundersley. *Essx* —3B **20**
Thurnham. *Kent* —3C **29**
Thursley. *Surr* —2A **34**
Ticehurst. *E Sus* —2A **38**
Tichborne. *Hants* —2B **32**
Tiddington. *Oxon* —1C **15**
Tidebrook. *E Sus* —3A **38**
Tidmarsh. *W Ber* —1A **28**
Tilbury. *Thur* —1A **28**
Tilbury Green. *Essx* —1B **10**
Tilbury Juxta Clare. *Essx* —1B **10**
Tilehurst. *Read* —1C **23**
Tilford. *Surr* —1A **34**
Tilgate Forest Row. *W Sus* —3A **36**
Tillingham. *Essx* —1D **21**
Tillington. *W Sus* —3B **34**
Tilmanstone. *Kent* —3D **31**
Tilsworth. *Beds* —2B **6**
Timsbury. *Hants* —3A **32**
Tingewick. *Buck* —1C **5**
Tingrith. *Beds* —1C **7**
Tinsley Green. *W Sus* —2A **36**
Tiptree. *Essx* —3C **11**
Tiptree Heath. *Essx* —3C **11**
Tisman's Common. *W Sus* —2C **35**
Titchfield. *Hants* —2B **42**
Titsey. *Surr* —3C **27**
Toddington. *Beds* —2C **7**
Tokers Green. *Oxon* —1D **23**
Tollesbury. *Essx* —3D **11**
Tolleshunt D'Arcy. *Essx* —3D **11**
Tolleshunt Knights. *Essx* —3D **11**
Tolleshunt Major. *Essx* —3D **11**
Tolworth. *G Lon* —2D **25**
Tonbridge. *Kent* —1D **37**
Tongham. *Surr* —1A **34**
Tonwell. *Herts* —3B **8**
Toot Baldon. *Oxon* —1B **14**
Toot Hill. *Essx* —1D **19**
Toot Hill. *Hants* —1A **42**
Toppesfield. *Essx* —1B **10**
Tortington. *W Sus* —2C **45**
Tottenham. *G Lon* —2B **18**
Totteridge. *G Lon* —2A **18**
Totternhoe. *Beds* —2B **6**
Totton. *Hants* —1A **42**
Touchenend. *Wind* —1A **24**
Tower Hill. *W Sus* —3D **35**
Towersey. *Oxon* —1D **15**
Town Littleworth. *E Sus* —1C **47**
Town Row. *E Sus* —2D **37**
Towns End. *Hants* —3B **22**
Townsend. *Herts* —1D **17**
Toy's Hill. *Kent* —3C **27**
Trash Green. *W Ber* —2C **23**
Treyford. *W Sus* —1A **44**
Trimley Lower Street. *Suff* —1C **13**
Trimley St Martin. *Suff* —1C **13**
Trimley St Mary. *Suff* —1C **13**
Tring. *Herts* —3B **6**
Trottiscliffe. *Kent* —2A **28**
Trotton. *W Sus* —3A **34**
Trowley Bottom. *Herts* —3C **7**
Trumps Green. *Surr* —2B **24**
Tubney. *Oxon* —2A **14**
Tudeley. *Kent* —1A **38**
Tuesley. *Surr* —1B **34**
Tufton. *Hants* —1A **32**
Tumbler's Green. *Essx* —2C **11**
Tunbridge Wells, Royal. *Kent* —2D **37**
Tunstall. *Kent* —2C **29**
Tunworth. *Hants* —1C **33**
Turgis Green. *Hants* —3C **23**

Turkey Island. *Hants* —1B **42**
Turners Hill. *W Sus* —2B **36**
Turnford. *Herts* —1B **18**
Turville. *Buck* —2D **15**
Turville Heath. *Buck* —2D **15**
Turweston. *Buck* —1C **5**
Tutts Clump. *W Ber* —1B **22**
Twickenham. *G Lon* —1D **25**
Twineham. *W Sus* —3A **36**
Twinstead. *Essx* —1C **11**
Twinstead Green. *Essx* —1C **11**
Twyford. *Buck* —2C **5**
Twyford. *Hants* —3A **32**
Twyford. *Wok* —1D **23**
Tye. *Hants* —2D **43**
Tye Green. *Essx* —2D **9**
(Bishop's Stortford)
Tye Green. *Essx* —2B **10**
(Braintree)
Tye Green. *Essx* —1D **9**
(Saffron Walden)
Tyler Hill. *Kent* —2B **31**
Tylers Green. *Buck* —2A **16**
Tyler's Green. *Essx* —1D **19**

U

Uckfield. *E Sus* —3C **37**
Udimore. *E Sus* —1C **49**
Ufton Nervet. *W Ber* —2C **23**
Ugley. *Essx* —2D **9**
Ugley Green. *Essx* —2D **9**
Ulcombe. *Kent* —1C **39**
Ulting. *Essx* —1C **21**
Underriver. *Kent* —3D **27**
Union Street. *E Sus* —2B **38**
Upchurch. *Kent* —2C **29**
Upham. *Hants* —3B **32**
Uplees. *Kent* —2D **29**
Up Marden. *W Sus* —1D **43**
Upminster. *G Lon* —3D **19**
Up Nately. *Hants* —3C **23**
Upper Arncott. *Oxon* —3C **5**
Upper Astrop. *Nptn* —1B **4**
Upper Basildon. *W Ber* —1B **22**
Upper Beeding. *W Sus* —1D **45**
Upper Bucklebury. *W Ber* —2B **22**
Upper Bullington. *Hants* —1A **32**
Upper Clatford. *Hants* —1A **32**
Upper Cokeham. *W Sus* —2D **45**
Upper Common. *Hants* —1C **33**
Upper Dicker. *E Sus* —2D **47**
Upper Dovercourt. *Essx* —1C **13**
Upper Dunsley. *Herts* —3B **6**
Upper Enham. *Hants* —1A **32**
Upper Farringdon. *Hants* —2D **33**
Upper Froyle. *Hants* —1D **33**
Upper Gravenhurst. *Beds* —1D **7**
Upper Green. *Essx* —1C **9**
Upper Green. *W Ber* —2A **22**
Upper Hale. *Surr* —1A **34**
Upper Halliford. *Surr* —2C **25**
Upper Halling. *Medw* —2A **28**
Upper Hartfield. *E Sus* —2C **37**
Upper Heyford. *Oxon* —2A **4**
Upper Horsebridge. *E Sus* —1C **49**
Upper Layham. *Suff* —1A **12**
Upper North Dean. *Buck* —2A **16**
Upper Norwood. *W Sus* —1B **44**
Upper Stondon. *Beds* —1D **7**
Upper Street. *Suff* —1B **12**
Upper Sundon. *Beds* —2C **7**
Upperton. *W Sus* —3B **34**
Upper Tooting. *G Lon* —1A **26**
Upper Upnor. *Medw* —1B **28**
Upper Weald. *Mil* —1D **5**
Upper Wellingham. *E Sus* —1C **47**
Upper Wield. *Hants* —2C **33**
Upper Winchendon. *Buck* —3D **5**
Upper Wootton. *Hants* —3B **22**
Upshire. *Essx* —1C **19**
Up Somborne. *Hants* —2A **32**
Upstreet. *Kent* —2C **31**
Upton. *Buck* —3D **5**
Upton. *Hants* —3A **22**
.(Andover)
Upton. *Hants* —1A **42**
(Southampton)
Upton. *IOW* —3B **42**
Upton. *Oxon* —3B **14**
Upton. *Slo* —1B **24**
Upton End. *Beds* —1D **7**
Upton Grey. *Hants* —1C **33**
Upwaltham. *W Sus* —1B **44**
Upwick Green. *Herts* —2C **9**
Uxbridge. *G Lon* —3C **17**

V

Valley End. *Surr* —2B **24**
Vange. *Essx* —3B **20**
Vernham Dean. *Hants* —3A **22**

Vernham Street. *Hants* —3A **22**
Vigo Village. *Kent* —2A **28**
Vinehall Street. *E Sus* —3B **38**
Vine's Cross. *E Sus* —1D **47**
Virginia Water. *Surr* —2B **24**

W

Waddesdon. *Buck* —3D **5**
Wadesmill. *Herts* —3B **8**
Wadhurst. *E Sus* —2A **38**
Wadwick. *Hants* —3A **22**
Wainscott. *Medw* —1B **28**
Wakes Colne. *Essx* —2C **11**
Walberton. *W Sus* —2B **44**
Waldersdale. *Medw* —2B **28**
Walderton. *W Sus* —1D **43**
Waldron. *E Sus* —1D **47**
Walkern. *Herts* —2A **8**
Wallands Park. *E Sus* —1C **47**
Wallcrouch. *E Sus* —2A **38**
Wallend. *Medw* —1C **29**
Wallingford. *Oxon* —3C **15**
Wallington. *G Lon* —2A **26**
Wallington. *Hants* —2B **42**
Wallington. *Herts* —1A **8**
Walliswood. *Surr* —2D **35**
Walmer. *Kent* —3D **31**
Walsworth. *Herts* —1D **7**
Waltham. *Kent* —1B **40**
Waltham Abbey. *Essx* —1B **18**
Waltham Chase. *Hants* —1B **42**
Waltham Cross. *Herts* —1B **18**
Waltham's Cross. *Essx* —1A **10**
Waltham St Lawrence. *Wind* —1A **24**
Walthamstow. *G Lon* —3B **18**
Walton. *Mil* —1A **6**
Walton. *Suff* —1C **13**
Walton-on-Thames. *Surr* —2D **25**
Walton on the Hill. *Surr* —3A **26**
Walton-on-the-Naze. *Essx* —2C **13**
Wanborough. *Surr* —1B **34**
Wandsworth. *G Lon* —1A **26**
Wannock. *E Sus* —2D **47**
Wanshurst Green. *Kent* —1B **38**
Wanstead. *G Lon* —3C **19**
Wantage. *Oxon* —3A **14**
Warbleton. *E Sus* —1A **48**
Warblington. *Hants* —2D **43**
Warborough. *Oxon* —2B **14**
Warden. *Kent* —1A **30**
Wardhedges. *Beds* —1C **7**
Wardley. *W Sus* —3A **34**
Ware. *Herts* —3B **8**
Ware. *Kent* —2C **31**
Warehorne. *Kent* —2D **39**
Wareside. *Herts* —3B **8**
Warfield. *Brac* —1A **24**
Wargrave. *Wok* —1D **23**
Warkworth. *Nptn* —1A **4**
Warlingham. *Surr* —3B **26**
Warminghurst. *W Sus* —1D **45**
Warners End. *Herts* —1C **17**
Warnford. *Hants* —3C **33**
Warnham. *W Sus* —2D **35**
Warningcamp. *W Sus* —2C **45**
Warninglid. *W Sus* —3A **36**
Warren Corner. *Hants* —1A **34**
(Aldershot)
Warren Corner. *Hants* —3D **33**
(Petersfield)
Warren Row. *Wind* —3A **16**
Warren Street. *Kent* —3D **29**
Warsash. *Hants* —2A **42**
Wartling. *E Sus* —2A **48**
Warwick Wold. *Surr* —3B **26**
Washbrook. *Suff* —1B **12**
Wash Common. *W Ber* —2A **22**
Washington. *W Sus* —1D **45**
Wasp Green. *Surr* —1B **36**
Waterbeach. *W Sus* —2A **44**
Water End. *Beds* —1C **7**
Water End. *Herts* —1A **18**
(Hatfield)
Water End. *Herts* —3C **7**
(Hemel Hempstead)
Waterford. *Herts* —3B **8**
Wateringbury. *Kent* —3A **28**
Waterlooville. *Hants* —2C **43**
Waterperry. *Oxon* —1C **15**
Watersfield. *W Sus* —1C **45**
Waterside. *Buck* —1B **16**
Waterstock. *Oxon* —1C **15**
Water Stratford. *Buck* —1C **5**
Watford. *Herts* —2C **17**
Watlington. *Oxon* —2D **15**
Watton at Stone. *Herts* —3A **8**
Wavendon. *Mil* —1B **6**
Waverley. *Surr* —1A **34**
Wealdstone. *G Lon* —2D **17**
Weedon. *Buck* —3A **6**
Weeke. *Hants* —2A **32**
Weeley. *Essx* —2B **12**

Weeley Heath. *Essx* —2B **12**
Welford. *W Ber* —1A **22**
Welham Green. *Herts* —1A **18**
Well. *Hants* —1D **33**
Well Hill. *Kent* —2C **27**
Wellhouse. *W Ber* —1B **22**
Welling. *G Lon* —1C **27**
Wellow. *IOW* —3A **42**
Wellpond Green. *Herts* —2C **9**
Welwyn. *Herts* —3A **8**
Welwyn Garden City. *Herts* —3A **8**
Wembley. *G Lon* —3D **17**
Wendens Ambo. *Essx* —1D **9**
Wendlebury. *Oxon* —3B **4**
Wendover. *Buck* —1A **16**
Wennington. *G Lon* —3D **19**
Wepham. *W Sus* —2C **45**
West Ashling. *W Sus* —2A **44**
Westbere. *Kent* —2B **30**
West Bergholt. *Essx* —2D **11**
West Blatchington. *Brig* —2A **46**
Westbourne. *W Sus* —2D **43**
West Brabourne. *Kent* —1A **40**
Westbrook. *Kent* —1D **31**
West Burton. *W Sus* —1B **44**
Westbury. *Buck* —1C **5**
West Byfleet. *Surr* —2C **25**
West Challow. *Oxon* —3A **14**
West Chiltington. *W Sus* —1C **45**
West Chiltington Common. *W Sus* —1C **45**
West Clandon. *Surr* —3C **25**
West Cliffe. *Kent* —1D **41**
Westcliffe-on-Sea. *S'end* —3C **21**
Westcot. *Oxon* —3A **14**
Westcott. *Buck* —3D **5**
Westcott. *Surr* —1D **35**
Westcott Barton. *Oxon* —2A **4**
Westdean. *E Sus* —3D **47**
West Dean. *W Sus* —1A **44**
West Drayton. *G Lon* —1C **25**
West End. *G Lon* —3A **18**
West End. *Hants* —1A **42**
West End. *Herts* —1A **18**
West End. *Kent* —2B **30**
West End. *Surr* —2B **24**
West End. *Wind* —1A **24**
West End Green. *Hants* —2C **23**
Westenhanger. *Kent* —2B **40**
Westergate. *W Sus* —2B **44**
Westerham. *Kent* —3C **27**
Westerton. *W Sus* —2A **44**
West Farleigh. *Kent* —3B **28**
Westfield. *E Sus* —1C **49**
West Firle. *E Sus* —2C **47**
Westgate on Sea. *Kent* —1D **31**
West Ginge. *Oxon* —3A **14**
West Green. *Hants* —2D **33**
West Grinstead. *W Sus* —3D **35**
West Hagbourne. *Oxon* —3B **14**
Westham. *E Sus* —2A **48**
West Ham. *G Lon* —3B **18**
Westhampnett. *W Sus* —2A **44**
West Hanney. *Oxon* —2A **14**
West Hanningfield. *Essx* —2B **20**
West Harting. *W Sus* —3D **33**
West Heath. *Hants* —3B **22**
(Basingstoke)
West Heath. *Hants* —3A **24**
(Farnborough)
West Hendred. *Oxon* —3A **14**
West Hill. *W Sus* —2B **36**
West Hoathly. *W Sus* —2B **36**
West Horndon. *Essx* —3A **20**
West Horsley. *Surr* —3C **25**
West Hougham. *Kent* —1C **41**
Westhumble. *Surr* —3D **25**
West Hyde. *Herts* —2C **17**
West Hythe. *Kent* —2B **40**
West Ilsley. *W Ber* —3A **14**
West Itchenor. *W Sus* —2D **43**
West Kingsdown. *Kent* —2D **27**
West Langdon. *Kent* —1D **41**
West Lavington. *W Sus* —3A **34**
West Leith. *Herts* —3B **6**
Westlington. *Buck* —3D **5**
West Malling. *Kent* —3A **28**
West Marden. *W Sus* —1D **43**
Westmarsh. *Kent* —2C **31**
West Meon. *Hants* —3C **33**
West Mersea. *Essx* —3A **12**
Westmeston. *E Sus* —1B **46**
Westmill. *Herts* —2B **8**
(Buntingford)
Westmill. *Herts* —1D **7**
(Hitchin)
Westminster. *G Lon* —1A **26**
West Molesey. *Surr* —2D **25**
West Norwood. *G Lon* —1B **26**
Weston. *Hants* —3D **33**
Weston. *Herts* —1A **8**
Weston. *W Ber* —1A **22**
Westoning. *Beds* —1C **7**
Weston-on-the-Green. *Oxon* —3B **4**
Weston Patrick. *Hants* —1C **33**

Weston Turville. *Buck* —3A **6**
West Peckham. *Kent* —3A **28**
West Stoke. *W Sus* —2A **44**
West Stourmouth. *Kent* —2C **31**
West Stratton. *Hants* —1B **32**
West Street. *Kent* —3D **29**
West Thorney. *W Sus* —2D **43**
West Thurrock. *Thur* —1D **27**
West Tilbury. *Thur* —1A **28**
West Tisted. *Hants* —3C **33**
West Town. *Hants* —3D **43**
Westwell. *Kent* —1D **39**
Westwell Leacon. *Kent* —1D **39**
West Wickham. *G Lon* —2B **26**
West Wittering. *W Sus* —3D **43**
Westwood. *Kent* —2D **31**
West Woodhay. *W Ber* —2A **22**
West Worldham. *Hants* —2D **33**
West Worthing. *W Sus* —2D **45**
West Wycombe. *Buck* —2A **16**
Wethersfield. *Essx* —1B **10**
Wexham Street. *Buck* —3B **16**
Weybourne. *Surr* —1A **34**
Weybridge. *Surr* —2C **25**
Whaddon. *Buck* —1A **6**
Wharley End. *Beds* —1B **6**
Whatlington. *E Sus* —1B **48**
Wheathampstead. *Herts* —3D **7**
Wheatley. *Hants* —1D **33**
Wheatley. *Oxon* —1B **14**
Wheelerstreet. *Surr* —1B **34**
Whelpley Hill. *Buck* —1B **16**
Wherstead. *Suff* —1B **12**
Wherwell. *Hants* —1A **32**
Whetsted. *Kent* —1A **38**
Whetstone. *G Lon* —2A **18**
Whippingham. *IOW* —3B **42**
Whipsnade. *Beds* —3C **7**
Whistley Green. *Wok* —1D **23**
Whitchurch. *Buck* —2A **6**
Whitchurch. *Hants* —1A **32**
Whitchurch Hill. *Oxon* —1C **23**
Whitchurch-on-Thames. *Oxon* —1C **23**
Whiteash Green. *Essx* —1B **10**
White Colne. *Essx* —2C **11**
Whitehall. *Hants* —3D **23**
Whitehall. *W Sus* —3D **35**
Whitehill. *Hants* —2D **33**
Whiteley. *Hants* —2B **42**
Whiteley Village. *Surr* —2C **25**
Whitemans Green. *W Sus* —3B **36**
Whitenap. *Hants* —3A **32**
White Notley. *Essx* —3B **10**
White Roding. *Essx* —3D **9**
Whitesmith. *E Sus* —1D **47**
Whitestreet Green. *Suff* —1D **11**
White Waltham. *Wind* —1A **24**
Whitfield. *Kent* —1D **41**
Whitfield. *Nptn* —1C **5**
Whitstable. *Kent* —2B **30**
Whitway. *Hants* —3A **22**
Whitwell. *Herts* —2D **7**
Whyteleafe. *Surr* —3B **26**
Wick. *W Sus* —2C **45**
Wichling. *Kent* —3D **29**
Wicken. *Nptn* —1D **5**
Wicken Bonhunt. *Essx* —1C **9**

Wicker Street Green. *Suff* —1D **11**
Wickford. *Essx* —2B **20**
Wickham. *Hants* —1B **42**
Wickham. *W Ber* —1A **22**
Wickham Bishops. *Essx* —3C **11**
Wickhambreaux. *Kent* —3C **31**
Wickham Heath. *W Ber* —2A **22**
Wickham St Paul. *Essx* —1C **11**
Wick Hill. *Wok* —2D **23**
Widdington. *Essx* —1D **9**
Widford. *Essx* —1A **20**
Widford. *Herts* —3C **9**
Widmer End. *Buck* —2A **16**
Wiggens Green. *Essx* —1A **10**
Wigginton. *Herts* —3B **6**
Wigginton. *Oxon* —1A **4**
Wiggonholt. *W Sus* —1C **45**
Wigmore. *Medw* —2C **29**
Wildern. *Hants* —1A **42**
Wildhern. *Hants* —3A **22**
Willen. *Mil* —1A **6**
Willesborough. *Kent* —1A **40**
Willesborough Lees. *Kent* —1A **40**
Willesden. *G Lon* —3A **18**
Willey Green. *Surr* —3B **24**
Willian. *Herts* —1A **8**
Willingale. *Essx* —1D **19**
Willingdon. *E Sus* —2D **47**
Willows Green. *Essx* —3B **10**
Wilmington. *E Sus* —2D **47**
Wilmington. *Kent* —1D **27**
Wilsley Green. *Kent* —2B **38**
Wilstead. *Beds* —1C **7**
Wilstone. *Herts* —3B **6**
Wimbish. *Essx* —1D **9**
Wimbish Green. *Essx* —1A **10**
Wimbledon. *G Lon* —1A **26**
Winchelsea. *E Sus* —1D **49**
Winchelsea Beach. *E Sus* —1D **49**
Winchester. *Hants* —3A **32**
Winchet Hill. *Kent* —1B **38**
Winchfield. *Hants* —3D **23**
Winchmore Hill. *Buck* —2B **16**
Winchmore Hill. *G Lon* —2B **18**
Windlesham. *Surr* —2B **24**
Windmill Hill. *E Sus* —1A **48**
Windsor. *Wind* —1B **24**
Wineham. *W Sus* —3A **36**
Wing. *Buck* —2A **6**
Wingfield. *Beds* —2C **7**
Wingham. *Kent* —3C **31**
Wingmore. *Kent* —1B **40**
Wingrave. *Buck* —3A **6**
Winkfield. *Brac* —1B **24**
Winkfield Row. *Brac* —1A **24**
Winklebury. *Hants* —3C **23**
Winnersh. *Wok* —1D **23**
Winslade. *Hants* —1C **33**
Winslow. *Buck* —2D **5**
Winterbourne. *W Ber* —1A **22**
Winterbrook. *Oxon* —3C **15**
Winter Gardens. *Essx* —3B **20**
Winton. *E Sus* —2D **47**
Wisborough Green. *W Sus* —3C **35**
Wisley. *Surr* —3C **25**
Wissenden. *Kent* —1D **39**
Wiston. *W Sus* —1D **45**

Witham. *Essx* —3C **11**
Witherenden Hill. *E Sus* —3A **38**
Witheridge Hill. *Oxon* —3C **15**
Withermarsh Green. *Suff* —1A **12**
Withyham. *E Sus* —2C **37**
Witley. *Surr* —1B **34**
Witney. *Oxon* —3A **4**
Wittersham. *Kent* —3D **39**
Wivelrod. *Hants* —2C **33**
Wivelsfield. *E Sus* —3B **36**
Wivelsfield Green. *E Sus* —3B **36**
Wivenhoe. *Essx* —2A **12**
Wix. *Essx* —2B **12**
Wixoe. *Suff* —1B **10**
Woburn. *Beds* —1B **6**
Woburn Sands. *Mil* —1B **6**
Woking. *Surr* —3C **25**
Wokingham. *Wok* —2A **24**
Woldingham. *Surr* —3B **26**
Wolvercote. *Oxon* —1A **14**
Wolverton. *Hants* —3C **23**
Wolverton. *Mil* —1A **6**
Wolverton Common. *Hants* —3B **22**
Womenswold. *Kent* —3C **31**
Wonersh. *Surr* —1C **35**
Wonston. *Hants* —2A **32**
Wooburn. *Buck* —3B **16**
Wooburn Green. *Buck* —3B **16**
Woodchurch. *Kent* —2D **39**
Woodcote. *Oxon* —3C **15**
Woodcott. *Hants* —3A **22**
Woodeaton. *Oxon* —3B **4**
Wood End. *Herts* —2B **8**
Woodend. *W Sus* —2A **44**
Woodend Green. *Essx* —2D **9**
Woodfield. *Oxon* —2B **4**
Woodford. *G Lon* —2C **19**
Woodford Green. *G Lon* —2C **19**
Woodgate. *W Sus* —2B **44**
Wood Green. *G Lon* —2A **18**
Woodham. *Surr* —2C **25**
Woodham Ferrers. *Essx* —2B **20**
Woodham Mortimer. *Essx* —1C **21**
Woodham Walter. *Essx* —1C **21**
Woodingdean. *Brig* —2B **46**
Woodlands. *Kent* —2D **27**
Woodlands Park. *Wind* —1A **24**
Woodlands St Mary. *W Ber* —1A **22**
Woodley. *Wok* —1D **23**
Woodmancote. *W Sus* —2D **43**
  (Chichester)
Woodmancote. *W Sus* —1A **46**
  (Henfield)
Woodmancott. *Hants* —1B **32**
Woodmansgreen. *W Sus* —3A **34**
Woodmansterne. *G Lon* —3A **26**
Woodnesborough. *Kent* —3D **31**
Wood's Green. *E Sus* —2A **38**
Woodside. *Brac* —1B **24**
Woodside. *Herts* —1A **18**
Woodstock. *Oxon* —3A **4**
Wood Street Village. *Surr* —3B **24**
Woolage Green. *Kent* —1C **41**
Woolbeding. *W Sus* —3A **34**
Woolhampton. *W Ber* —2B **22**
Woolmer Green. *Herts* —3A **8**
Woolston. *Sotn* —1A **42**

Woolton Hill. *Hants* —2A **22**
Woolverstone. *Suff* —1B **12**
Woolwich. *G Lon* —1C **27**
Wootton. *IOW* —3B **42**
Wootton. *Kent* —1C **41**
Wootton. *Oxon* —1A **14**
  (Abingdon)
Wootton. *Oxon* —3A **4**
  (Woodstock)
Wootton Bridge. *IOW* —3B **42**
Wootton Common. *IOW* —3B **42**
Wootton St Lawrence. *Hants* —3B **22**
Worcester Park. *G Lon* —2A **26**
Workhouse Green. *Suff* —1D **11**
Worlds End. *Hants* —1C **43**
World's End. *W Ber* —1A **22**
World's End. *W Sus* —1B **46**
Wormingford. *Essx* —1D **11**
Worminghall. *Buck* —1C **15**
Wormley. *Herts* —1B **18**
Wormley. *Surr* —2B **34**
Wormshill. *Kent* —3C **29**
Worplesdon. *Surr* —3B **24**
Worth. *Kent* —3D **31**
Worth. *W Sus* —2B **36**
Worthing. *W Sus* —2D **45**
Worting. *Hants* —3C **23**
Wotton. *Surr* —1D **35**
Wotton Underwood. *Buck* —3C **5**
Wouldham. *Kent* —2B **28**
Wrabness. *Essx* —1B **12**
Wraysbury. *Wind* —1C **25**
Wrecclesham. *Surr* —1A **34**
Wright's Green. *Essx* —3D **9**
Writtle. *Essx* —1A **20**
Wrotham. *Kent* —3A **28**
Wrotham Heath. *Kent* —3A **28**
Wroxton. *Oxon* —1A **4**
Wyatt's Green. *Essx* —2D **19**
Wych Cross. *E Sus* —2C **37**
Wyck. *Hants* —2D **33**
Wycombe Marsh. *Buck* —2A **16**
Wyddial. *Herts* —1B **8**
Wye. *Kent* —1A **40**
Wyfold Grange. *Oxon* —3C **15**
Wyke. *Surr* —3B **24**
Wymering. *Port* —2C **43**
Wytham. *Oxon* —1A **14**

Y

Yalding. *Kent* —3A **28**
Yapton. *W Sus* —2B **44**
Yarmouth. *IOW* —3A **42**
Yarnton. *Oxon* —3A **4**
Yateley. *Hants* —2A **24**
Yattendon. *W Ber* —1B **22**
Yeading. *G Lon* —3D **17**
Yelford. *Oxon* —1A **14**
Yelsted. *Kent* —2C **29**
Yiewsley. *G Lon* —3C **17**
Yorkletts. *Kent* —2A **30**
Young's End. *Essx* —3B **10**

CITY & TOWN CENTRE PLANS

Brighton & Hove	62	Guildford	66	Portsmouth	68
Canterbury	63	London	64-65	Reading	68
Dover	63	Medway Towns	66	Southampton	69
Eastbourne	63	Milton Keynes	67	Winchester	69
Folkestone	68	Oxford	67	Windsor	69

Airport Plans

✈ London Gatwick _____ 70   ✈ London Luton _____ 71

✈ London Heathrow _____ 70   ✈ London Stanstead _____ 71

Port Plans

Harwich _____ 72

Newhaven _____ 72

Reference to Town Plans

MOTORWAY	**M1**
MOTORWAY UNDER CONSTRUCTION	
MOTORWAY PROPOSED	
MOTORWAY JUNCTIONS WITH NUMBERS	
Unlimited Interchange	4
Limited Interchange	5
PRIMARY ROUTE	A41
DUAL CARRIAGEWAY	
CLASS A ROAD	A129
CLASS B ROAD	B177
MAJOR ROAD UNDER CONSTRUCTION	
MAJOR ROAD PROPOSED	
MINOR ROAD	
RESTRICTED ACCESS	
PEDESTRIAN ROAD & MAIN FOOTWAY	
ONE WAY STREET	

TOLL	
RAILWAY AND B.R. STATION	
UNDERGROUND, D.L.R. & METRO STATION	DLR
LEVEL CROSSING AND TUNNEL	
TRAM STOP AND ONE WAY TRAM STOP	
BUILT UP AREA	
ABBEY, CATHEDRAL, PRIORY ETC.	†
AIRPORT	✈
BUS STATION	
CAR PARK (Selection of)	P
CHURCH	†
CITY WALL	
FERRY (Vehicular)	
(Foot only)	
GOLF COURSE	
HELIPORT	

HOSPITAL	H
INFORMATION CENTRE	i
LIGHTHOUSE	
MARKET	
NATIONAL TRUST PROPERTY (Open)	NT
(Restricted opening)	NT
(National Trust of Scotland)	NTS NTS
PARK & RIDE	P+
PLACE OF INTEREST	
POLICE STATION	▲
POST OFFICE	★
SHOPPING AREA (Main street and precinct)	
SHOPMOBILITY	
TOILET	▽
VIEWPOINT	

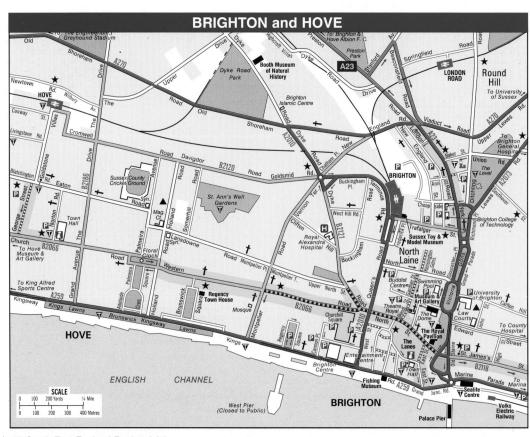

BRIGHTON and HOVE

DOVER

To: Buckland Hospital & Dover Ath. F.C.
Connaught Park
Langdon Cliffs Picnic Site
Langdon Cliffs
TOLL
Coaches Only
Bleriot Memorial
A2
Dover Castle
PWRR & Queen's Regt. Mus.
The Pharos
St. Mary-in-Castro Saxon Church
Tower Hamlets
Maison Dieu
Maison Dieu Liby.
Pencester Gds.
Dover College
Old St. James Church Ruins
Moat Bulwark
Hellfire Corner & Underground Hospital
Car Ferry Terminal
EASTERN DOCKS
DOVER PRIORY
Sports Centre & Swimming Pool
Roman Painted House
Dover Mus.
Bureau de Change
C.S. Rolls Statue
Captain Webb Memorial
Clarendon
Drop Redoubt
Western Heights
Grand Shaft
Wellington Dock
OUTER HARBOUR
Calais 1hr. 10mins.
Dunkirk 2hrs.
Zeebrugge 4hrs. 30mins.
Knights Templar Church
WESTERN DOCKS
Car Ferry Terminal
Prince of Wales Pier
Southern Breakwater
Aycliff
To Shakespeare Cliff
A20
INNER HARBOUR
Calais 50mins. (Fast Ferry)
Ostend 2hrs. (Fast Ferry)
Cruise Liner Terminal
Admiralty Pier
SCALE
0 100 200 Yards ¼ Mile
0 100 200 300 400 Metres

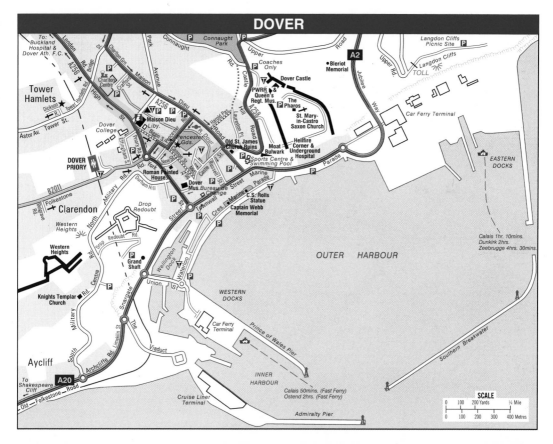

CANTERBURY

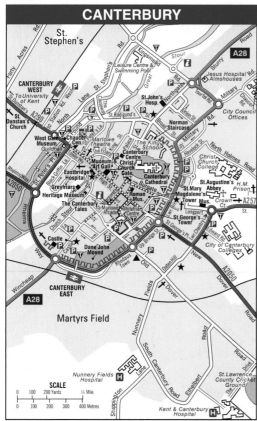

EASTBOURNE

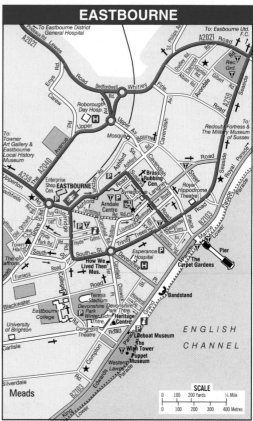

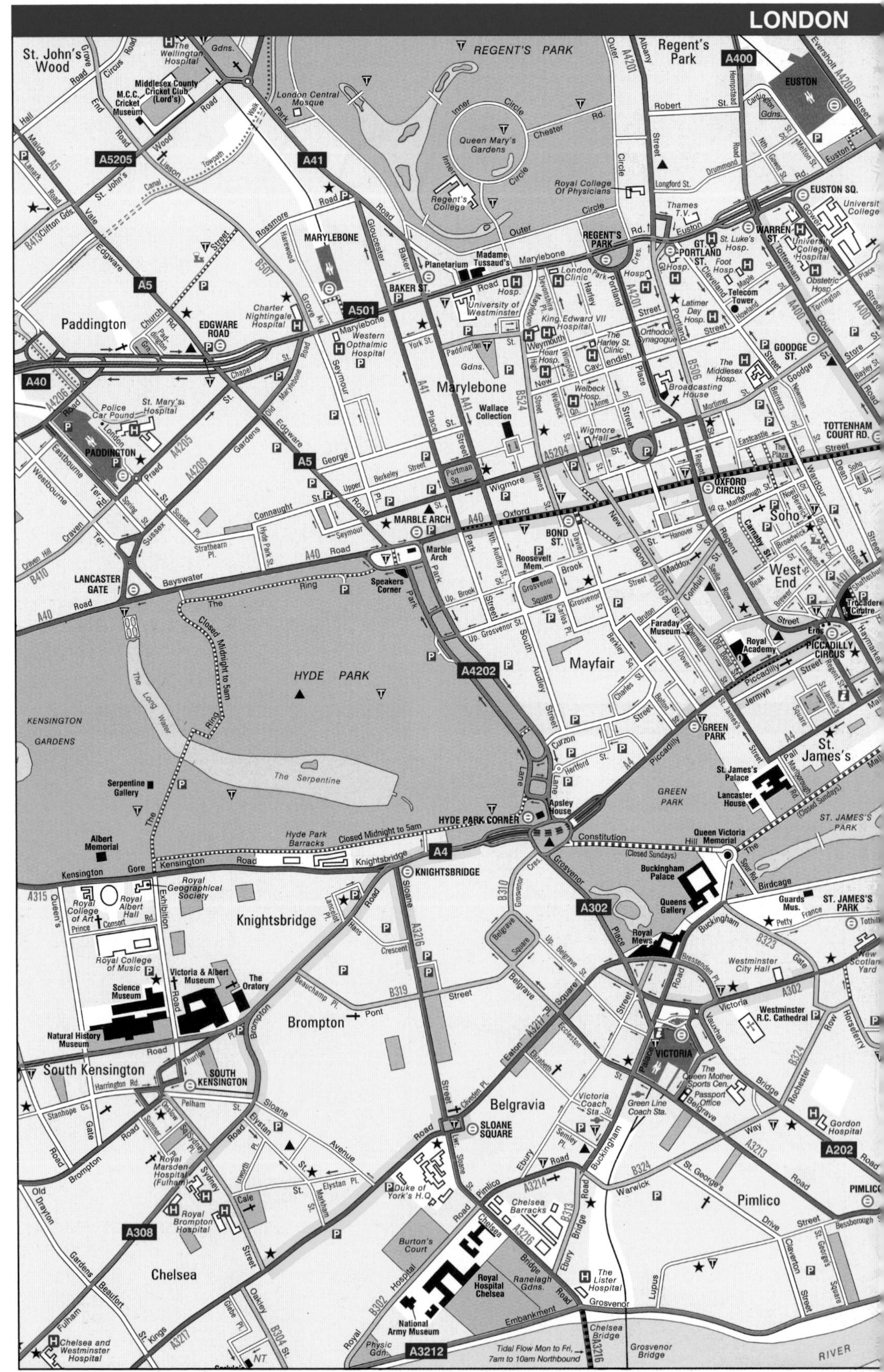
St. John's Wood
REGENT'S PARK
Regent's Park
EUSTON
London Central Mosque
Queen Mary's Gardens
Middlesex County Cricket Club (Lord's)
M.C.C. Cricket Museum
The Wellington Hospital
Regent's College
Royal College Of Physicians
EUSTON SQ.
University College
MARYLEBONE
Planetarium
Madame Tussaud's
REGENT'S PARK
WARREN ST.
GT. PORTLAND ST.
St. Luke's Hosp.
Thames T.V.
BAKER ST.
University of Westminster
London Clinic
Telecom Tower
Charter Nightingale Hospital
Western Opthalmic Hospital
King Edward VII Hospital
The Harley St. Clinic
Orthodox Synagogue
Latimer Day Hosp.
GOODGE ST.
Paddington
EDGWARE ROAD
The Middlesex Hosp.
Marylebone
Broadcasting House
St. Mary's Hospital
Police Car Pound
PADDINGTON
Wallace Collection
Welbeck Hosp.
Wigmore Hall
TOTTENHAM COURT RD.
OXFORD CIRCUS
Soho
MARBLE ARCH
BOND ST.
Roosevelt Mem.
Grosvenor Square
West End
LANCASTER GATE
Speakers Corner
Faraday Museum
Royal Academy
Trocadero Centre
Eros
PICCADILLY CIRCUS
HYDE PARK
Mayfair
KENSINGTON GARDENS
The Long Water
Closed Midnight to 5am
GREEN PARK
St. James's
The Serpentine
Serpentine Gallery
St. James's Palace
Lancaster House
GREEN PARK
HYDE PARK CORNER
Apsley House
Albert Memorial
Hyde Park Barracks
Closed Midnight to 5am
Queen Victoria Memorial
ST. JAMES'S PARK
(Closed Sundays)
KNIGHTSBRIDGE
Buckingham Palace
Royal Geographical Society
Royal College of Art
Royal Albert Hall
Knightsbridge
Queens Gallery
Guards Mus.
ST. JAMES'S PARK
Royal Mews
Royal College of Music
Victoria & Albert Museum
The Oratory
Westminster City Hall
New Scotland Yard
Science Museum
Brompton
Westminster R.C. Cathedral
Natural History Museum
South Kensington
SOUTH KENSINGTON
VICTORIA
The Queen Mother Sports Cen.
Passport Office
Victoria Coach Sta.
Green Line Coach Sta.
Belgravia
SLOANE SQUARE
Gordon Hospital
Royal Marsden Hospital (Fulham)
Duke of York's H.Q.
Chelsea Barracks
Pimlico
PIMLICO
Royal Brompton Hospital
Burton's Court
Chelsea
The Lister Hospital
Royal Hospital Chelsea
Ranelagh Gdns.
National Army Museum
Chelsea and Westminster Hospital
Physic Gdn.
Chelsea Bridge
Grosvenor Bridge
Tidal Flow Mon to Fri, 7am to 10am Northbound
RIVER
A5205
A41
A5
A501
A40
A4202
A4
A302
A308
A202
A3212
A400

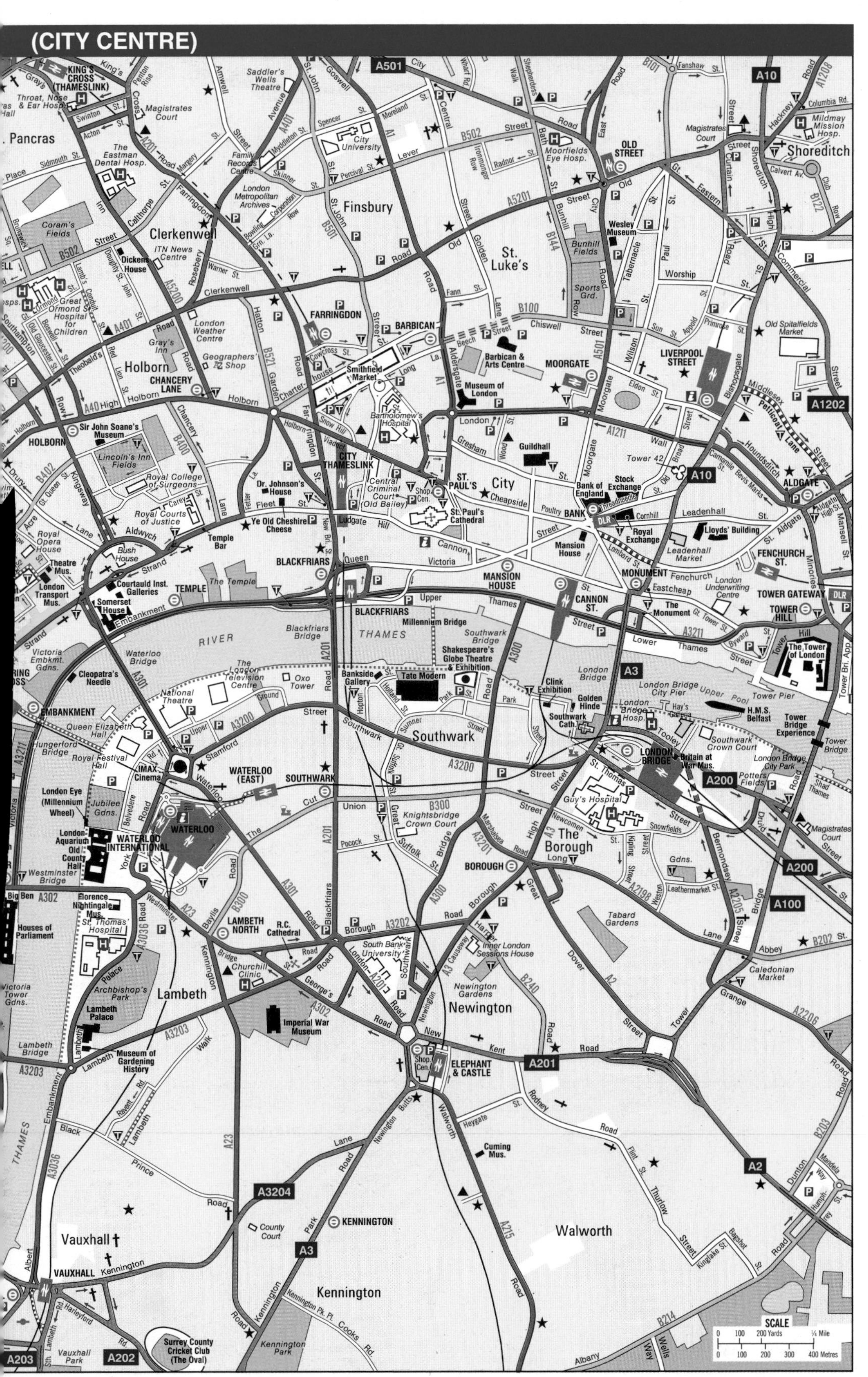
KING'S CROSS (THAMESLINK)
Pancras
Magistrates Court
Saddler's Wells Theatre
City University
Finsbury
Clerkenwell
Coram's Fields
The Eastman Dental Hosp.
Family Records Centre
London Metropolitan Archives
ITN News Centre
Dickens House
Great Ormond St. Hospital for Children
London Weather Centre
Geographers' A-Z Shop
Holborn
CHANCERY LANE
HOLBORN
Sir John Soane's Museum
Lincoln's Inn Fields
Royal College of Surgeons
Royal Courts of Justice
Aldwych
Bush House
Royal Opera House
Theatre Mus.
London Transport Mus.
Courtauld Inst. Galleries
Somerset House
TEMPLE
The Temple
Temple Bar
Ye Old Cheshire Cheese
Dr. Johnson's House
Central Criminal Court (Old Bailey)
FARRINGDON
BARBICAN
Smithfield Market
St. Bartholomew's Hospital
Barbican & Arts Centre
Museum of London
CITY THAMESLINK
ST. PAUL'S
St. Paul's Cathedral
City
Guildhall
MOORGATE
Bank of England
Stock Exchange
BANK
Royal Exchange
Mansion House
MANSION HOUSE
Lloyds' Building
Leadenhall Market
MONUMENT
The Monument
London Underwriting Centre
CANNON ST.
FENCHURCH ST.
TOWER GATEWAY
TOWER HILL
The Tower of London
ALDGATE
LIVERPOOL STREET
Old Spitalfields Market
OLD STREET
Moorfields Eye Hosp.
Wesley Museum
Bunhill Fields
St. Luke's
Shoreditch
Mildmay Mission Hosp.
BLACKFRIARS
Blackfriars Bridge
Millennium Bridge
Southwark Bridge
Shakespeare's Globe Theatre & Exhibition
Tate Modern
Bankside Gallery
RIVER THAMES
Waterloo Bridge
Cleopatra's Needle
Victoria Embkmt. Gdns.
EMBANKMENT
Hungerford Bridge
Queen Elizabeth Hall
Royal Festival Hall
National Theatre
The London Television Centre
Oxo Tower
IMAX Cinema
London Eye (Millennium Wheel)
Jubilee Gdns.
London Aquarium
Old County Hall
WATERLOO INTERNATIONAL
WATERLOO
WATERLOO (EAST)
SOUTHWARK
Southwark
Clink Exhibition
Golden Hinde
Southwark Cath.
London Bridge
London Bridge City Pier
Upper Pool
Hay's Galleria
H.M.S. Belfast
Tower Pier
Tower Bridge Experience
Tower Bridge
LONDON BRIDGE
Britain at War Mus.
Southwark Crown Court
London Bridge City Park
Potters Fields
Guy's Hospital
Knightsbridge Crown Court
The Borough
BOROUGH
Westminster Bridge
Big Ben
Houses of Parliament
Florence Nightingale Mus.
St. Thomas' Hospital
LAMBETH NORTH
R.C. Cathedral
Churchill Clinic
South Bank University
Inner London Sessions House
Tabard Gardens
Caledonian Market
Archbishop's Park
Lambeth
Lambeth Palace
Imperial War Museum
Newington Gardens
Newington
Lambeth Bridge
Museum of Gardening History
ELEPHANT & CASTLE
Cuming Mus.
Walworth
KENNINGTON
County Court
Vauxhall
VAUXHALL
Kennington
Kennington Park
Surrey County Cricket Club (The Oval)
Vauxhall Park
SCALE
0 100 200 Yards ¼ Mile
0 100 200 300 400 Metres

GUILDFORD

MEDWAY TOWNS

STROOD
Strood Pier
Bridge Reach
Henley Business Park
Enterprise Business Centre
Neptune
To: World Naval Base Entrance
Khyber
Lower Lines
Road
To The Strand
Central Business Park
Neptune Industrial Estate
Historic Dockyard
Kent Police Museum
World Naval Base
Dock
Brompton
Royal School of Military Engineering
Road
Road
Arthur
Rochester Bridge
Lake
Wood
War Memorial
Pasley Rd.
Royal Engineers Museum
B2004
Prince Arthur Park
Ryl. Victoria & Bull Hotel
ROCHESTER
Frindsbury Peninsula
Chatham Reach
St. Prince
To Civic Centre
Guildhall Museum
Limehouse Reach
Sir Thomas
Longley
Close
Medway City Estate
Road
Black Lion Leisure Centre
Esplanade
Corporation
Liby.
Brompton
To Station & Gillingham F.C.
Castle
Hill
A231
Rd.
Inner Lines
A231
Mill
Sports Ground
Road
Six Poor Travellers Ho.
Riverside Estate
Liby.
High
Boley
Cathedral
A2
GILLINGHAM
St.
Blue Boar Pier
Medway Heritage Centre
Dock
Fort Amherst
Charles Dickens Cen. (Eastgate Ho.)
Street
The Vines
Crow La.
St. Margaret's
Restoration House
RIVER MEDWAY
Riverside Gardens
The Brook Theatre
Canterbury
Vines
La.
East Row
ROCHESTER
Library
Town Hall Gdns.
Victoria
High
Sun Pier
Magistrates Court
Great Lines
King Edward Rd.
Rd.
Union St.
Star
Ship Pier
Medway
St.
War Memorial
King
St.
Hill
Sir John Hawkins Hospital
Street
A231
Pentagon Centre
The
Cross
CHATHAM
Marlborough
Watts
New
A2
St. Bartholomew's Hospital
Manor Rd.
Rd.
High
Troy Town
Delce
Road
New
Av.
Best
Brook Pumping Mus.
Street
City
Central Theatre
Clover
Richard St.
Brook
York
Av.
Kent Institute of Art & Design
Victoria Gdns.
CHATHAM
New Cut
New
St.
St.
Av.
B2097
Fort Pitt
Hill
Albany T.
Old
High
Rd.
Windmill Rd.
Street
Street
Road
Rd.
Road
Medway Maritime Hospital
A2
Mid Kent College of Higher and Further Education
Otway
Magpie
Luton
Chatham
Cecil
Road
A229
A230
Jenkins Dale
Salisbury Rd.
Hall
A2
Cemetery
To: Rochester Airport, M2 Junc. 3 & Buckmore Park
SCALE
0 100 200 Yards ¼ Mile
0 100 200 300 400 Metres
Hill
Maidstone
St.
Catherine
Way
Maidstone
Road
Holcombe Rd.
Rd.
Listmas Rd.
Castle R.
Road
To Fort Luton
To Ski Centre
To Ice Bowl

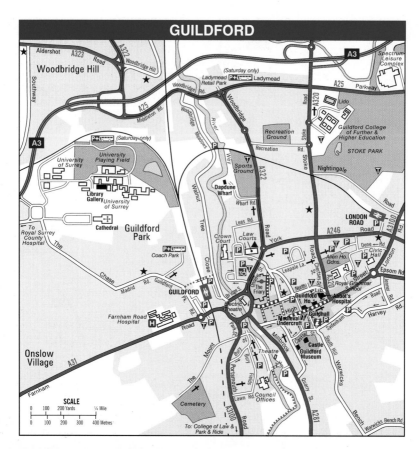

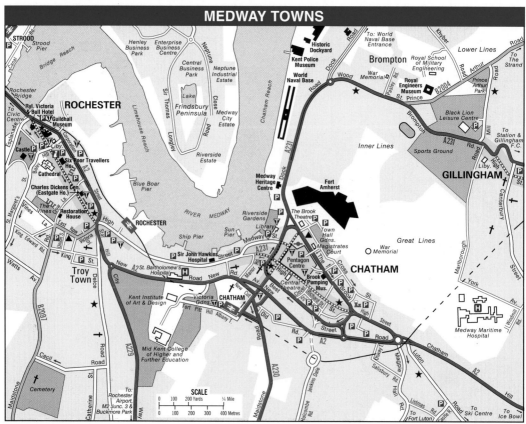

MILTON KEYNES

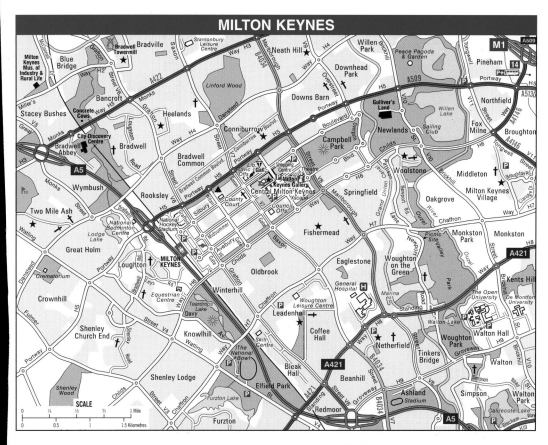

OXFORD

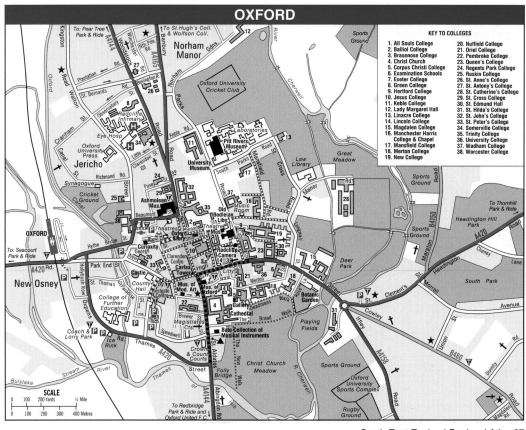

KEY TO COLLEGES

1. All Souls College
2. Balliol College
3. Brasenose College
4. Christ Church
5. Corpus Christi College
6. Examination Schools
7. Exeter College
8. Green College
9. Hertford College
10. Jesus College
11. Keble College
12. Lady Margaret Hall
13. Linacre College
14. Lincoln College
15. Magdalen College
16. Manchester Harris College & Chapel
17. Mansfield College
18. Merton College
19. New College
20. Nuffield College
21. Oriel College
22. Pembroke College
23. Queen's College
24. Regents Park College
25. Ruskin College
26. St. Anne's College
27. St. Antony's College
28. St. Catherine's College
29. St. Cross College
30. St. Edmund Hall
31. St. Hilda's College
32. St. John's College
33. St. Peter's College
34. Somerville College
35. Trinity College
36. University College
37. Wadham College
38. Worcester College

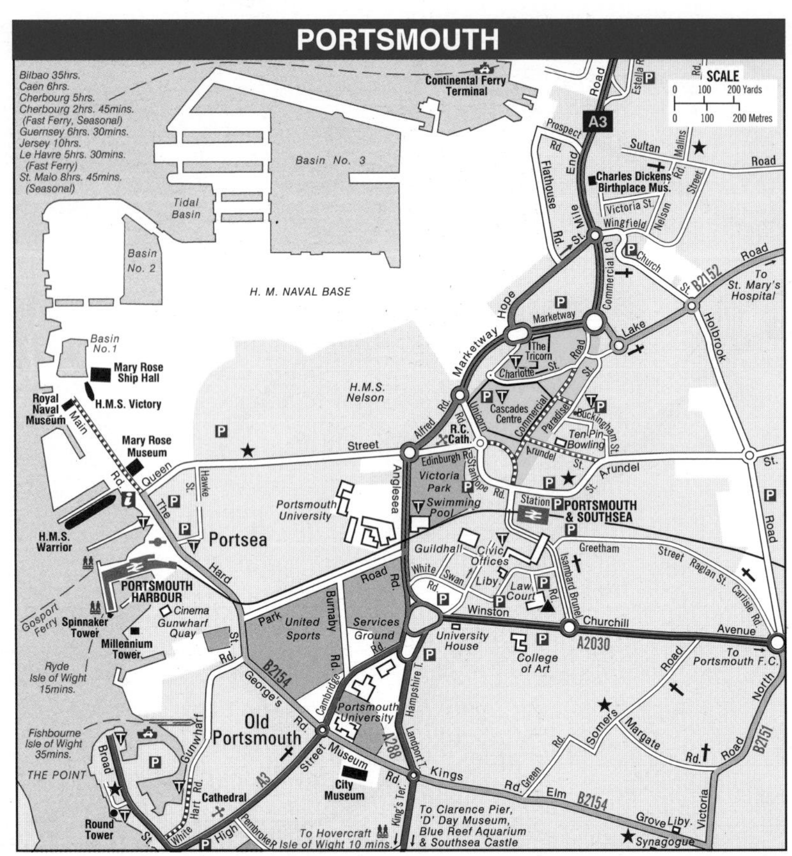
PORTSMOUTH
Bilbao 35hrs.
Caen 6hrs.
Cherbourg 5hrs.
Cherbourg 2hrs. 45mins. (Fast Ferry, Seasonal)
Guernsey 6hrs. 30mins.
Jersey 10hrs.
Le Havre 5hrs. 30mins. (Fast Ferry)
St. Malo 8hrs. 45mins. (Seasonal)
Continental Ferry Terminal
SCALE
0 100 200 Yards
0 100 200 Metres
A3
Basin No. 3
Tidal Basin
Basin No. 2
Basin No.1
H. M. NAVAL BASE
H.M.S. Nelson
Mary Rose Ship Hall
H.M.S. Victory
Royal Naval Museum
Mary Rose Museum
H.M.S. Warrior
PORTSMOUTH HARBOUR
Cinema
Gunwharf Quay
Spinnaker Tower
Millennium Tower
Gosport Ferry
Ryde Isle of Wight 15mins.
Fishbourne Isle of Wight 35mins.
THE POINT
Round Tower
Cathedral
Old Portsmouth
Portsea
Portsmouth University
United Sports
Services Ground
University House
College of Art
City Museum
Charles Dickens' Birthplace Mus.
Sultan
Road
Malins Rd.
Nelson Street
Victoria St.
Wingfield
Prospect Rd.
Flathouse Rd.
Mile End Rd.
Commercial Rd.
Church
Lake
B2152
Holbrook
To St. Mary's Hospital
Marketway
Hope
The Tricorn
Charlotte St.
Cascades Centre
Buckingham St.
Ten Pin Bowling
Paradise St.
Arundel St.
R.C. Cath.
Edinburgh Rd.
Victoria Park
Swimming Pool
Station
PORTSMOUTH & SOUTHSEA
Greetham Street
Raglan St.
Carlisle Rd.
Guildhall
Civic Offices
Liby.
Law Court
Winston Churchill Avenue
A2030
Isambard Brunel Rd.
White Swan Rd.
To Portsmouth F.C.
Somers Road
Margate Rd.
North Road
B2151
Kings Rd.
Green Rd.
Elm Grove
B2154
Grove Liby.
Synagogue
Victoria Road
Alfred Rd.
Anglesea Rd.
Unicorn Rd.
Stanhope Rd.
Queen Street
Hawke St.
The Hard
Main Rd.
Park Rd.
Burnaby Rd.
St. George's Rd.
Cambridge Rd.
Hampshire Ter.
Landport T.
A288
Museum Rd.
King's Ter.
High Street
Pembroke Rd.
White Hart Rd.
Gunwharf Rd.
Broad St.
To Hovercraft Isle of Wight 10 mins.
To Clarence Pier, 'D' Day Museum, Blue Reef Aquarium & Southsea Castle

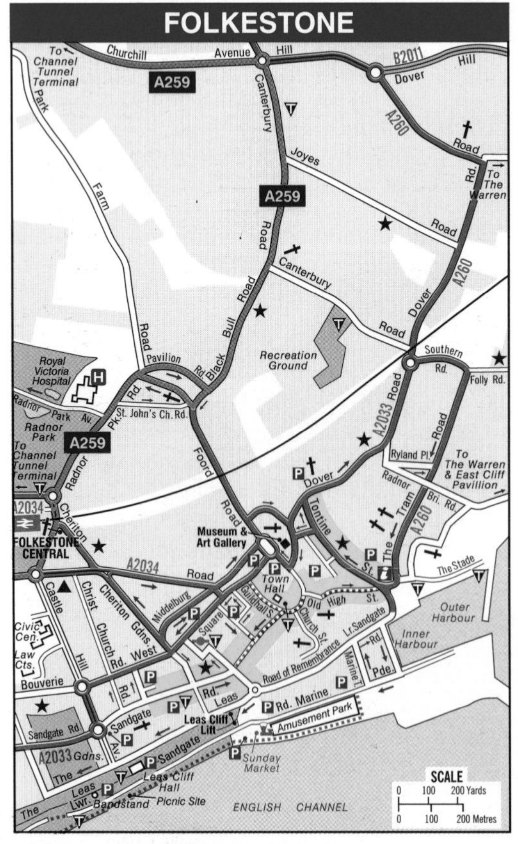
FOLKESTONE
To Channel Tunnel Terminal
Churchill Avenue
Hill
B2011
Dover Hill
A259
Canterbury Road
A260
Joyes Road
Canterbury Road
Dover Road
To The Warren
Park Farm Road
Bull Road
Black Rd
Pavilion Rd
Recreation Ground
Southern Rd.
Folly Rd.
A2033 Road
Royal Victoria Hospital
Radnor Park Av.
Radnor Park
St. John's Ch. Rd.
Radnor Pk.
To Channel Tunnel Terminal
Foord Road
Dover St.
Ryland Pl.
Radnor Bri. Rd.
Tram Road
Tontine St.
To The Warren & East Cliff Pavillion
The Stade
A2034
FOLKESTONE CENTRAL
Cheriton Road
Museum & Art Gallery
Town Hall
Old High St.
Outer Harbour
Inner Harbour
Middelburg Sq.
Guildhall St.
Church St.
Lr. Sandgate Rd.
Road of Remembrance
Castle Hill
Christ Church Rd.
Cheriton Gdns.
West
Civic Cen.
Law Cts.
Bouverie
Leas
Rd. Marine
Marine T.
Pde.
Leas Cliff Lift
Amusement Park
Sandgate Rd.
Sandgate Av.
A2033 Gdns.
The Leas
Leas Cliff Hall
Lwr. Sandgate
Bandstand
Picnic Site
Sunday Market
ENGLISH CHANNEL
SCALE
0 100 200 Yards
0 100 200 Metres

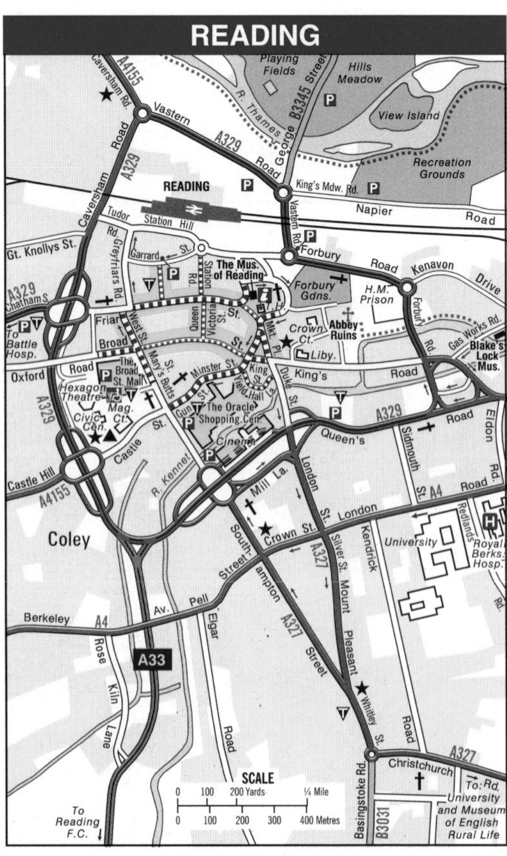
READING
Caversham Rd.
A4155
Playing Fields
R. Thames
B3345 George Street
Hills Meadow
View Island
Recreation Grounds
Vastern Road
A329
King's Mdw. Rd.
READING
Napier Road
Tudor Rd.
Station Hill
Vastern Rd.
Forbury Road
Kenavon Drive
Gt. Knollys St.
Garrard St.
Greyfriars Rd.
Station Rd.
The Mus. of Reading
Forbury Gdns.
H.M. Prison
A329 Chatham St.
To Battle Hosp.
Friar St.
Queen Victoria St.
Mkt. Pl.
Abbey Ruins
Crown Ct.
Liby.
Gas Works Rd.
Blake's Lock Mus.
Broad St.
West St.
Minster St.
King's Road
Oxford Road
Hexagon Theatre
Broad St. Mall
St. Mary's Butts
Mag. Ct.
Gun St.
The Oracle Shopping Cen.
Cinema
Duke St.
Queen's Road
A329
Sidmouth St.
Eldon Rd.
Civic Cen.
Castle St.
R. Kennet
Mill La.
London St.
A4
London Road
Castle Hill
A4155
Coley
Crown St.
South Street
Southampton Street
A327
Silver St.
Mount Pleasant
Kendrick Rd.
University
Redlands Rd.
Royal Berks. Hosp.
Berkeley Av.
A4
Pell St.
Elgar Road
Rose Kiln Lane
A33
Whitley St.
Christchurch Road
A327
To Rd. University and Museum of English Rural Life
Basingstoke Rd.
B3031
SCALE
0 100 200 Yards ¼ Mile
0 100 200 300 400 Metres
To Reading F.C.

SOUTHAMPTON

WINCHESTER

WINCHESTER
Fulflood
B3044
B3049
B3040
B3045
B3047
B3420
B3330
B3335
B3404
Bereweeke
Stockbridge
Romsey
Coach Park
Recreation Ground
Hyde Abbey Gatehouse
Historic Resources Centre
River Park Leisure Centre
School of Art
Winchester Gallery
Theatre Royal
Libraries
Oram's Arbour
H.M.P. Winchester
Royal Greenjackets & Light Infantry Mus.
Westgate
County Offices
The Brooks Experience
Castle Great Hall
Law Cts.
Gurkhas & Royal Hussars Museum
Royal Hampshire Regiment Museum
County Hospital
Cemetery
Old Guildhall
City Mus.
Gall.
King Alfred's Statue
City Mill
Guildhall Gallery
Abbey Gds.
Cathedral
The Deanery
Triforium Gallery
Wolvesey Palace
Wolvesey Castle
King Alfred's College
Winchester College
Ridding Meads
To St. Cross Hospital
SCALE
0 100 200 Yards
0 100 200 Metres

WINDSOR

SCALE
0 100 200 Yards ¼ Mile
0 100 200 300 400 Metres
Eton College
Museum of Eton Life
Eton
South Meadow
The Brocas
RIVER THAMES
WINDSOR & ETON RIVERSIDE
Windsor Bri.
Leisure Centre
Clewer St.Stephen
Playing Field
Alexandra Gdns.
Coach
WINDSOR & ETON CENTRAL
Windsor Castle
St. George's Chapel
Guildhall
Brass Rubbing Cen.
King Edward Ct. Cen.
Town & Crown Exhibition
Library
Municipal Offices
Victoria Barracks
H.R.H. Princess Christian Hosp.
Sports Ground
Magistrates Court
Windsor & Maidenhead College
Princess Margaret Hosp.
New Windsor
Household Cavalry Museum
Combermere Barracks
King Edward VII Hospital
Berkshire Yeomanry Museum
To Racecourse
To Legoland
To Savill Garden
The Home Park
A332
A308
B3022
B3026
B3173
B470

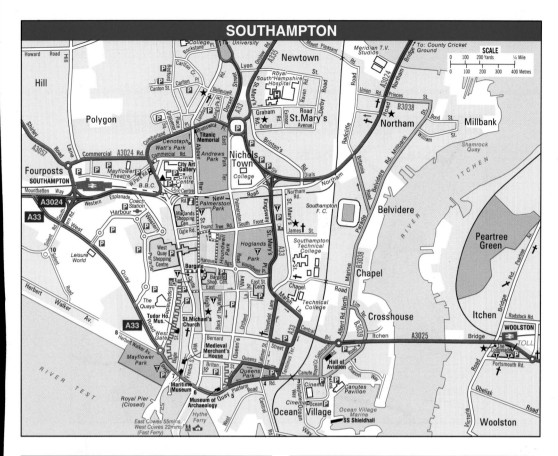

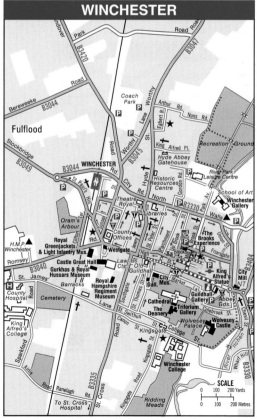

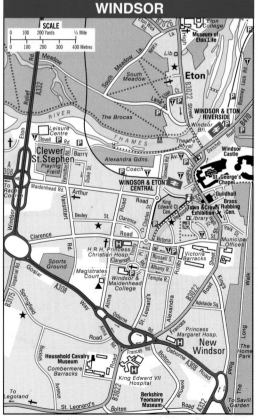

AIRPORT PLANS

LONDON GATWICK

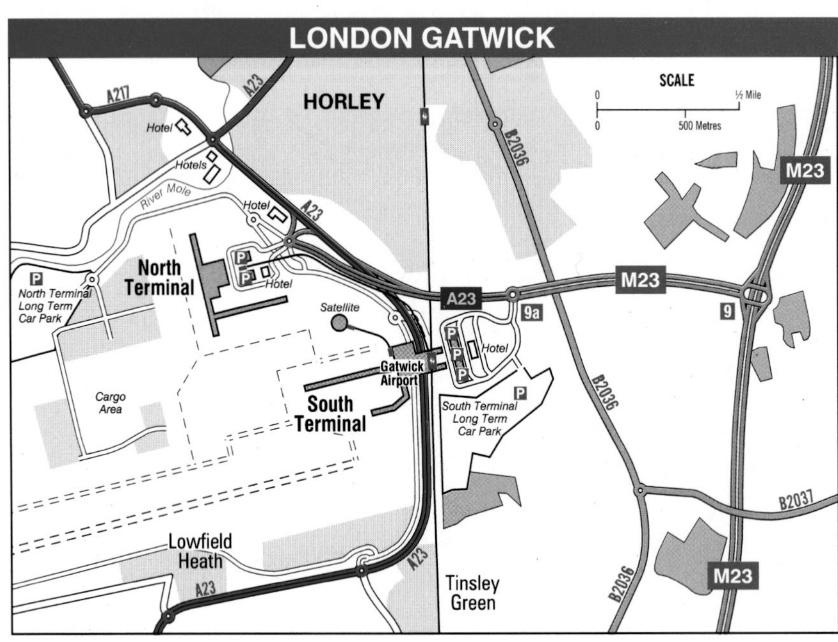

HORLEY
SCALE
0
½ Mile
500 Metres
A217
A23
Hotel
Hotels
River Mole
North Terminal
North Terminal Long Term Car Park
Hotel
Satellite
Gatwick Airport
South Terminal
Cargo Area
South Terminal Long Term Car Park
M23
9a
9
B2036
B2037
Lowfield Heath
Tinsley Green

LONDON HEATHROW

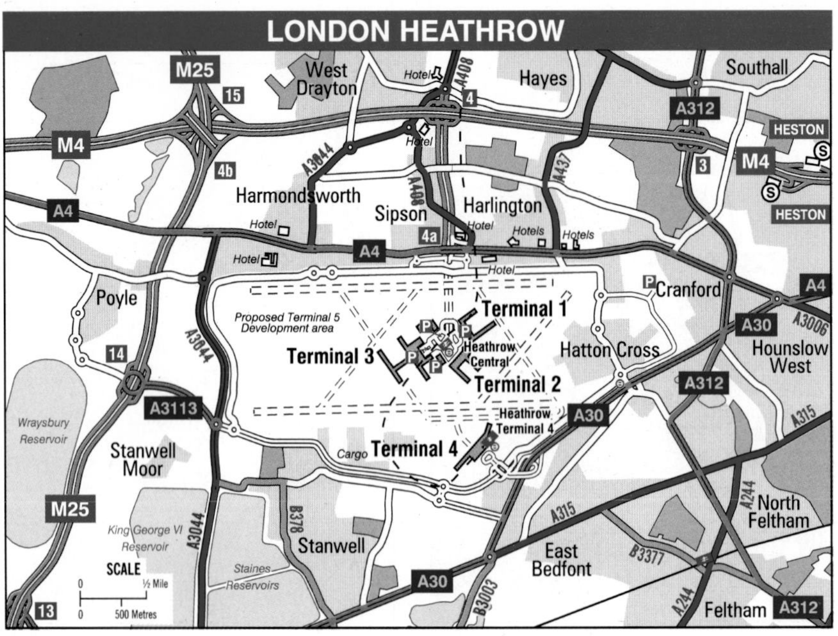

M25
15
West Drayton
Hotel
A408
4
Hayes
Southall
A312
HESTON
M4
3
4b
A3044
A437
Harmondsworth
Sipson
Harlington
A4
4a
Hotels
Cranford
Poyle
Proposed Terminal 5 Development area
Terminal 1
Terminal 3
Heathrow Central
Terminal 2
Hatton Cross
A30
A3006
Hounslow West
14
A3113
Heathrow Terminal 4
Wraysbury Reservoir
Stanwell Moor
Cargo
Terminal 4
A315
North Feltham
A244
B378
Stanwell
King George VI Reservoir
SCALE
0
½ Mile
500 Metres
Staines Reservoirs
East Bedfont
B3377
B3003
13
Feltham

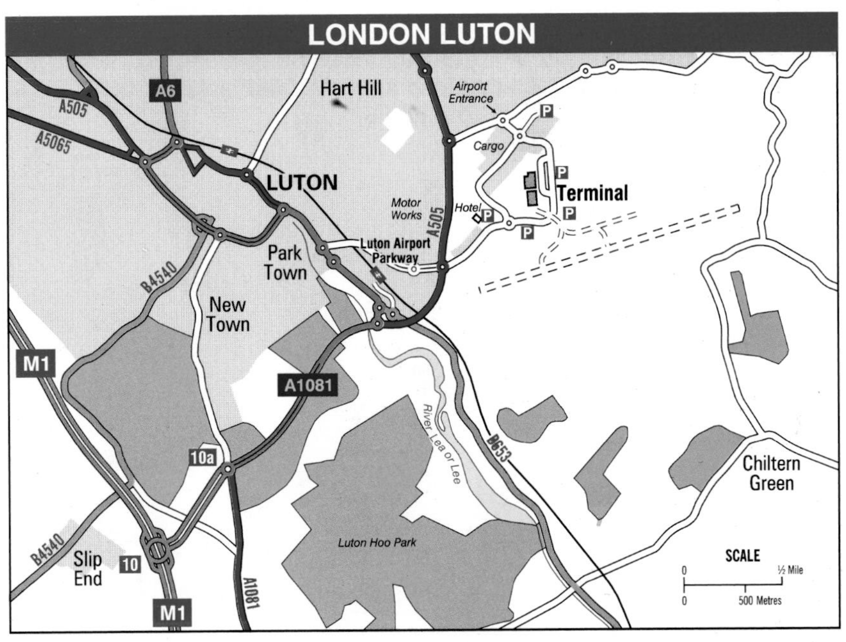

LONDON LUTON

Hart Hill

Airport Entrance

A6

A505

A5065

Cargo

LUTON

Motor Works

Hotel

P

P

Terminal

P

A505

Luton Airport Parkway

Park Town

New Town

M1

A1081

River Lea or Lee

B653

Chiltern Green

10a

Luton Hoo Park

B4540

A1081

Slip End

10

M1

B4540

SCALE

0 ½ Mile

0 500 Metres

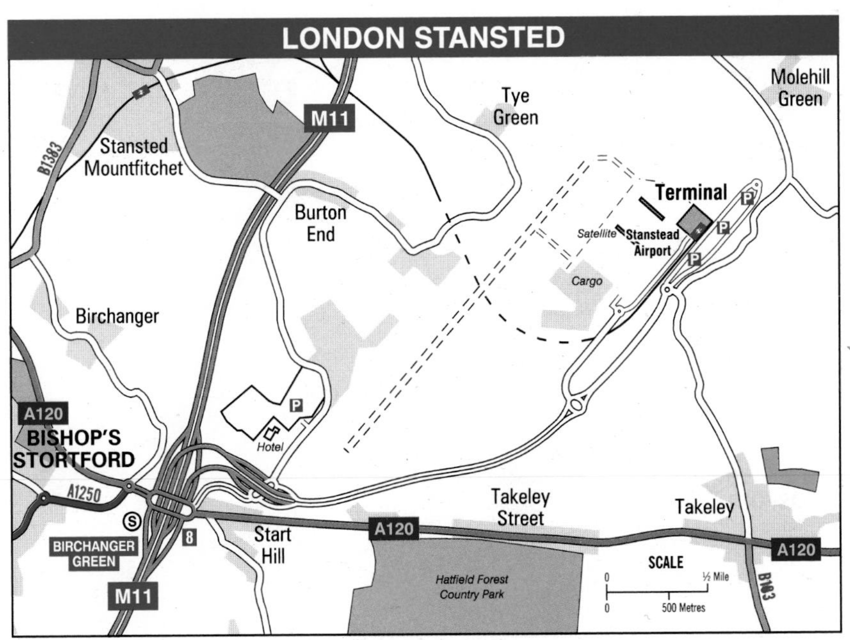

LONDON STANSTED

Molehill Green

B1383

Stansted Mountfitchet

M11

Tye Green

Burton End

Terminal

Satellite Stanstead Airport

P

P

Cargo

Birchanger

A120

P

BISHOP'S STORTFORD

Hotel

A1250

S

8

Start Hill

A120

Takeley Street

Takeley

A120

B183

BIRCHANGER GREEN

M11

Hatfield Forest Country Park

SCALE

0 ½ Mile

0 500 Metres

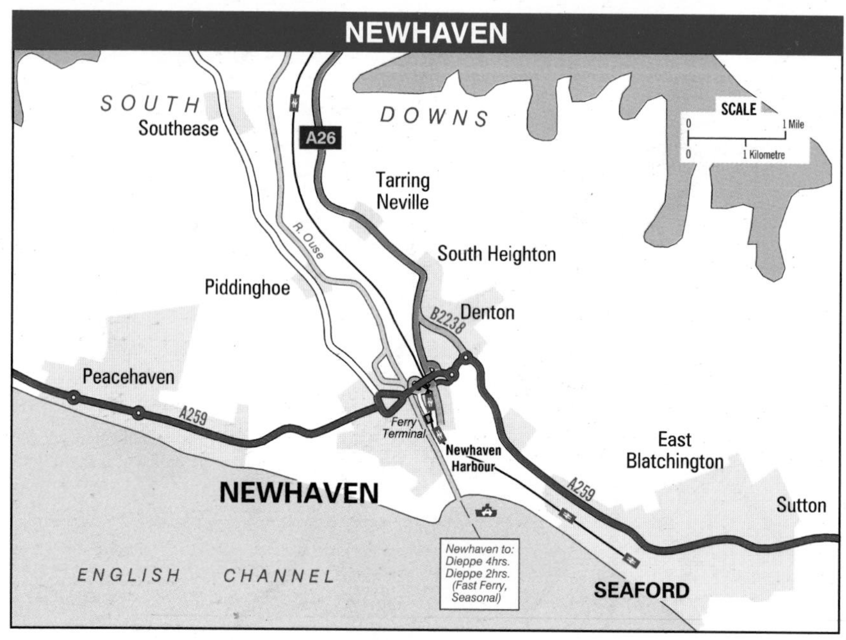

NEWHAVEN

SOUTH
Southease
DOWNS
A26
Tarring
Neville
South Heighton
Piddinghoe
B2238
Denton
Peacehaven
A259
Ferry
Terminal
Newhaven
Harbour
East
Blatchington
NEWHAVEN
A259
Sutton
ENGLISH CHANNEL
Newhaven to:
Dieppe 4hrs.
Dieppe 2hrs.
(Fast Ferry,
Seasonal)
SEAFORD

SCALE
0   1 Mile
0   1 Kilometre

R. Ouse

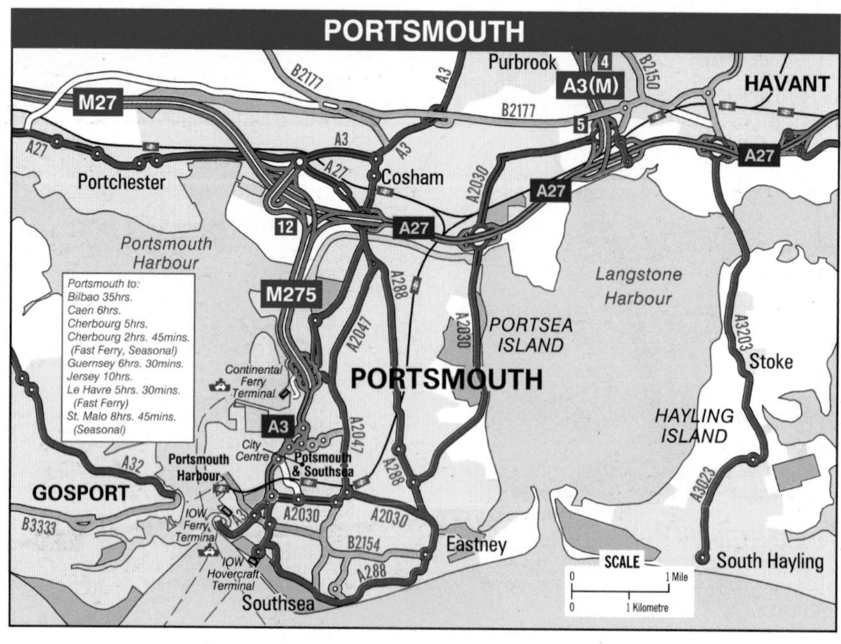

PORTSMOUTH

B2177
A3
Purbrook
4
B2150
M27
A3(M)
HAVANT
A27
B2177
5
Portchester
A3
A3
A27
Cosham
A27
A2030
A27
A27
12
A27
Portsmouth
Harbour
M275
A288
Langstone
Harbour
A3203
Portsmouth to:
Bilbao 35hrs.
Caen 6hrs.
Cherbourg 5hrs.
Cherbourg 2hrs. 45mins.
(Fast Ferry, Seasonal)
Guernsey 6hrs. 30mins.
Jersey 10hrs.
Le Havre 5hrs. 30mins.
(Fast Ferry)
St. Malo 8hrs. 45mins.
(Seasonal)
A2047
A2030
PORTSEA
ISLAND
Stoke
Continental
Ferry
Terminal
PORTSMOUTH
HAYLING
ISLAND
A3
City
Centre
A2047
A288
Portsmouth
Harbour
Portsmouth
& Southsea
A30230
GOSPORT
A32
IOW
Ferry
Terminal
A2030
A2030
A288
B3333
B2154
IOW
Hovercraft
Terminal
A288
Eastney
South Hayling
Southsea

SCALE
0   1 Mile
0   1 Kilometre